Enron and World Finance

Also by Observatoire de la Finance

From Bretton Woods to Basel
Finance & the Common Good/Bien Commun, no. 21, Spring 2005

Ethics of Taxation and Banking Secrecy
Finance & the Common Good/Bien Commun, no. 12, Autumn 2002

Will the Euro Shape Europe?
Finance & the Common Good/Bien Commun, no. 9, Winter 2001–2

Dommen, E. (ed.) *Debt Beyond Contract*
Finance & the Common Good/Bien Commun, Supplement no. 2, 2001

Bonvin, J.-M. *Debt and the Jubilee: Pacing the Economy*
Finance & the Common Good/Bien Commun, Supplement no. 1, 1999

Dembinski, P. H. (leading contributor) *Economic and Financial Globalization: What the Numbers Say*
United Nations, Geneva, 2003

Enron and World Finance

A Case Study in Ethics

Edited by

Paul H. Dembinski
Carole Lager
Andrew Cornford
and
Jean-Michel Bonvin

palgrave
macmillan

in association with the
Observatoire de la Finance

First published 2006 by
PALGRAVE MACMILLAN
Houndmills, Basingstoke, Hampshire RG21 6XS and
175 Fifth Avenue, New York, N.Y. 10010
Companies and representatives throughout the world.

PALGRAVE MACMILLAN is the global academic imprint of the Palgrave
Macmillan division of St. Martin's Press, LLC and of Palgrave Macmillan Ltd.
Macmillan® is a registered trademark in the United States, United Kingdom
and other countries. Palgrave is a registered trademark in the European
Union and other countries.

ISBN-13: 978–1–4039–4763–5
ISBN-10: 1–4039–4763–5

This book is printed on paper suitable for recycling and made from fully
managed and sustained forest sources.

A catalogue record for this book is available from the British Library.

Library of Congress Cataloging-in-Publication Data
    Enron and world finance : a case study in ethics / edited by Paul H.
Dembinski ... [et al.].
      p. cm.
    Includes bibliographical references and index.
    ISBN 1–4039–4763–5
      1. Enron Corp.—Corrupt practices—Case studies. 2. Energy industries—
Corrupt practices—United States. 3. Corporations—Corrupt practices—United
States—Case studies. 4. Business ethics—United States—Case studies.
    5. Corporate governance—United States—Case studies. 6. Corporate culture—
United States—Case studies. I. Dembinski, Pawel H., 1955–
HD9502.U54E57367 2005
333.79'0973—dc22   2005051354

10 9 8 7 6 5 4 3 2 1
15 14 13 12 11 10 09 08 07 06

Printed and bound in Great Britain by
Antony Rowe Ltd, Chippenham and Eastbourne

Contents

List of Tables and Boxes

Tables

Boxes

Acknowledgements

The editors and publishers wish to thank the *Villanova Law Review* for permission to use Frank Partnoy's article, 'A Revisionist View of Enron and the Sudden Death of "May" '; the *Phi Kappa Phi Forum* for permission to use John R. Boatright's article, 'Ethics for a Post-Enron America'; and Andrew Cornford and the International Group of Twenty-Four on International Monetary Affairs, UNCTAD, for permission to use Andrew Cornford's paper, 'Enron and Internationally Agreed Principles for Corporate Governance and the Financial Sector'.

Every effort has been made to trace all copyright-holders, but if any have been inadvertently overlooked the publishers will be pleased to make the necessary arrangement at the first opportunity.

Notes on the Contributors

Henri-Claude de Bettignies holds the AVIVA Chair in Leadership and Responsibility, and is Professor of Asian Business and Comparative Management at INSEAD. Since 1988, he has had a joint appointment as Visiting Professor of International Business at Stanford University. He started and developed INSEAD's activities in Japan and the Asia Pacific region, which led in 1980 to the creation of the Euro-Asia Centre, and in 2000 to the creation of the INSEAD campus in Asia. He is currently engaged in the development of the Ethics initiative at INSEAD, and is pioneering a new approach (AVIRA) to enlighten business leaders. AVIRA encourages very senior executives to explore their responsibilities as leaders, and the responsibility of their organization, in an uncertain and fast-changing global environment. The programme enhances understanding of the complex interdependency between responsibility and decision-making and the implementation process, taking action at the top. H.-C. de Bettignies is on the Editorial Board of several journals, including *The Journal of Asian Business*, *The International Journal of Business Governance and Ethics*, *Finance & the Common Good/Bien Commun*. Among the books published under his name is *The Changing Business Environment in the Asia Pacific Region* (London: International Thomson Business, 1997). He has published more than sixty articles in business and professional journals.

Hans J. Blommestein is the Head of the Capital Markets Programme at the OECD, and the PricewaterhouseCoopers Professor of Finance at Tilburg University, The Netherlands. He has published widely on banking issues, the transformation of financial systems and financial institutions, new financial instruments, risk management, the impact of ageing populations and institutional investors on financial markets, the development of securities markets, ethics and finance, and public debt management.

John R. Boatright is the Raymond C. Baumhart, S.J., Professor of Business Ethics in the Graduate School of Business at Loyola University Chicago. He currently serves as the Executive Director of the Society for Business Ethics, and is a past president of the Society. He is the author of the books *Ethics and the Conduct of Business* (Upper Saddle River: Prentice Hall, 2003) and *Ethics in Finance* (Oxford: Blackwell Publishing, 2002). He received his PhD in Philosophy from the University of Chicago.

Jean-Michel Bonvin has a PhD in Sociology from the University Paris IV-Sorbonne, and is Professor of the Department of Sociology of the University of Geneva. His main fields of interest are the sociology of justice and social theory, the sociology of financial activities, employment and social protection. Among his books are *L'Organisation internationale du travail. Etude sur une agence productive de normes* (Paris: PUF, 1998) and *Gemeinwohl. Ein kritisches Plädoyer* (with G. Kohler and B. Sitter-Liver) (Fribourg: Academia Press, 2004). He also publishes extensively in leading national and international reviews on issues related to social justice and social theory.

Andrew Cornford had been for several years Senior Economic Adviser specialising in financial markets and financial services in the division of UNCTAD dealing with macroeconomics and finance, whose responsibilities included assistance to developing countries participating in negotiations in GATT/WTO. He is now Research Fellow for the Financial Markets Center, a non-profit institute providing research, policy development and education resources.

Paul H. Dembinski is a Professor at the University of Fribourg, where he teaches International Competition and Strategy. He is also the initiator and Director of the Foundation of the Observatoire de la Finance (*http://www.obsfin.ch*) and the founder and editor of the bilingual journal *Finance & the Common Good/Bien Commun*. A political scientist and economist by training, he has written a dozen books and some sixty scientific articles in the field of the internationalisation of enterprises, the globalisation of enterprises, competition, ethics and finance. His main books include *Financial Markets. Mission Impossible?* (Paris: FPH, 1993); *L'internationalisation des PME suisses à l'horizon de l'an 2000* (Geneva: Georg, 1994); *La privatisation en Europe de l'Est* (Paris: PUF, 1995); *Economie et Finance* (Berne: BPS, 1995); *Economic and Financial Globalization: What the Numbers Say* (New York/Geneva: United Nations, 2003); *Les PME suisses: profils et défis* (Geneva: Georg, 2004; also in German – Zurich: Rüegger Verlag, 2004).

John Dobson received a BSc in Economics from the University of Lancaster, in 1979, before coming to the USA to pursue graduate work at the University of South Carolina, where he earned a Master's degree in Economics in 1981, and a PhD in Finance in 1988. Since completing his PhD, he has become increasingly interested in business ethics, and in particular how the theory of ethics relates to financial side of business activity. He has published articles on ethics and finance in various academic journals, and written two books, both of which investigate the synthesis of finance and ethics. His current research focuses on the connections between psychology, finance theory and moral philosophy.

Edward Dommen, a specialist in economic ethics, is President of the Scientific Committee of the Geneva International Academic Network. His recent publications include *How Just Is the Market Economy?* (Geneva: World Council of Churches, 2003).

Robert G. Kennedy is a Professor in the Departments of Management and Catholic Studies at the University of St Thomas, Saint Paul, Minnesota. He earned his doctorate at the University of Notre Dame (USA). His areas of academic specialisation are professional ethics and the Christian social tradition. Recent papers include 'Wealth Creation within the Catholic Social Tradition', 'The Professionalization of Work' and 'The Practice of Just Compensation'.

Beth Krasna is an independent Board member of Vaud Cantonal Bank, Swiss Federal Institutes of Technology; Raymond Weil SA; and a former vice-chairman of the Swiss Railways. She has ten years' experience as a CEO in the turnaround of industrial companies (Valtronic, Secheron and Symalit), and prior to that ten years' experience in venture capital. She holds a MSc in Chemical Engineering from the Swiss Federal Institute of Technology in Zurich, and a MSc in Management from the Sloan School, Cambridge, USA.

Carole Lager has a PhD in Political Science from the University of Geneva. She is a scientific collaborator at the Observatoire de la Finance in Geneva and the editorial officer of the review *Finance & the Common Good/Bien Commun*. Her main research interests and areas of expertise focus on the European Union and on the socio-political aspects of money. Among her publications are: *La face cachée de l'euro* (Brussels: PIE-Peter Lang, in Press), 'L'euro, symbole d'identité européenne?' *Etudes internationales*, March 2005; *L'Europe en quête de ses symboles* (Berne: Peter Lang, 1995).

François-Marie Monnet is a holder of a Diploma of the Institute for Political Studies in Paris (1970) and of an Arts Degree of the Sorbonne in Paris (German language), he became the foreign correspondent of the French newspaper *Le Monde* in Canada before switching in 1976 to a banking career at Banque Nationale de Paris and subsequently Morgan Stanley & Co., where he rose to be Vice-president of Corporate Finance through several assignments in Paris, New York and London. He left London for Geneva in 1987 to head the Swiss capital markets unit of Crédit Commercial de France (now part of HSBC). In 1991, he created an independent bond broker, Bridport & Co., and six years later joined MultiPlus Finance, an independent financial adviser specialising in monitoring management mandates for a limited number of large investors. Elected in 1999 to chair the Swiss Bond Commission of the European Federation of Financial Analysts' Societies (EFFAS) and Secretary of the European Bond Commission in 2001; selected as member of the Swiss Stock Exchange Bond Index commission set up in 2004. Sits on the Board of Directors of the Sicav 'Dexia Ethique-Gestion Obligataire', created in April 2000 to respond to the needs of various institutional investors.

Frank Partnoy is a Professor of Law at the University of San Diego, where he teaches courses on corporations, corporate finance, deals, financial market regulation and white collar crime. He is the author of more than a dozen law review articles and book chapters on various topics in law and finance, and has written two books about financial markets: *Infectious Greed: How Deceit and Risk Corrupted the Financial Markets* (New York: Henry Holt & co., 2003) and *FIASCO: Blood in the Water on Wall Street* (New York: W.W. Norton & co. 1997). Prior to teaching, he was an attorney at Covington & Burling, and an investment banker at Morgan Stanley and CS First Boston. He is a graduate of Yale Law School.

Etienne Perrot is an economist specialising in the phenomena of economic rent and corruption, a Jesuit and editor of the Paris-based journals *Etvdes* and *Projet*. His most recent book is *L'argent* (Paris: Editions Salvator, 2002) and his most recently published article 'L'arma monetaria', *La Civiltà Cattolica*, 18 September 2004.

Catherine Sauviat is a senior economist at IRES (Institut de Recherches Economiques et Sociales, France). She has published numerous articles in academic journals and written chapters in collective books (notably on professional services). She is currently working on financial globalisation and its implications at macro and micro levels. She teaches International Economics in Service Industries at Paris-XIII Villetaneuse University.

Domingo Sugranyes Bickel graduated in economics from the University of Fribourg, Switzerland, in 1969. He is a member of the Executive Board of MAPFRE, a Spanish mutual insurance group with a publicly listed 'downstream holding' subsidiary; the group is the number one insurer in Spain and operates in thirty-eight countries, with a significant position in Latin America, has 19,000 employees and more than 25,000 agents. He has been involved since the 1970s in the work of UNIAPAC (the International Christian Union of Business Executives), of which he was General Secretary from 1974 to 1981, and President in 1997–2000.

Anthony Travis is a UK chartered accountant and former partner in PricewaterhouseCoopers, Geneva, and is responsible for auditing and regulatory issues at a number of Swiss-based international banking groups. His professional career has involved working on virtually every continent. He is a former chairman of the British–Swiss Chamber of Commerce in Geneva and for fifteen years was a founding board member of the Family Business Network, Lausanne. He is a member of the board of L'Observatoire de la Finance, Geneva.

List of Abbreviations

AC	Andersen Consulting
AICPA	American Institute of Certified Public Accountants
CalPERS	California Public Employees' Retirement System
CAO	Chief Accounting Officer
CEO	Chief Executive Officer
CFMA	Commodity Futures Modernization Act
CFO	Chief Financial Officer
CFTC	Commodity Futures Trading Commission
CLN	Credit-linked note
COO	Chief Operating Officer
CPA	Certified public accountant
CSR	Corporate social responsibility
EDF	Electricité de France
EIB	European Investment Bank
EMH	Efficient market hypothesis
EU	European Union
FAS	Financial Accounting Standard
FASB	Financial Accounting Standards Board
FERC	Federal Energy Regulatory Commission
GAAP	Generally Accepted Accounting Principles
GAO	General Accounting Office
IAIS	International Association of Insurance Supervisors
IAS	International Accounting Standards
IASB	International Accounting Standards Board
IASC	International Accounting Standards Committee
IASCF	International Accounting Standards Committee Foundation
IFAC	International Federation of Accountants
IFRS	International Financial Reporting Standards
IMF	International Monetary Fund
IOSCO	International Organization of Securities Commissions
IPO	Initial public offering
ISO	Independent System Operator
JEDI	Joint Energy Development Investments
LIFFE	London International Financial Futures Exchange
LLP	Limited liability partnership
MAS	Management Advisory Services
MBA	Master of Business Administration
MD&A	Management Discussion and Analysis

NGO	Non-governmental organisation
NPV	Net present value
NRSRO	Nationally Recognized Statistical Rating Organization
NYMEX	New York Mercantile Exchange
OECD	Organisation for Economic Co-operation and Development
OTC	Over-the-counter
PCAOB	Public Company Accounting Oversight Board
POB	Public Oversight Board
PRC	Performance Review Committee
PSG	Professional Standards Group
ROSCs	Reports on Standards and Codes
SEC	Securities and Exchange Commission
SFAS	Statement of Financial Accounting Standards
SOX	Sarbanes-Oxley Act
SPE	Special purpose entity
SPV	Special purpose vehicles
TNPC	The New Power Company
UBS	Union des Banques Suisses
VAR	Value at risk
VPP	Volumetric production payments
WTO	World Trade Organization

1

Overview of the Book

Andrew Cornford

This book ranges widely over the different aspects of corporate practice and governance, law and ethics involved in the Enron case, and of the policy responses to the recent corporate scandals in the USA and internationally. Broadly, they can be classified under the following headings:

- *Transactions and institutional structure.* Major subjects here are Enron's use of transactions such as derivatives and of institutions such as special purpose entities (SPE) to restrict the transparency of its operations. These practices have posed a major challenge to corporate governance.
- *Accounting and auditing.* This heading is closely related to the first, since the opaqueness of Enron's operations was reflected in its financial reports and the accounting firm, Arthur Andersen, also served as adviser and consultant regarding the design and conformity with regulations of many of its transactions.
- *Corporate governance.* High-quality accounting and auditing are necessary for good corporate governance, but other parties – such as the firm's Board of Directors its regulators, its banks and investors, credit rating agencies and investment analysts – all have essential roles here. These so-called 'gatekeepers' fell short in the performance of their duties in the Enron case. Failures under this heading have helped to shape recent reforms.
- *Corporate culture and ethics.* These dimensions of a firm overlap with corporate governance, since good corporate governance will not be achieved in the absence of an ethical corporate culture. The dividing line between corporate governance and corporate ethics is difficult to specify. Roughly, the first concerns major rules and norms related to a firm's management and operations, and the relations between the main parties, (including those external to the firm, that assure, or are significantly affected by, its functioning); and the second concerns features of a firm's organisation and functioning that are conducive to the observance of good corporate governance and ethical behaviour. Subjects under the

latter heading include not only the conduct of senior executives and other employees, but also business education and conceptualisation of the firm in management thought.

- *Ethical foundations (meta-ethics).* Not only corporate culture but also many other rules and norms governing business operations are related directly or indirectly to more fundamental values and moral principles. These are not a universal datum for different cultures and value systems, and the discussion in this book is inevitably highly selective.

The overview of the chapters that follow focuses on salient features of the contributions under these different headings, and on their mutual relations. It also points to questions that the contributions raise which merit, and will no doubt receive, more detailed consideration by others in the future.

Enron: origins, character and failure

Several of the chapters describe aspects of Enron's history and the collapse of Arthur Andersen. An overall account is to be found in Andrew Cornford's Chapter 2. This describes the use by Enron of transactions and institutional structures to manipulate the firm's financial reports and to avoid regulation. It documents the failings of Andersen, Enron's auditors, of the Board of Directors, of the other 'watchdogs' or 'gatekeepers' mentioned above, and of the firm's different regulators. The subject of Enron's corporate culture is broached through a review of its hiring practices and its unusually rigorous but ultimately counter-productive system of incentives and sanctions for its employees. This serves as an introduction to more detailed discussions in other contributions of particular aspects of Enron's operations and culture, as well as analogous features of other businesses in the contributions by the other authors.

Transactions and institutional structure

It is now a commonplace of financial engineering that its instruments can be used to get round regulations and other operational constraints, such as banks' credit limits to particular borrowers. Enron made extensive use of derivatives for these purposes, and perhaps more importantly to reduce the transparency of its financial reports. Derivatives are the linchpin of Frank Partnoy's review of Enron in Chapter 3, and are central to his critique of the regulatory response in the USA. He brings out the extent to which Enron became a derivatives firm whose main source of profits was its trading of these instruments.[1] SPEs played a subordinate role in Partnoy's view, providing institutional structures that enabled Enron to exploit fully the potential of derivatives. As a trading firm, Enron absolutely required an investment-grade rating from the credit-rating agencies. As its ability to avoid regulations applicable to debt financing, derivatives and transparency broke down in 2001, its rating was threatened and eventually its stock price collapsed. Crucial to this story is Partnoy's view that weaknesses in the transactional regulation of Enron's trading and position-taking, particularly in over-the-counter (OTC) as opposed to exchange-traded derivatives, provided the firm with the scope it needed, and that the regulatory oversight of Enron as a firm (which, as Cornford pointed out, was in any case not carried out to a reasonable standard) was no substitute. In his analysis of the Sarbanes-Oxley Act (SOX), Partnoy emphasises that firms' standards of transparency for derivatives and other off-balance-sheet risks have not properly been addressed in key rules for the Act's implementation. This means that they continue to have the possibility of using 'financial engineering as a kind of plastic surgery' to make themselves look better than they really are.[2]

François-Marie Monnet also devotes much attention in Chapter 4 to derivatives and their impact on transparency, and his graphic analogy is between Enron and '*l'escamoteur*', whose skill lies in diverting the attention of the audience from the hand or other place where the trick is performed. Monnet is also concerned with a more general issue raised by derivatives use, the growth in the financial system's dependence on tradable instruments, and the associated reduction in face-to-face relations between creditors or investors and those they finance. These developments have various consequences, such as the increased difficulty for analysts to identify firm's true exposures to financial risks and the continuous need for liquidity in the markets for the instruments of the new finance. The implications for business ethics of the greater anonymity now characteristic of relations between parties in financial markets are also discussed in contributions by other authors. Taken to an extreme, this trend could have consequences highlighted in the following quotation from an authoritative treatise on derivatives law:

> Banks may cease thinking of themselves as traditional bank lenders, in the sense of making loans funded primarily through deposits and incurring long-term credit risk ... Going a step further, the technology may now be in place for 'notional banks'. A notional bank would be an institution that is exposed to all the risks of a commercial bank which has deposits, loans, trading accounts and the like, with a difference: the notional bank will not take deposits and will not make (or arrange) loans. The risk and return profile of a traditional commercial bank would be replicated notionally, but would need to be supported by substantially less office space, personnel and capital. (Henderson, 2003, pp. 120–1)

Accounting and auditing

The transparency which is an essential part of models of corporate governance depends crucially on the satisfactory performance of accountants and auditors, as is emphasised by both Cornford and Partnoy. A number of issues bearing more specifically on this performance in the Enron case and other recent corporate scandals, as well as on the future of accountants and auditors, are taken up in the chapters by Catherine Sauviat (Chapter 8) and Anthony Travis (Chapter 9) and more peripherally by other contributors. Sauviat describes major features of the legal and institutional environment as well as of Andersen as an institution, which frame the firm's failings regarding Enron, while Travis focuses more on longer-term pressures in the practice of auditing and on accounting firms. These pressures underlie his views as to the shortcomings of reform initiatives so far.

Sauviat describes the sharp rise in the number of restatements of earnings in the USA from 1997 onwards, the conflicts of interest associated with the growing importance to accounting firms' earnings of non-auditing services, the limits on the legal liabilities of auditors in the USA introduced in 1995 and 1998, the length of audit tenures in major US firms, and shortcomings in accounting firms' systems of peer reviewing. She also focuses on aspects of Andersen that she regards as contributing to the firm's involvement in some other major auditing failures as well as the Enron case. From the point of view of business ethics, her reference to the emphasis in Andersen's in-house training on 'the one firm concept' is particularly interesting: this involved the drilling of staff in a single set of methodologies and types of specific knowledge, and tended to instil robotic approaches to problems.[3] From the point of view of the economics of Andersen's business, also very interesting is her description of the exclusive relationship with Enron of the firm's lead auditor in the Houston office, David Duncan, who did not deal with any other client. Sauviat also raises the political dimension of Andersen's indictment, linked in her view to the Bush Administration's need for a scapegoat to deflect public indignation. As Travis emphasises, this indictment was effectively Andersen's death-warrant because of the likelihood of a consequent suspension by the Securities and Exchange Commission (SEC) of Andersen's rights to practice – a situation of which those who decided to prosecute were fully aware. Andersen's demise followed the haemorrhage of its clients to other firms even before a 'guilty' verdict.

As a practising auditor, Travis believes that his profession is held to exacting legal standards that are becoming increasingly difficult to meet, to a significant extent because of the internationalisation of business – of both firms and their auditors. The increasing involvement of auditing firms in the provision of non-auditing services he views as being to a great extent a response to increasing downward competitive pressures on auditing fees[4] so that the issue of ensuring the adequacy of such fees may need to be revisited as part of the reforms now being undertaken in Europe as well as the USA in the aftermath of recent corporate scandals. Regarding problems raised by internationalisation, he points to the difficulty of achieving satisfactory cross-border co-operation in auditing in the face of different national rules.

In their discussion of the policy response in the USA to recent corporate scandals, Sauviat and Travis express different views as to the part that should be played by the public sector in the regulation of auditing. Sauviat accepts the direction of policy towards greater official involvement implicit in the creation by SOX of the Public Company Accounting Oversight Board (PCAOB), but would like to go further, supporting the selection of firms' auditors by a public agency financed by the contributions of audit clients. By contrast, Travis is wary of greater intrusion of the public sector into auditing, raising questions as to the possibility of breaches in the confidentiality of the auditing process and as to the liability of the government if audits are seen to carry some measure of official endorsement. Similar questions were raised in the debates in the USA at the time of the New Deal Acts of 1933–35 which reformed the securities business and accounting practice after the speculative excesses of the 1920s.[5]

In his observations on the way forward, Travis devotes more attention to the basic characteristics of accounting and auditing than to particular failures in recent corporate scandals. His discussion includes widespread illusions as to the exactitude and precision of financial statements and the need for greater flexibility in both the preparation of financial statements (which will thus be capable of accommodating new business practices) and in audit attestation standards; the debate over rules-based versus principles-based accounting (a subject also taken up by John Boatright in a later chapter) which Travis believes fails to pay sufficient attention to the inextricable links between the two approaches in accounting standards; and auditor liability, which currently serves as an impediment to the greater emphasis on judgement as opposed to rules.

In Chapter 11, Hans Blommestein approaches accounting and auditing failures through the theory of efficient financial markets in which market participants' use of reliable information plays an essential role. A business world characterised by rapid innovation has interacted with a moral climate of overweening individualism to undermine the observance of ethical standards, and thus the trust and integrity on which market efficiency depends. For their restoration, he would depend as far as possible on the price exacted by the financial markets themselves for unacceptable business conduct. However, he would also like to see speedier incorporation in accounting standards of new financial instruments, and the introduction of ethical audits to supplement traditional audits. Regarding the latter, some firms are already producing audits of this kind. However, if ethical audits were to become part of normal practice, further thought would need to be given to their contents, their target audiences, and the identity of those who would produce them.

Strengthening corporate governance

Corporate governance covers relations between a firm and the different parties that have an influence on its functioning or that are affected significantly by its operations. Reforms in response to recent corporate scandals have been directed at remedying weaknesses in the performance of management, Boards of Directors, and the other 'gatekeepers' listed above, including firms' auditors. Cornford's account of international initiatives focuses principally on the main set of international standards, the OECD Principles of Corporate Governance, whose flouting in the Enron case was particularly striking with respect to shareholder rights, disclosure and transparency, the performance of the Board of Directors, and abusive self-dealing. Cornford also notes the way in which the Enron case has highlighted difficulties of regulating conglomerate firms supplying goods and services subject to various different regulatory regimes. Regulatory failures here were evident principally at the national level, but cases can be envisaged in which the challenges to cross-border regulation and supervisory co-operation assume greater importance. Initiatives to deal with these problems are still in their infancy. And further progress will inevitably be gradual, not only because of the complexity of the issues involved and the limitations of existing forums for the formulation of international standards but also because of the difficulty of achieving a consensus for standards concerning subjects whose treatment in countries' company and insolvency law reflects different national histories.

In Chapter 10, Beth Krasna examines the requirements for successful performance of their role by a firm's Board of Directors in the light of the failure in the Enron case. These include both organisational issues and competences, and her discussion of the fiduciary failures of Enron's directors concerns a subject where corporate governance overlaps corporate ethics and culture. She also raises the important but sometimes overlooked question of the monitoring of the Board's own performance, which she would entrust to evaluations by the Board itself.

Several authors take up different aspects of SOX, the most important national reform adopted in response to recent scandals. As already noted, Partnoy provides a detailed explanation of his view that the Act will not redress the weaknesses in the regulation of derivatives, which he views as the central feature of the Enron case. And Travis raises the Act's failure to address in a satisfactory manner underlying problems of accounting and auditing. SOX relies to a significant extent on criminal penalties for senior managements' failures to fulfil their responsibilities. Such reliance does not figure prominently in the contributions to this book, whose authors would clearly prefer to rely primarily on changes in incentives and in business culture, better rules and standards, and improvements in observance of them. SOX, however, builds on a regime in the USA in which historically criminal punishment for business misdeeds has played an especially important role. Both the Enron case and other recent corporate scandals have been followed by prosecutions of major participants and substantial fines in cases already resolved (see Box 1.1).

Box 1.1   Selected legal proceedings connected to the Enron case[6]

As of early 2005, charges had been brought against thirty-three people or firms connected to the Enron case:

- fifteen of these people had pleaded guilty;
- five people and one firm had been convicted;
- one person had been acquitted; and
- eleven people had been charged, of whom eight were awaiting trial and three (British bankers) were fighting extradition.

Among these, a number are of particular interest because of their prominent roles in events that have been the subject of special attention in commentary on the Enron case.

Of Enron's senior managers, Kenneth Lay, Jeffrey Skilling and Richard Causey were awaiting trial. Lay was Chief Executive Officer (CEO) and Chairman of the Board of Directors of Enron from its formation in 1986 until February 2001, when he stepped down as CEO but continued as Chairman. On the resignation of Skilling in August 2001, he resumed his position as CEO. Skilling was either a consultant to or an employee of Enron from the late 1980s until December 2001. First hired in 1990, he held various management positions until being appointed President and Chief Operating Officer (COO) in 1997. In February 2001, he became President and CEO, positions from which he resigned in August 2001. Causey was a certified public accountant who joined Enron from Arthur Andersen in 1991 and became the firm's Chief Accounting Officer (CAO) in 1998.

- Lay, Skilling and Causey have all been indicted on charges related to the manipulation of the firm's reported financial results, and making false and misleading statements about Enron's financial performance and results;
- Causey also faces charges of money laundering (participation in financial transactions involving the proceeds of unlawful activity);
- Skilling and Causey also face charges of insider trading in Enrons stock; and
- Lay also faces charges of bank fraud in the form of misrepresentations to banks in connection with borrowing to finance securities operations.

Other senior Enron managers who have pleaded guilty under plea agreements include Andrew Fastow, Ben Glisan, Michael Kopper and David Delainey. Fastow was Enron's Chief Financial Officer (CFO) during most of 1998–2001, having previously served as a Managing Director. Glisan was Treasurer of Enron from the spring of 2000 until October 2001. Kopper was a financial officer of Enron from 1994 until July 2001. From the beginning of 2000 until July 2001 he was involved in the management of one of the SPEs controlled by Enron and used for transactions designed to manipulate its financial statements. On his resignation from Enron he bought Fastow's interest in this SPE. Delainey was a former head of two large Enron divisions, Enron North America and Enron Energy Services.

- Fastow pleaded guilty to charges related to his involvement in the manipulation of Enron's financial statements through transactions with SPEs under his control, and to self-enrichment in violation of his duties to Enron's shareholders through transactions with such SPEs. Fastow's guilty plea was conditioned upon that of his wife, Lea Fastow, to tax fraud in connection with profits received by the Fastow family from an SPE controlled by Enron (which led to a one-year prison sentence).

- Kopper pleaded guilty to charges related to transactions arising out of his involvement in the SPE controlled by Enron (see above).
- Glisan pleaded guilty to involvement in the creation and use of an SPE for illegal transactions intended to manipulate Enron's financial statements, and was sentenced to a prison term of up to five years.
- Delainey pleaded guilty to charges that he used profits from Enron's energy trading to conceal losses in other activities that the firm was promoting to investors, and that he engaged in insider trading in the firm's stock.

With the exception of Glisan and Lea Fastow, those who have pleaded guilty are still at the time of writing awaiting sentencing. Such sentences generally include a fine and forfeiture of the proceeds of illegal acts of which the accused are found quilty or plead guilty. The latter sums can be large. For example, Andrew Fastow forfeited approximately US$24 million, and in the case of Skilling the prosecution is seeking more than US$50 million. In the case of Lay, forfeitures sought include 'a sum of money equal to the amount of the proceeds obtained as a result of the conspiracy, and securities and wire fraud offenses, for which the defendants [Skilling and Causey as well as Lay] are jointly and severally liable', an amount for which no estimate is given but which will also be large.

Daniel Bayly, James Brown, William Fuhs, and Robert Furst, bankers from Merrill Lynch, and Daniel Boyle, an Enron Vice-President in Global Finance, were found guilty of involvement in parking Enron's interest in some Nigerian barges mounted with electricity generators which Enron had been planning to sell to another investor in a deal that fell through. The parking enabled Enron to record US$12 million in earnings and US$28 million in cash flow required to meet the firm's 1999 targets. Merrill Lynch participated in this transaction on the basis of a secret oral promise that within six months it would be able to sell its interest at a profit – in the event to an SPE controlled by Enron.

Arthur Andersen, auditor and provider of consultancy services to Enron, was convicted in a June 2002 jury trial of the single felony count of obstruction of justice by impeding the government's investigation of Enron. The fine imposed was less damaging than the obstruction-of-justice indictment itself in mid-March 2002, which led to the haemorrhaging of Andersen's client list. David Duncan, the Andersen partner in Houston in charge of the firm's Enron account, had earlier, in April 2002, pleaded guilty to a charge of obstruction of justice and agreed to co-operate in the case against Andersen. The Supreme Court has agreed to hear Andersen's appeal, in which a key issue is likely to be whether the destruction of documents before the receipt of a subpoena from the SEC provided valid grounds for the firm's conviction.

Corporate culture and incentive systems

In a recent article, John Kay looked at different aspects of the question of whether there is such a thing as corporate personality:[7]

> Many economists and business people think this anthropomorphisation of the company is sentimental tosh. A company is a nexus of contracts defined by its charter or articles of association. Lawyers have tried to resolve the issue in a different way. They search for a 'directing mind', whose thoughts and desires can be detected in everything the organisation does ... But neither the nexus of contracts nor the directing mind describes the reality of modern corporate life. If a business was no more than a nexus of contracts, you could establish an equally successful business by reproducing the nexus of contracts. You cannot because an effective organisation relies on the social context surrounding its nexus of contracts ... So in both good and bad companies, corporate personality is a commercial reality, not just a legal construct. And if the company has its own distinctive character, like an individual, that refutes the claim that the company is necessarily amoral, that it has no ethics only interests ... Companies have no immortal soul but, like human beings, they live and die. While they live, they prosper by the attributes of their personality.

Kay's examples of psychopathic companies include Enron and Arthur Andersen. And corporate culture and ethics are covered in several of the chapters in this volume. Character, especially that of business leaders, is a recurring theme of the contributors – see, for example, the remarks of Boatright (Chapter 15), Henri-Claude de Bettignies (Chapter 14), John Dobson (Chapter 12), and Robert Kennedy (Chapter 13). This character in turn needs to be harnessed to good goals. Here the focus of much of the authors' attention is the shortcomings of firms' goals, recently all too evident in conduct such as the maximisation of short-term shareholder value. Boatright and Kennedy both underline failures involving the fiduciary duty of firms' managers in recent scandals. Kennedy would like to see a movement towards the observance of a genuine professional ethic by the managers and specialised workers upon whom the modern corporation depends. Part of the responsibility for promoting such an ethic would devolve upon business schools. For de Bettignies, the guiding principle of corporate ethics should be acknowledgement of the corporation as society's most important value-creation mechanism, this term being understood to entail contributions transcending shareholder value. The two ideas are perhaps nicely encapsulated in Peter Drucker's statement that 'it is to supply the consumer that society entrusts wealth-producing resources to the business enterprise' which, as a commentator notes, is intended not so much as a working assumption as a moral starting-point for his thought (Beatty, 1998, p. 106).

In his extended discussion of the contents of business education Dobson pays considerable attention to the underlying model of the firm used in teaching. The reductionist concept of a firm as a nexus of contracts mentioned in Kay's article and excessive emphasis on narrow financial rationality receive special criticism. In his view, these lead too easily to a perspective according to which observance of ethical guidelines is a constraint that should be circumvented or ignored as far as possible, so that the contribution of such observance to healthy internal working relations and the long-term prospects of the firm has little value as such. But how far will those responsible for education in business schools be prepared to take such criticism in the present intellectual climate? The emphasis on narrow financial rationality is, after all, in accord with the model of the economically rational person that has been an essential element of mainstream postwar economic theory. Ability to use this model in both theoretical and empirical work is widely regarded within academy as providing a more-or-less objective criterion for the evaluation of professional competence, and thus plays an important part in hiring and promotion in economics faculties and business schools.

Primarily on the basis of his first-hand experience of insurance in Latin America, Domingo Sugranyes Bickel views in Chapter 7 improvements in corporate culture, enhanced transparency and better corporate governance, and a more successful and humane process of economic development as recently being subject to mutually reinforcing trends. Sugranyes see progress in transparency and corporate governance as being linked to greater financial openness – for example, in the form of opening stock markets to external investors. Questions raised by his optimism relate to a generalisation from what is only one stage in a much longer-term process. In emerging-market countries there are generally several basic and often almost self-evident reforms to both financial markets and corporate governance which can improve economic performance and render economies less vulnerable to financial instability and crisis. But more advanced financial sectors can be expected to bring a new set of problems linked to the new kinds of transactional and organisational complexity that usually accompany them (and that are exemplified to an extreme degree by Enron). For example, a number of legal cases involving firms in developed and emerging-market countries as counter-parties indicate that problems already posed by derivatives in the former – their use to avoid financial regulation, misrepresentation and abuse of fiduciary responsibilities – are becoming more common in the latter.[8]

Economic incentives unavoidably have a key role in a firm's culture. This role involves a two-way process, since not only does this culture reflect a firm's system of incentives but it is itself also a major influence on the design of the system. Many of the contributors emphasise the incentives to disinformation when management's remuneration is linked closely to the price of the firm's stock. Broader issues related to the remuneration of top management are now also looming larger in public debate. One topic here with ethical implications is the recent rapid increase in the gap between this remuneration and that of other categories of a firm's employees, a tendency that has been particularly marked in the USA, but which has begun to spread to other countries. This is a subject not covered directly in the contributions here that deal with firms' ethics, but the connection between exceptionally high levels of remuneration for top management and the maximisation of shareholder value as a firm's overriding goal is increasingly difficult to avoid as part of corporate governance, even though it does not figure in the policy initiatives discussed above – no doubt owing the divergence of norms in different countries and the likelihood of political resistance to any attempt to set principles in this area internationally.

Ethical foundations

Corporate culture and ethics opens up questions concerning the deeper foundations that underlie its values and rules, and help to provide their meta-ethical legitimacy. Some might argue that, because of inevitable differences regarding the subject, probing such philosophical frameworks serves no useful purpose in discussions of corporate ethics and culture. As long as the values and rules are well established, capable of adaptation as necessary, and supported by 'durable public opinion', their use requires no further justification.[9] However, most people probably expect something more than this, and in view of the extent to which observed differences in principles of good corporate governance and in good business practices are linked to differences in systems of moral principles, they would appear to be justified in this expectation. Contributors to this volume raise a number of points that belong to the domain of the meta-ethical.

Perceived connections between moral principles and good business practice are manifold and complex. One set of problems here results from variations in these principles among places and over time. Such problems become important as soon as discussion of the implications of Enron for principles of corporate governance and corporate ethics transcends a purely US context.

Other problems concern the indirect or often tenuous relationship of moral principles to many business rules and behavioural norms. In most cultures there is some convergence between ethical principles, legal rules, and norms. Murder, robbery and – in business – the more egregious forms of opportunistic conduct and self-dealing are not only regarded as immoral but also are illegal. But the convergence is less apparent regarding several other subjects. Think, for example, of mergers and acquisitions and anti-trust, insider trading on securities markets, prudential rules for banks and investment firms, accounting standards, and the admissibility of derivatives transactions. Much of the breakdown of corporate ethics and governance in the Enron case involves such subjects as these. Indeed, Partnoy, writing about Enron in

2003 has even characterised much of Enron's behaviour as 'alegal' rather than 'illegal', in that it involved transactions increasingly accepted by many of Enron's peers, and for which regulations were often still hazy (Partnoy, 2003, p. 298).

The rules and norms of business can be characterised as a tissue with features reflecting many different determinants such as best and customary practice, compatibility with the rest of a country's legal framework, more general social norms, accommodation of innovation of different kinds, and prerequisites for fair dealing between different participating parties. As noted above, only some of these rules and norms have a close connection to moral principles. The justification for many others is the greater good of society because of their place in a larger system that contributes to enabling and facilitating good management and the interactions between economic agents upon which economic activity and material welfare depend. In some cases, moral principles usefully supplement or reinforce such rules and norms, and help to foster their observance. But their very generality often mean that they are an inappropriate starting-point for detailed prescription, as do the ambivalence and socially counter-productive nature of their implications for conduct in certain situations.[10] Moreover, basing business rules and norms on moral principles would often render them less adaptable, and thus less responsive to changes in the situations with which they are designed to deal.

But while too close and too comprehensive connections between business rules and norms, on the one hand, and moral principles on the other are neither feasible nor desirable, at a certain remove the influence of the latter is still powerful. A key concept here is fair dealing (even though historically and in different cultures there has been considerable variation in what is accepted as 'fair'). Essential to fair dealing is trust, and trust in turn is important in enhancing the quality of economic agents' mutual relations and thus also of business practices.

Etienne Perrot acknowledges in Chapter 5 that different possible ethical principles and frameworks can be applied to participants in the Enron case and serve as pointers to improved standards for business conduct. These include the attribution of special importance to trust and to frameworks incorporating group conventions and solidarity. The latter he views as being an inadequate source of improved standards because of the precariousness of the behavioural equilibrium thus achieved and to the probability of consequent over-emphasis on procedure rather than substance and the consequences of actions. He would rather base the ethical framework for good business practice in what he calls the ethics of individual conviction. This in turn should incorporate the capacity to perceive the different dimensions of situations (their complexity) and different possible approaches to them as well as an understanding of the interests of and the effects of actions on others (not only those belonging to one's own group or culture but also broader communities). If such a framework is to become effective, the reminding people of ethical principles on its own will not be sufficient. A deeper exercise on the self will be required – what Perrot calls 'training in self-esteem'.

In Chapter 6, Edward Dommen tackles issues raised by the increased anonymity of much business life (which is also a concern of Monnet with regard to many of the products of financial innovation) and the trust essential to good practice. For this purpose he deploys a taxonomy of different meanings of anonymity, showing the ways in which it can have positive as well as negative effects. Drawing on his knowledge of Quaker history, he points to the way in which the shared values of a community can guarantee trust and the associated sense of fairness in business activity, obviously first and foremost among the community's own members but also to varying degrees among those drawn into its orbit as the members' counter-parties.

This general point has ample support from other evidence. In his fascinating history of derivatives, beginning with their origins in the second millenium BC, Edward Swan, a pioneer practitioner of derivatives law, documents the analogous role played at various times by other communities and communal institutions in ensuring fair dealing (Swan, 2000, sections 2.4.1, 2.4.3, 4.6.1). These have included temples as clearing houses for commodity trading and the institution of a *karu* or community of foreign merchants beyond the gates of cities in ancient Mesopotamia, separate merchant communities called *pandokien* in Ptolemaic Egypt, and the self-governing *fondachi* serving similar purposes in Italian mercantile cities of the Middle Ages. However, as Dommen notes, communitarianism provides only a partial basis for an ethical framework of business life, where distance has become an unavoidable characteristic of both transactions and other interactions among different parties, including the weakest and most disadvantaged, who are clearly a part of the ethics of individual conviction advocated by Perrot.

Variation in moral frameworks for business ethics helps to explain the complexity of the task of reaching international consensus on the principles of corporate governance and ethics needed for global business and finance, and the slowness with which the process moves forward. Different ethical and religious beliefs, as well as different histories and legal systems, are inputs to this process. Achieving acceptability for the results of such a consensus is a prerequisite for its effectiveness, and slow progress is surely a price worth paying.

Notes

1 This point is made still more starkly in Partnoy's testimony to the United States Senate in early 2002, where he shows from an analysis of the consolidated income statement of Enron and its subsidiaries for 1998–2000 that its positive operating income was largely made up of profits from its derivatives business. See Testimony

of Frank Partnoy, 'Hearings before the United States Senate Committee on Governmental Affairs', 24 January 2002, pp. 27–9.

2   The phrase is from Partnoy's testimony, ibid., p. 11.

3   A more detailed description of these features of Andersen's culture can be found in the book by a former employee (Toffler and Reingold, 2003).

4   A report by Arthur Young on the intensification of competition among accounting firms from the late 1970s onwards (quoted in Berenson, 2004, p. 114) brings out graphically the consequences of Travis's point, as follows: 'No longer do accountants compete solely on the strength of their capabilities. Today, every accounting firm ... competes with every other accounting firm in its market area for clients present and future, for attention, for exposure. Accounting firms compete with each other presentation for presentation, press release for press release, speech for speech, seminar for seminar, and increasingly, ad for ad.'

5   These debates are usefully summarised in Flegm (1984).

6   For the summary totals see *Houston Chronicle*, 27 January 2005. The principal sources consulted for individuals mentioned were the superseding indictment of Lay, Skilling and Causey of 7 July 2004; the superseding indictment of Bayly, Boyle, Brown, Fuhs and Furst of 14 October 2003; the indictment of Fastow of 31 October 2002; the indictment of Arthur Andersen of 7 March 2002; the SEC complaint against Kopper of August 2002; the plea agreements of the Fastows of 14 January 2004; the plea agreement of Glisan of September 2003; and the plea agreement of Duncan of 10 April 2002. Other sources used were 'Andersen the fallout', *Financial Times*, 17 June 2002; 'Skilling indictment', *Financial Times*, 20 February 2004; J. Chaffin, 'Enron executive expected to plead guilty', *Financial Times*, 31 October 2003 (on Delainey); 'L'ancien numéro deux d'Enron inculpé par la justice américaine', *Le Monde*, 21 February 2004 (on Skilling); 'Le premier procès pénal d'anciens dirigeants d'Enron débute à Houston, au Texas', *Le Monde*, 22 September 2004 (on the Merrill Lynch bankers, Boyle and Fastow); K. Scannell and J. Weil, 'Supreme Court to hear Andersen's appeal of conviction', *The Wall Street Journal*, 10 January 2005; R. F. Duska and B. S. Duska, 'Enron, Arthur Andersen, and the financial markets: a chronology of *Wall Street Journal* articles', *Accounting Ethics* (Oxford: Blackwell, 2003); Toffler and Reingold (2003), ch. 9.

7   J. Kay, 'Corporate character is not just a legal construct', *Financial Times*, 7 December 2004.

8   See, for example, '*Bankers Trust International* v. *PT Dharmala Sakti Sejahtera*' (a case involving an Indonesian entity in 1994), '*Lehman Brothers Commercial Corp and Lehman Brothers Special Financing Inc* v. *Minmetals International Non-Ferrous Metals Trading Co.*' (a case involving a Chinese entity in 2000), and '*Korea Life Insurance Company* v. *Morgan Guaranty Trust Company of New York*' (2003). Because of their complexity, the merits of these cases are hard to evaluate, but noteworthy features were allegations of misrepresentation and breaches of fiduciary. In '*Korea Life*' the transactions were structured with the intention of avoiding supervisory scrutiny, and the multi-firm institutional arrangements included SPEs in Malaysia and the Channel Islands.

9   The phrase 'durable public opinion' is that of Richard Posner (1999) who uses it in the different but analogous context of the philosophical framework underpinning the legitimacy of law.

10 S. Shavell, to whom the discussion here of relations between law and morality owes much, exemplifies this point with certain breaches of contract (Shavell, 2004, p. 630).

References

Beatty, J. (1998) *The World According to Peter Drucker: The Life and Work of the World's Greatest Management Thinker* (London: Orion Business Books).

Berenson, A. (2004) *The Number: How the Drive for Quarterly Earnings Corrupted Wall Street and Corporate America* (New York: Random House).

Flegm, E. H. (1984) *Accounting: How to Meet the Challenges of Relevance and Regulation* (New York: John Wiley).

Henderson, S. K. (2003) *Henderson on Derivatives* (London: Lexis/Nexis).

Partnoy, F. (2003) *Infectious Greed: How Deceit and Risk Corrupted the Financial Markets* (New York: Times Books).

Posner, R. A. (1999) *The Problematics of Moral and Legal Theory* (Cambridge, Mass.: Belknap Press of Harvard University Press).

Shavell, S. (2004) *Foundations of Economic Analysis of Law* (Cambridge, Mass.: Belknap Press of Harvard University Press).

Swan, E. J. (2000) *Building the Global Market: 4000 Year History of Derivatives* (The Hague: Kluwer Law International).

Toffler, B. L. and J. Reingold (2003), *Financial Accounting: Ambition, Greed, and the Fall of Arthur Andersen* (New York: Broadway Books).

Part 1
Enron: Origins, Character and Failure

2
Enron and Internationally Agreed Principles for Corporate Governance and the Financial Sector[1]

Andrew Cornford[2]

Introduction

Recent corporate scandals in the USA and elsewhere have led to a wide-ranging re-examination of standards for corporate governance with repercussions that extend also to financial regulation. The key standards for financial systems whose application is a major component of current initiatives to strengthen the so-called international financial architecture include three that are pertinent to this re-examination, and will themselves be affected by the policy response: the Organisation for Economic Co-operation and Development (OECD) Principles of Corporate Governance, and the initiatives concerning International Financial Reporting Standards (IFRS) (see Box 2.1) and International Standards on Auditing (see Box 2.2).

This chapter gives an account of the breakdown of corporate governance in the most baroque of recent scandals, that involving the collapse of Enron, which involved not only conflicts with standards for good corporate governance but also unusually extensive use of sophisticated techniques and transactions to manipulate the firm's financial reports. This account serves as a backdrop to a discussion of policy initiatives in the aftermath of Enron's collapse, and of implications for the development and reform of corporate governance in emerging-market and other developing countries. This is a vast area and the discussion here is limited largely to the general principles of corporate governance and pertinent parts of financial regulation. The remarks on auditing and accounting are restricted to topics closely related to these subjects in the Enron case, and to the relationship of progress in the elaboration of internationally agreed principles under these two headings to that on standards for corporate governance, and do not address more specialised issues under these two headings.

Box 2.1   International Financial Reporting Standards (IFRS)

IFRS cover requirements for recognition, measurement, presentation and disclosure for transactions and events that are important in general-purpose financial statements. They may also set out such requirements for transactions and events that arise mainly in specific industries or sectors. This initiative is carried out under the auspices of the International Accounting Standards Committee Foundation (IASCF), an organisation established in 2000. Since 2001, the International Accounting Standards Board (IASB), whose members are appointed by the Trustees of the IASCF, has had the responsibility of developing, in the public interest, a single set of high-quality, global accounting standards that require transparent and comparable information in general-purpose financial statements, co-operating for this purpose with national accounting standard-setters and also being advised and otherwise assisted in its work by other bodies operating under the auspices of the IASCF. At its inception, the IASB adopted the then existing body of International Accounting Standards (IAS) issued by its predecessor, the Board of the International Accounting Standards Committee (IASC).

Box 2.2   International Standards on Auditing

International Standards on Auditing are issued by the International Federation of Accountants (IFAC), a body established in 1977 to promulgate international standards in auditing and closely related subjects, and which nominates five of the nineteen Trustees of the IASCF. The standards of IFAC are directed at international harmonisation of external auditing (in areas such as auditors' responsibilities, audit planning, assessment of internal controls, audit evidence, using the work of other auditors or experts, and audit conclusions and reporting), a task complicated by variations in countries' company law with respect to such subjects as qualifications, the respective authority of the profession and the government, and the degree of local control in countries with federal systems.

A sketch of Enron

At the time of its filing for bankruptcy in December 2001, the complex industrial structure of Enron was fully understood by few outsiders, and more complete information as to the true levels of its assets, liabilities and off-balance-sheet positions was still unfolding. An idea of the firm's complexity can be obtained from such features as its 2,800 offshore units and the 54 pages required to list people and companies owed money by Enron. This was a far cry from the firm which, in the 1980s, specialized in the provision of natural gas pipelines and related services. But from these origins Enron expanded relentlessly into trading activities in 1,800 products or contracts and thirteen currencies (which included bandwidth, pulp and paper, and contracts such as weather and credit derivatives), the great majority of which were not subject to the regulatory oversight of the United States Commodity Futures Trading Commission (CFTC). It was in connection with expansion into trading that Enron engaged in increasingly aggressive and creative accounting, and in other transactions and techniques described in more detail below.

Part of the motivation behind Enron's conduct was similar to that of many other firms in the 1990s, deriving from the links between stock prices and executives' remuneration and wealth, above all through stock options. But in Enron's case, the factor of its credit rating was also crucial. The firm's rapid expansion required access to large amounts of financing; and as its involvement in trading activities grew, so did the importance of its credit rating, since this determined its financing costs – and crucially, the willingness of its counter-parties to trade with it. A favourable earnings picture and the avoidance of excessive leverage on Enron's balance sheet were perceived by its management as being essential to maintain the firm's credit rating.

The means used to achieve these objectives involved extraordinary departures from transparency, which affected the firm's relations with investors and creditors, its own Board of Directors (and thus an important part of its internal control), and other stakeholders of the corporation. The firm's use of special purpose entities (SPE) was part and parcel of the practices employed to manipulate the firm's earnings figures and balance sheet, as was recourse to hedging and the use of derivatives in conflict with reporting rules or business logic (or both). Many of the transactions associated with this manipulation were also associated with self-dealing by Enron executives, leading to substantial personal enrichment.

Accounting and transactional techniques used by Enron

Seven accounting and transactional techniques were used extensively by Enron and provide an idea of the ways in which the firm pushed against or overstepped the limits imposed by regulation.[3] Not all of Enron's use of these techniques was in conflict with accepted accounting rules and practice; nevertheless, a great deal of what has been classified as questionable or improper in investigations since the firm's bankruptcy belongs under these seven headings.[4]

Financial Accounting Standards (FAS) 140 transactions

FAS 140 governs the sale of financial assets and specifies the conditions that must be fulfilled if their transfer is to be considered a sale. FAS 140 transactions were used by Enron to monetize liquid assets on (and thus remove them from) its balance sheet, while in fact retaining control over them. This was achieved by the sale of the assets through a number of steps to an SPE not consolidated in its financial statements. The resources of the SPE consisted of borrowings and equity in the proportions of 97 per cent and 3 per cent, respectively. Enron's continuing control over the assets (and thus also its continuing assumption of financial obligations linked to them) was typically achieved by a Total Return Swap, a credit derivative through which Enron retained most of the economic benefits and risks of ownership of the assets and committed itself to meeting the costs of the SPE's borrowings. Thus transactions classified as sales were closer to financing and part of Enron's debt. Enron also recognised as income the difference between the cash proceeds of the 'sale' and the carrying value of the assets in question.

Tax transactions

These transactions typically boosted reported income through the creation of future tax deductions, sometimes several years hence, and the recording in the current period of the projected benefits associated with them.

Non-economic hedges with SPE and other related parties

Under this technique, Enron hedged the value of investments marked to market (see below) by entering into derivative contracts with counter-parties related to itself. The acceptability of a hedge from the point of view of accounting rules or business logic turns on the correlation between two mutually offsetting positions, or on the existence of an unrelated party prepared to assume through a contract part or all of the economic risk of the position being hedged. These conditions are not fulfilled if one of the counter-parties to the contract is closely related to the firm, or if the value of the two positions depend on the same underlying assets. These conditions were thus not fulfilled for a number of important hedges entered into by Enron since, first, the counter-parties to the hedges were entities in which Enron employees participated and over which they exercised managerial control; and, second, the resources of these entities were largely Enron stock, forward contracts to purchase such stock, and warrants on the stocks of firms in which Enron had controlling investments.

Share trust transactions

Under this technique, Enron established entities for the purpose of removing assets and liabilities from its balance sheet. One of the entities (the issuer) issued securities of which the proceeds were received by another entity (the holding entity) that also held assets contributed by Enron itself. The assets of the holding entity were then used to meet obligations on the issuer's securities and to purchase assets from Enron or repay its debt. The capacity of the issuer to meet its obligations was effectively guaranteed by Enron, which also retained control over, and the benefits of, the holding entity's assets. This rendered questionable the moving of assets and liabilities from Enron's consolidated balance sheet by use of this technique.

Minority interests

This technique enabled Enron to raise money that was classified on its balance sheet as 'minority interests', a category of financing treated by credit rating agencies as hybrid equity rather than debt. A majority-owned subsidiary was established by Enron with a minority interest being taken by another entity, financed by debt and equity in the proportions of 97 per cent and 3 per cent, respectively. The minority shareholder in the subsidiary was not consolidated with Enron for accounting purposes, and the financing for Enron from this source was not counted as debt, with the result that key credit ratios of the firm were improved.

Prepays

The technique of prepaid swaps was used by Enron to disguise the nature of financial transactions between the firm and major banks. In prepays, one counter-party is paid a fixed sum in advance in return for a stream of future payments (the receipts and payments in this case being linked to the oil price and being made partly through an offshore conduit SPE). The cash flows of the prepay mimic those of a loan, but as long as the swap meets certain conditions, now judged not to have been met in Enron's case, the transaction can be accounted for as a hedge (see Box 2.3). As such, prepays can boost operating cash flows, while also keeping down debt.

Box 2.3   Prepays precedents and applicable law

Major features of prepays in the Enron case resemble those of 'pre-export financing' used in certain international trade transactions. In a model of 'pre-export financing', simplified for the purpose of exposition, a bank lends to a SPE which uses the money to prepay a producer of a commodity under a forward contract and enters into another contract to sell the commodity to a buyer at the future spot price. The SPE also enters into a commodity swap with a dealer, under which the proceeds of the sale of the commodity are converted into a stream of payments matching those on the interest and principal of the loan. Such financing may be used when the producer is restricted in its borrowing possibilities, and is attractive to the counter-parties through reducing market and credit risks associated with the transaction. The question of whether Enron's prepays were forward purchase contracts or disguised loans became an issue in a court case involving JPMorgan Chase and insurance companies that had issued to SPEs surety bonds guaranteeing the obligations of Enron entities under forward purchase contracts for oil and natural gas. The insurance companies claimed that they had been fraudulently committed to providing guarantees on transactions that were loans rather than bona fide forward purchase contracts, the significance of the distinction being that, under the law of New York, the relevant jurisdiction, insurance companies are not permitted to guarantee loans. Under a settlement reached during the trial the insurance companies agreed to pay US$600 million of the claim that exceeded US$1 billion. As an authority on the law of derivatives succinctly commented, 'this case is unlikely to improve the reputation of at least certain insurers as credit enhancers in the structured finance markets, nor to increase the public's admiration for the ingenuity of the arrangers of structured financings' (Henderson, 2003, sections 8.7, 10.8).

Mark-to-market/mark-to-model accounting

Mark-to-market accounting, which enabled Enron to value its longer-term and some of its more complex contracts, involves the revaluation of assets on a regular basis. Such accounting can be relatively straightforward – for example, when unambiguous market prices are available for the assets and liabilities in question. But it is less so when applied to non-standardised, over-the-counter (OTC) transactions and to complex, long-term contracts. In the latter case, recourse is typically had to models for valuation (a process known as mark-to-model), which depend on assumptions about an inherently uncertain future and provide scope for judgement. Such accounting can be (and in Enron's case *was*) a major generator of reported earnings. However, it can be the source of divergences between reported earnings and cash flow, a problem Enron addressed by combining mark-to-market accounting with techniques for monetising assets, some of which are part of other transactions already described.

Enron's court-appointed bankruptcy examiner has made estimates of the impact of these techniques other than mark-to-market accounting on Enron's financial statements for 2000, the last year for which Enron issued an audited annual financial statement, as well as on components of Enron's key credit ratios and on the key credit ratios themselves for 31 December 2000. These are shown in Tables 2.1 and 2.2, and the results are frequently dramatic. Note, in particular, the more than doubling of Enron's debt and the drastic falls in net income and in funds flow from operations.

Yet even these estimates understate the magnitude of the divergence between Enron's reported debt and a truer picture just before its insolvency. In its filing for the third quarter of 2001, Enron's debt reported according to Generally Accepted Accounting Principles (GAAP) was US$12.97 billion. But in a presentation to bankers on the day on which this figure was released, Enron's own executives acknowledged that this did not take into account off-balance-sheet obligations of US$25.116 billion – US$14 billion of which were incurred through structured-finance transactions involving SPEs – so that a truer figure for its debt was US$38.094 billion.[5]

Enron's financial reports

Coverage of many of Enron's operations in its financial returns to the Securities and Exchange Commission (SEC) and in its proxy statements to shareholders was frequently skimpy. Commenting on coverage of Enron's related-party transactions, the Powers Committee (appointed by Enron's Board to look into the firm's accounting in October 2001) concluded that 'while it has been widely reported that the related-party transactions ... involved "secret" partnerships and other SPEs, we believe that is not generally the case' but also that 'Enron could have, and we believe in some respects should have, been more expansive under the governing standards in

Table 2.1 Effects of application of six accounting techniques on Enron's financial statements for 2000

| | Funds flow (in millions US$) | | | |
	Net income	From operations	Total assets	Debt
As reported	979.0	3,010.0	65,503.0	10,229.0
Adjustments for:				
1 FAS 140 transactions	(351.0)	(1,158.3)	812.5	3,353.4
2 Tax transactions	(269.1)	(60.6)	—	—
3 Non-economic hedges	(345.7)	—	(867.0)	(150.0)
4 Share trusts	29.7	(418.0)	4,178.0	4,871.0
5 Minority interests	—	—	—	1.740
6 Prepays	—	(1,527.0)	—	4,016.3
Total adjustments	(936.7)	(3,163.9)	4,123.5	11,830.7
Total after adjustments	42.3	(153.9)	69,626.5	22,059.7
Adjustments as percentage of amount originally reported	(96)	(105)	6	116

Source: United States Bankruptcy Court Southern District of New York, *Second Interim Report of Neal Batson, Court-Appointed Examiner*, 'In re: Enron Corp. *et al.*, Debtors', 21 January 2003, pp. 48–9.

Table 2.2 Adjusted components of Enron's key credit ratios

| Credit ratio component | As reported | As adjusted | Percentage change |
	(in millions US$)		
Funds flow from operations	3,010.0	(153.9)	(105)
Debt	10,229.0	22,059.7	116
Total obligations	10,466.0	22,297.0	113
Shareholders' equity and other items	14,788.0	10,342.0	(31)
Earnings for credit analysis	2,492.0	1,793.0	(28)
Interest	944.0	1,567.0	66

Source: United States Bankruptcy Court Southern District of New York, *Second Interim Report of Neal Batson, Court-Appointed Examiner*, 'In re: Enron Corp. *et al.*, Debtors', 21 January 2003, pp. 48–9.

its descriptions of these entities and Enron's transactions with them' (Powers *et al.*, 2002, pp. 201–2). Indeed, arguably only with the report of the Powers Committee itself and other subsequent investigations triggered by the firm's decline and bankruptcy in late 2001 did it become possible to develop a reasonably wide-ranging picture of the functioning of the complex network which by then constituted Enron and its closely related entities.[6]

Some other examples of Enron's activities

Many other activities of Enron have been the special focus of attention of commentators. One was a particularly aggressive and targeted the use of political lobbying – backed by large financial contributions – which, *inter alia*, enabled Enron to avoid proper regulatory oversight for much of its trading. Another, generator of controversy and a source of much unfavourable publicity for the firm, was its 'gaming'[7] of California's system of energy supply during the state's energy crisis.

Enron's questionable practices in the California energy market took place after the market's deregulation in 1996. Under the new regime, the state's utilities sold their own power plants and bought their electricity from a single wholesale pool, the California Power Exchange. They were forbidden from entering into long-term supply contracts. Ironically, in view of subsequent events, the reason for this prohibition was the perceived danger that the utilities would be locked into higher prices. But the new regime left the utilities exposed to fluctuations in the spot market for electricity. At first the system functioned reasonably well, but there was a change in 2000 as the effects of a hot summer were superimposed on an economic boom of which a major feature was an increase in demand caused by the expanding use of power-hungry computer equipment. The consequent rises in prices generated considerable ill will towards electricity traders, of which Enron was the largest.

Although people were quickly suspicious that energy traders were gaming the market, only later was the scale of Enron's use of such practices disclosed.[8] There was eventually concern within Enron itself as to the resulting danger of regulatory sanctions, and in a memorandum of December 2000 from an outside law firm to an in-house Enron lawyer, the firm's practices are described in some detail.[9] This concern led Enron to cease such operations later that month. Some of the practices described in the memorandum consisted of legitimate arbitraging of interstate price differentials resulting from differences in regulatory frameworks. The more questionable practices involved the earning of Congestion Fees paid by California's Independent System Operator (ISO) to firms to reduce the power scheduled for delivery over the state's transmission lines during periods when these lines were overloaded. Enron traders found a number of ways to earn Congestion Fees by creating such overloading or the appearance of such overloading (phantom congestion). The practices were often given picaresque names such as 'Death Star', 'Get Shorty' and 'Fat Boy'.

Different parties and non-observance of good corporate governance

Corporate governance is concerned with the relationships between a business's management and its Board of Directors, its shareholders and lenders, and its other stakeholders such as employees, customers, suppliers, and the community of which it is a part.[10] The subject thus concerns the framework through which business objectives are set, the means of attaining them, and of determining performance monitoring. Good corporate governance follows principles that still vary significantly among countries, and are currently the subject of various initiatives designed to achieve agreement on an acceptable framework of basic standards in which a central role is attributed to the OECD's Principles of Corporate Governance (discussed at length below). Implementation of good corporate governance requires satisfactory performance on the part of several different parties from both the private and public sectors. Those from the private sector include the firm's own Board of Directors and auditors, but also other so-called private-sector 'watchdogs' such as credit rating agencies, lenders and investors, and financial analysts. The role of these parties must be complemented by effective regulation, which in the case of a firm with operations as complex as Enron's includes not only major regulators of the financial sector but also the regulator of the energy sector.

Much of the commentary on failures of corporate governance in the Enron case has tended to focus on the performance of the Board of Directors and the external 'private-sector watchdogs'. However, good corporate governance depended no less on the conduct of the firm's management and other employees internally, and thus crucially on its system of incentives and sanctions, the first of the subjects taken up in what follows.

Enron's system of incentives and sanctions

While Enron's system of remuneration and other incentives to its employees and the closely related subjects of hiring and staff evaluation was in major respects specific to Enron, many of its features can be found in other firms, though not pushed to the same extremes.

The influence of the firm's stock price on the incentive system for Enron's employees became increasingly important during the long financial boom of the 1990s. In the case of senior staff, this reflected a remuneration system of which a key part consisted of stock options. For other staff, much of their savings was invested in Enron stock, with the active encouragement of Enron's own management. An important part of this process consisted of retirement savings plans under which staff members' own contributions were topped up by contributions from Enron itself.

Enron's corporate culture has been widely described as cut-throat.[11] It combined pressure on employees to accept a very high degree of subordination of personal objectives to those of the firm – pressure for the creation of Enron Men and Enron Women – with fierce internal competition, especially between the units of the corporation, and within the units.

Enron's hiring practices were rigorous and targeted, with an emphasis on top graduates and undergraduates recently out of universities rather than more experienced employees. This produced a flexible workforce more easily moulded to the firm's goals as well as a relatively inexpensive one. Once on board, Enron's employees were subject to a system of incentives and sanctions characterised by continuing pressures related to the risk of being fired under a process that came to be known as 'rank and yank'. At the centre of this process was a twice-yearly Performance Review Committee (PRC), an exercise taking several days for managers gathered in a hotel for the purpose.[12] For many years, employees were evaluated on a bell curve, the resulting ranking placing them in categories 1 to 5. Those placed in category 1, the lowest, risked being 'yanked'. They were given six months to improve their performance: during this period they had to spend about an hour a day documenting their activities and their contributions to Enron. The consequent pressures led many employees to accept severance packages in short order. Those in categories 2 and 3 were made aware that they were susceptible to 'yanking' in a slightly more distant future if their performance did not improve.

Systems of such 'yanking' are not limited to Enron among major companies but Enron's version does seem to have been extreme, and this aspect probably explains the failure of other US energy firms to copy Enron. Apparently, these firms believed that the PRC system was not conducive to good teamwork. According to Sherron Watkins, the Enron 'whistle blower', Enron's management eventually realised that the system was proving to be counter-productive. As she puts it, 'Enron Gas Services was developing a reputation as a predatory place where people would sell each other out to survive. People outside the company got the word, too, and blue-chip recruits became leery of signing on' (Schwartz and Watkins, 2003, p. 61). Ratings based on the bell curve ceased from 1995, though the PRC process continued.

Another noteworthy outcome of the corporate culture of Enron was to contribute to the insertion of a specific provision in the Sarbanes-Oxley Act. As mentioned earlier, many Enron employees had invested substantial sums in Enron's own stock, and the active encouragement of this practice by Enron's own management continuing as late as the autumn of 2001. But at the same time, Enron officers and a few directors were themselves selling the firm's stock on a massive scale – to the tune of US$1.1 billion between January 1999 and July 2001, sales no doubt partly a result of normal portfolio diversification but also likely to have been increasingly influenced by insider knowledge of the growing precariousness of Enron's real situation.[13] By contrast, sales of Enron stock in employees' retirement plans were subject to restrictions and in fact became impossible during the period from 17 October to 19 November 2001 (when Enron's position was becoming increasingly critical) because of a change in the plans' administrators. The latter restrictions were an example of a 'blackout period', namely one of more than three business days during which there is a suspension of the right to sell the firm's equity for 50 per cent or more of the participants in, and beneficiaries of, individual-account retirement plans.

Board of Directors

A fundamental role in the achievement of good corporate governance is attributed to actors in the Board of Directors and independent external auditors. Key functions of the Board of Directors, which were particularly relevant in the case of Enron, include the selection and remuneration of executives, being alert to potential conflicts of interest adversely affecting the firm, and ensuring the integrity of the company's systems of accounting and financial reporting. Prerequisites for satisfactory performance include access to accurate and timely information bearing on the fulfilment of these responsibilities. The role of the Board in the area of conflicts of interest clearly includes the monitoring needed to avoid self-dealing by management.

The primary finding of a report to a committee of the United States Senate on the role of the Enron's Board in its collapse is damning (United States Senate, 2002, p. 11):

> The Enron Board of Directors failed to safeguard Enron shareholders and contributed to the collapse of the seventh largest public company in the United States, by allowing Enron to engage in high risk accounting, inappropriate conflict of interest transactions, extensive undisclosed off-the-books activities, and excessive executive compensation. The Board witnessed numerous indications of questionable practices by Enron management over several years, but chose to ignore them to the detriment of Enron shareholders, employees and business associates.

In a review of this finding, the experience and credentials of the Enron Board should be borne in mind: in 2001 this consisted of fifteen members, many of them with fifteen or more years of experience on the Board of Enron and its predecessor companies, and many of them also members of the Boards of other companies. Of the five committees of the Enron Board, the key Audit and Compliance Committee (the primary liaison body with the external auditors) had six members, of whom two had formal accounting training and professional experience and only one had limited familiarity with complex accounting principles; and the Compensation Committee had five members, three with at least fifteen years of experience with Enron (United States Senate, 2002, pp. 1–2, 9).[14]

Acknowledgement is due that for a number of key decisions the Board of Directors did not have access to the information required for them to perform their monitoring role in an informed way. None the less, the Board approved or acquiesced in several decisions with problematic features (major examples are transactions discussed in Annex 1 on page 40), and were aware of Enron's recourse to questionable accounting. The record is replete with developments (such as an increase in revenues from US$40 billion in 1999 to US$101 billion in 2000) which would appear to have deserved more questioning by the Board than was in fact occasioned. Moreover, Arthur

Andersen provided regular briefings to the Board concerning Enron's accounting practices, at which Andersen pointed to features that were novel and involved a serious risk of non-compliance with generally accepted accounting principles. The increase in the complexity of Enron's corporate structure does not seem to have led to questioning or critical review by the Board. For example, Enron's annual filings for 1999 and 2000, which were approved and signed by Board members without any indication of concern, listed almost 3,000 related entities, with over 800 in offshore jurisdictions – 120 in the Turks and Caicos Islands and 600 in the Cayman Islands (United States Senate, 2002, p. 23).

The report to the Committee of the United States Senate cited above criticised the Board's Compensation Committee for exercising inadequate oversight over compensation for Enron executives. For example, it drew special attention to the fact that, in 2001, executives received almost US$750 million in cash bonuses for performance in the year 2000, a period in which the company's entire net income amounted to US$979 million (United States Senate, 2002, p. 54). Moreover, the Board's approval of partnerships (discussed in Annex 1) which were likely to lead to conflicts of interest involving Enron's employees or to be associated with abusive self-dealing point to serious weaknesses in its performance regarding these two subjects.

One widely accepted principle of good corporate governance is that the Board is independent of management. The finding of the report to the Senate Committee concerning the effect on Enron's Board of financial ties between the company and certain Board members suggests that this requirement was not met in the case of Enron. Economic ties between the Board and Enron took such forms as retainers or payments for consultancy services (or both) to two Board members; another Board member's service on the Board of directors of a company making substantial sales of oilfield equipment and services to Enron subsidiaries; donations by Enron to medical and educational institutions with which Board members were associated; hedging transactions between Enron and an oil company of which a Board member was a former chairman and chief executive officer; and payments for services and other contributions to organisations engaged in governmental relations, tax consulting and lobbying where a former Board member had ownership interests or otherwise played a prominent role (United States Senate, 2002, pp. 54–6). It should also be mentioned here that, of the compensation paid to the Board, a substantial proportion was in the form of stock options, a practice capable of exerting pressure on the Board to approve decisions likely to have a favourable influence on the firm's stock price, similar to those also exerted on management.

Accountants/auditors

Regarding auditing, good corporate governance requires high quality standards for preparation and disclosure, and independence for the external auditor. Enron's external auditor was Arthur Andersen, which also provided the firm with extensive internal auditing and consulting services. Some idea of its relative importance in these different roles during the period leading up to Enron's insolvency is indicated by the fact that in the year 2000, consultancy fees (at US$27 million) accounted for more than 50 per cent of the approximately US$52 million earned by Andersen for work on Enron. The history of relations between Enron and Arthur Andersen suggests that they were frequently characterised by tensions due to the latter's misgivings concerning several features of Enron's accounting.[15] However, overall, Andersen's performance, revelations concerning which were to lead to the break-up of the firm, led to the following assessment by the Powers Committee: 'The evidence available to us suggests that Andersen did not fulfil its professional responsibilities in connection with its audits of Enron's financial statements, or its obligation to bring to the attention of Enron's Board (or the Audit and Compliance Committee) concerns about Enron's internal contracts over the related-party transactions' (Powers *et al.*, 2002, p. 24). Both the Powers Committee and bodies of the United States Senate that have investigated Enron's collapse have taken the view that lack of independence linked to its multiple consultancy roles was a crucial factor in Andersen's failure to fulfil its obligations as Enron's external auditor (United States Senate, 2002, pp. 57–8).[16]

Banks

Enron's banks were deeply involved in the firm's recourse to techniques for the manipulation of its reported earnings and balance sheet under the seven major transactional and accounting headings described earlier. A typical summary of the role played by banks in Enron's way of doing business in the report of the court-appointed bankruptcy examiner reads as follows:

> The Examiner concludes that there is evidence that: (i) [the bank] had actual knowledge of the wrongful conduct in the transactions giving rise to the breaches of fiduciary duty [by Enron's officers]; (ii) [the bank] gave substantial assistance to certain of [Enron's] officers by participating in the structuring and closing of such transactions; and (iii) injury to [Enron] was the direct or reasonably foreseeable result of such conduct.[17]

Financial analysts

Most financial analysts covering Enron stock continued to recommend it to investors well into the autumn of 2001, even as revelations concerning Enron's accounting and management failings began to proliferate. Many of the analysts made this recommendation even though they admitted that they did not fully understand the firm's operations and structure. The overall verdict of the staff report to the United States Senate cited earlier is that 'Wall Street analysts [were] far less focussed on accurately assessing a company's performance than on other factors related to their own employers' businesses', citing here the employment of many of them by banks that derived large investment-banking fees from Enron transactions, that were investors in Enron's off-balance-sheet partnerships, and that had credit exposure to Enron.[18] Concerning this failure, the report draws attention not only to the links between analysts' bonuses and the profitability of the firms employing them, but also to more general pressures for favourable recommendations on a stock such as complaints and even legal threats from firms evaluated negatively, and restrictions on the access of analysts responsible for such evaluations to the information required for their work.[19]

Credit rating agencies

The major credit rating agencies enjoy great power by virtue of the influence of their ratings over firms' access to capital markets and over the cost of their financing. Their influence is associated with the granting to them since 1975 by the SEC of the status of Nationally Recognised Statistical Ratings Organisation (NRSRO). Their reliability has been called into question by a number of events in recent years, one of which was the failure of three major agencies to lower Enron's rating to below investment grade until a few days before the firm's bankruptcy despite a series of unfavourable disclosures. Here the report to the United States Senate cited above attributes the agencies' shortcomings to lack of inquisitiveness (despite the indications in Enron's financial reports of a propensity to engage in manipulation) and excessive attention to the firm's cash flow, the confidence of its counterparties, and the announcement shortly before its bankruptcy of a possible merger with Dynegy, another large trader of gas and electricity.[20]

SEC

In the Enron case, the SEC, the regulatory body responsible for reviewing firms' financial statements, missed warning signs concerning Enron's misconduct.[21] This failure partly reflected resource constraints. The SEC's stated goal was to review every company's annual report at least once every three years. However, in practice the annual returns of less than 50 per cent of public companies had been reviewed in the previous three years at the time of Enron's bankruptcy, and no review of Enron's returns had taken place after that of 1997, despite the warning signs.

Federal Energy Regulatory Commission (FERC)

Enron was also subject to the oversight of the FERC, the body responsible for regulation of the interstate transmission and wholesaling of electricity and natural gas, licensing of hydroelectric projects, and oil transmission by interstate pipelines. Under these headings the FERC is concerned with rate levels, the maintenance of competition and the construction of pipelines. The FERC's oversight did not concern Enron as a corporation *per se*, but affected various activities of the firm. A report to the United States Senate on the

FERC's oversight focused on areas where Enron is now known to have engaged in questionable transactions (such as the California energy crisis), and on financial risks to which it was exposed by its trading activities. For example, in May 2001 the FERC conducted an investigation into Enron Online, the firm's electronic platform for transactions in electricity and natural gas, with the objective of discovering whether it was associated with abusive market practices. In the view of a report to the United States Senate, the FERC failed to follow through on various concerns raised during this investigation, including some with a bearing on the firm's eventual bankruptcy, such as a trading model exposing it to large financial risks and the dependence of its trading capability on its creditworthiness. The overall verdict of the report to the Senate is that FERC 'was no match for a determined Enron' and 'has yet to prove that it is up to the challenge of proactively overseeing changing markets'.[22]

Corporate governance and the OECD Principles

As mentioned earlier, the main standards for corporate governance agreed at international intergovernmental level at the time of recent corporate scandals were the 1999 OECD Principles of Corporate Governance.[23] These Principles provided the principal overall framework within which international discussions on this subject took place, including that of policy responses to the Enron case.

The 1999 OECD Principles cover five basic subjects: (i) protection of the rights of shareholders; (ii) equitable treatment of shareholders, including full disclosure of material information and the prohibition of abusive self-dealing and insider trading; (iii) recognition, and protection of the exercise, of the rights of other stakeholders (a somewhat imprecise term denoting not only those directly involved in a firm's process of wealth creation but also other parties sufficiently strongly affected by this process); (iv) timely and accurate disclosure and transparency with respect to matters material to company performance, ownership and governance, which should include an annual audit conducted by an independent auditor; and (v) a framework of corporate governance ensuring strategic guidance of the company and effective monitoring of its management by the Board of Directors as well as the Board's accountability to the company and its shareholders.

The models of corporate governance found in reality belong to a spectrum not characterised everywhere by clear-cut breaks. At the extremes of the spectrum there are none the less important differences in such characteristics as the regulatory framework for management and Boards of Directors, the priority attributed to the interests of different stakeholders in the firm, and the prevalent systems of business financing. Financial systems that have progressed beyond the rudimentary level in the main incorporate the same major features as building blocks but differ in the relative importance of these blocks and in the links between them. At one extreme is often placed the German model, with its emphasis on multiple stakeholders and the influence exerted by banks through their shareholdings on firms' decision-making; and at the other is the Anglo-Saxon model, with its attribution of a major role in the efficient use of resources to the discipline imposed by open financial markets and its institutionalisation of priority for shareholder value.[24] Between the two extremes are many other variants typically including features from one or the other extreme (and often from both).

The preamble to the 1999 OECD Principles acknowledges that there is no single model of good corporate governance, and the Principles largely avoid detailed prescriptive rules in an area where rules unsupported by consensus would be likely to seem intrusive. But the generality and flexibility of the Principles have the consequence that potential inconsistencies among them, as well as other problems likely to arise in their application, are glossed over. Importantly for the Enron case, the Principles pay little attention to the issues of management incentives and remuneration. This matter is taken up – to the extent that it is – primarily under various headings covering the role of the Board of Directors and transparency. Under the headings of disclosure and transparency, companies are enjoined to include in the former material information on the remuneration of key executives. But nowhere do the 1999 OECD Principles address the problem of too close a link between executive remuneration and the reporting of financial results, especially short-term results.

The flouting of these Principles in the Enron case was particularly evident in the four areas of shareholders rights, disclosure and transparency, the execution of its responsibilities by the Board of Directors, and the prohibition of abusive self-dealing. Failures under these different headings were linked in various ways, perhaps most importantly through inadequate disclosure and transparency.

The revised version of the OECD Principles issued in 2004 fleshes out those of 1999 in various ways and includes within their coverage a number of new subjects, while continuing to avoid endorsement of any single model of corporate governance. The influence of recent corporate scandals is visible at several points.[25] A new first Principle is devoted to the connection between the basis for an effective corporate governance framework and its legal, regulatory and institutional foundation. There are references here to the need for regulators to have adequate authority and resources, to possible conflicts between the requirements of different legal and regulatory domains, both nationally and internationally, and the need for international dialogue and co-operation. Moreover, there are now references in this and other Principles to the role in good corporate governance of corporate ethics. For example, under Principle VI the responsibilities of the Board of Directors now include the application of high ethical standards; and there is a mention of the way in which a company code of ethics can encourage employees and others to report unethical and illegal behaviour ('whistle-blowing'), another feature of the new Principles likely to have been influenced by the Enron case. Under the same Principle there is also a reference to Board members' fiduciary duties, the duties of care and loyalty under this heading being spelt out at length.

Principle V on disclosure and transparency has been expanded substantially in comparison with the 1999 version. The expansion includes a fuller specification of the duties, selection and oversight of external auditors, and a reference to the responsibilities of other 'gatekeepers' such as stock-market research analysts, credit rating agencies and investment banks. The remuneration of key executives and of Board members continues to be covered under the heading of disclosure and transparency, with an additional reference now in Principle II (rights of shareholders and ownership functions) to disclosure's role in enabling shareholders to express their views on the subject. However, Principle VI also takes up the need to align the remuneration of key executives and the Board with the longer-term interests of the firm.

The policy response to recent corporate scandals

International: corporate governance and financial regulation

The Enron case and other recent corporate scandals have, unsurprisingly, led to widespread calls for changes in accounting standards and the strengthening of other features of regimes of corporate governance, and the discussion that follows is necessarily selective.

The OECD has committed itself to a drive to strengthen corporate governance worldwide. The focus of a meeting in Paris in November 2002 to discuss national and international initiatives addressing weaknesses in market foundations and improving market integrity included not only the 1999 OECD Principles of Corporate Governance but also other relevant OECD instruments such as the OECD Guidelines for Multinational Enterprises, and the Anti-Bribery Convention.[26] OECD ministers decided to bring forward to 2004 their comprehensive review of the OECD Principles, with the results discussed above.

International initiatives on financial regulation can also be expected to reflect policy responses to techniques for risk transfer and reducing transparency evidenced in recent corporate scandals. This is likely to have been true of the treatment of securitisation in the New Basel Capital Accord for Banks. This includes the definition of different categories of securitisation which serves as the basis for setting conditions as to the degree of risk transfer achieved by a securitisation. These now comprise not only the transfer to SPEs of underlying assets themselves ('traditional securitisation') but also of guarantees or credit derivatives linked to these assets ('synthetic securitisation').[27] Regulatory wariness concerning the possibility of shifting risks between different parts of corporate structures is also a feature of the rules for cases where a bank conducts an internal hedge in its banking book through a credit derivative in its trading book.[28]

International: regulatory gaps and conglomerate firms

It might also be hoped that, under international initiatives, there will eventually be an extension and intensification of work on regulatory problems posed by large conglomerate firms supplying goods and services. These are currently often subject to regimes involving several different regulators, which may none the less leave significant gaps. Issues connected to the regulation of financial conglomerates supplying traditional banking, securities and insurance services through the same corporate structure have become a subject for international initiatives in their own right, the body established for this purpose being the Joint Forum on Financial Conglomerates. The Joint Forum has the task of facilitating the exchange of information between supervisors within and between sectors, and to study legal and other impediments to such exchange. Beyond this, the Forum will also examine possible assignments of roles to different supervisors as part of improving their co-ordination and to develop principles for more effective supervision of financial conglomerates. The issues covered under these headings include not only supervisory methods and capital levels for such firms but also intragroup exposures, management structures, the suitability of managers, shareholder ownership, and intra-group conflicts of interest.[29]

The latter group of subjects seems pertinent to the case of Enron, and many of the principles enunciated by the Joint Forum in fact cover failings in the firm's functioning identified since its bankruptcy. However, even for the entities covered by the Joint Forum's work, namely financial conglomerates, application of these principles in practice is still at a preliminary stage, depending as it does on their incorporation in rules and standards set by other regulatory forums such as the Basel Committee on Banking Supervision, the International Organization of Securities Commission (IOSCO), and the International Association of Insurance Supervisors (IAIS), their eventual embodiment in national laws and regulations, and further development of co-operation between supervisors in different sectors and countries. As things stand, these initiatives do not cover firms such as Enron, with its extensive participation in activities outside specialised regulation.[30] There is an argument for reconsidering this lacuna for conglomerates which cannot be characterised as financial but which trade in several different organised and OTC markets, because of the possibility of contagion effects and systemic risks associated with their practices.

International: reconciling the different dimensions of reform

A successful outcome of international initiatives on corporate governance and related subjects of financial regulation faces considerable difficulties. Some of these are because of the interrelated character of the initiatives, which means that impediments to speedy progress in one area – such as agreement on international accounting standards – can also slow movement overall. Others are caused by the problem of reconciling with national legal regimes any increasingly detailed rules that may be enunciated as part of the initiatives through a process widely considered to lack representativeness.

The effects of the interrelated nature of ongoing initiatives bearing on corporate governance is particularly evident in the case of accounting standards. While additional impetus has been given to the negotiation of international accounting standards by recent corporate scandals, many of the outstanding issues remain extremely contentious among the different parties involved.[31] One of the issues is that of SPEs, which, as the Enron case illustrates, can be used to manipulate financial reports. Other difficult issues include the way in which gains on the investments in companies' pension funds should be included in earnings, the extent to which assets and liabilities should be valued on the basis of mark-to-market, and the appropriate balance in accounting standards between dependence on highly prescriptive, detailed and voluminous rules (the approach traditionally favoured by the USA), on the one hand, or on more general, principles-based regulations (the approach more favoured by European countries), on the other.[32]

Movement from the enumeration of general principles for corporate governance, of which the largely checklist approach of the 1999 OECD Principles is an example, to more detailed core rules is likely to be gradual as well as constrained by considerations of national sovereignty. Corporate governance is a subject linked to several parts of countries' private, company, and insolvency law.

Here we should also raise the issue of the representativeness of the process of enunciating more detailed, globally applicable rules for corporate governance. So far this process has been carried out within the OECD, an organisation that has extended its membership beyond its founding and mainly industrialised original member countries but still falls well short of being universal, or even of including all countries with developed or rapidly developing systems of company law. Resolving the issue of representativeness may well slow international agreement on detailed rules for corporate governance but it is a problem that will not go away.

National: the USA

The reverberations of recent corporate scandals for regimes of corporate governance and financial regulation are understandably proving particularly far-reaching in the USA.

One of the responses has been by the Financial Accounting Standards Board (FASB), which has issued new rules governing conditions under which avoidance of accounting consolidation of SPEs is permitted.[33] This is an area where hitherto standards have not been clear-cut: according to prevailing practice, based partly on no more than remarks of a senior SEC accountant,

Amando Pimentel, at an annual American Institute of Certified Public Accountants (AICPA) conference in 1997, consolidation was not required if independent third parties made an equity investment of no more than 3 per cent of the fair value of the SPE's assets, and if the equity was at risk during the entire term of the SPE.[34] Enron had exploited the latitude provided by this rule up to and beyond its permissible limits.

But the most important policy response so far, especially for the cross-border financial relations of the USA has been the Sarbanes-Oxley Act, passed in the summer of 2002.[35] This Act is directed at a wide range of the abuses revealed in recent scandals, and prescribes stringent penalties under several of its headings. Provisions of the Act affecting directors and senior executives include a requirement for certification of reports filed with the SEC, prohibition of insider lending to a firm's executives and directors, penalties for accounting restatements reflecting misconduct, bans on trading by executives and directors in the firm's stock during certain 'blackout periods' for retirement plans,[36] and a requirement for independence for members of audit committees. Enhanced disclosure is to be achieved by various provisions, including the following: the requirement that the SEC review a firm's periodic financial reports at least once every three years; the obligation on directors, officers and others owning 10 per cent or more of the firm's securities to report changes in their ownership within a specified (short) period new requirements for disclosure concerning subjects such as off-balance-sheet transactions, internal controls, and the existence or absence of a code of ethics for a firm's senior financial officers;[37] and timely disclosure of material changes in a firm's financial condition (so-called real time disclosure). Auditor independence is to be strengthened by limiting the scope of non-audit and consulting services for audit clients, and by requiring that a firm's audit committee pre-approve non-audit services provided by the firm's auditor. Under the same heading, an audit firm will not be permitted to provide audit services to a client if the lead or co-ordinating partner with primary responsibility for the audit or the partner responsible for reviewing the audit has performed audit services for that client in the five previous fiscal years.

The Act also establishes a Public Company Accounting Oversight Board (PCAOB) with wide-ranging authority to ensure compliance. The PCAOB will be responsible for setting standards for auditing, and this role will constitute a radical strengthening of public control over auditors and accountants.

Other provisions of Sarbanes-Oxley include rules to strengthen the independence of research analysts, lengthening the statute of limitations for litigation involving the violation of certain securities laws, the establishment of new securities-related offences and increases in certain criminal penalties, and new protection for employee 'whistle-blowers'. And section 302 prohibits entities incorporated in the USA from reincorporating abroad to avoid or lessen the legal force of the Act's provisions.

Sarbanes-Oxley does not generally distinguish between US and non-US firms, covering as it does all those to which the Securities Exchange Act of

1934 applies. This Act, whose primary objective is to assure the public availability of company information, applies not only to firms with publicly
traded stocks but also to those (in the USA) with more than a threshold number of shareholders and value of assets. In the rules adopted for the application of Sarbanes-Oxley there have been some concessions to foreign issuers
involving accommodation of structures for Boards of Directors elsewhere
based on concepts different from those of the USA and different rules for
auditors and exemption from some rules for stock exchange listing.[38]

The requirements of Sarbanes-Oxley have already been the source of legal
action against a large foreign firm and are leading others to consider the
option of delisting (though this is not straightforward, since it requires a
reduction in the number of US shareholders to less than a specified limit).[39]
As far as firms from developing countries are concerned, the direct impact
will be on non-US issuers of securities in US financial markets, and consequent
difficulties are likely to involve features of legal regimes in other jurisdictions
not conforming to Sarbanes-Oxley. Such features may include insider loans
(since many legal regimes permit loans to executives and directors), the code
of ethics for senior financial officers, and rules for the conduct of auditors
and for the oversight of audit committees. The indirect impact will depend
on the extent to which the provisions of Sarbanes-Oxley are incorporated
into rules of corporate governance elsewhere. Another area where revelations concerning Enron may eventually lead to further legislative action is
taxation. The revelations in a recent lengthy report to the Finance Committee
of the United States Senate by Congressional tax experts, which has not
been reviewed for this chapter, document complex transactions structured
for the purpose of tax avoidance and use for the same purpose of offshore
subsidiaries which were part of the extensive network of such entities
described above in this chapter ('A sketch of Enron').[40] Here too, Enron was
provided with assistance by accountancy firms and investment banks.
Tax matters are not ignored in Sarbanes-Oxley: under title X, section 1001, it
is stated that 'it is the sense of the Senate that the Federal income tax return
of a corporation should be signed by the chief executive officer of such
corporation'.

Corporate governance and key financial standards

A major lesson of the Enron case and other recent corporate scandals is that,
as with other social constructs, regimes of corporate governance and the financial systems to which they are inextricably linked are susceptible to the
effects of flaws and fault lines that are the product of financial innovation,
human ingenuity (not all of it necessarily legal), and other changes in mores,
and in the social and economic context. Many (but not all) of the problems
revealed by recent corporate scandals are more pertinent to the corporate
governance of developed countries than of emerging-market or other developing countries. However, in view of the pressures exerted on architects of

corporate governance in developing countries, they may take comfort from the confirmation by recent revelations that there is no nirvana for such governance, and no blueprint providing an alternative to step-by-step improvement, which may draw lessons from the experience of countries with more developed regimes but which attributes national conditions and history an integral role in the framework for system design.

The OECD Principles are one of the twelve financial standards that have been identified as being essential to the soundness and stability of financial systems and as having a key role in measures to strengthen the so-called international financial architecture.[41] Observance of these standards is now a subject covered by International Monetary Fund (IMF) Article IV surveillance. From the first there have been queries as to the suitability of corporate governance as a subject for the application of the incentives and sanctions envisaged as part of the global promotion of key financial standards. The grounds for such queries have included many already discussed: the summary nature of the OECD Principles; the complexity of the subject and the potential intrusiveness of international initiatives; and the non-representativeness of the process that has so far enunciated these Principles. To these queries there will now be added others reflecting acknowledgement that in important respects the state of the art, even in regimes considered the most developed, has recently demonstrated shortcomings hitherto unrecognised or only partially recognised.

Corporate governance so far has in fact been one of the less scrutinised subjects in the Reports on Standards and Codes (ROSCs) of the IMF and World Bank assessing countries' progress regarding key financial standards.[42] This seems understandable in the light of the subject's difficulty. Much good can eventually result from a patient process of development and reform in which international co-operation through exchange of experience and technical assistance can play a significant part. But this process should also incorporate acknowledgement of the proven limitations – illustrated graphically by the Enron case and other recent corporate scandals – as well as the strengths of all known models of corporate governance. Progress regarding such governance requires practical experimentation, and this experimentation in turn can only take place if national policy-makers are left considerable discretion as to choices regarding their route to development and reform.

Annex 1   Illustrations of Enron's accounting and transactional techniques

VPPs

Early recourse by Enron to SPEs included arrangements (volumetric production payments or VPPs) to finance the operations of small oil and gas companies. VPPs were used to lend to producers in exchange for agreed amounts of oil or gas, the finance being secured by the production fields and not by the producing company. The VPP itself was already a form of SPE, but Enron then took the process a step further by securitisation, pooling securities backed by the VPPs in limited partnerships called Cactus Funds and using derivatives to smooth the earnings from sales of the oil and gas in the VPPs. Some of the securities so created were placed in SPEs, which were used to meet the obligations due to bank loans incurred by Enron in connection with the VPPs, and others were sold directly to financial institutions. In both cases, the financial exposure of Enron resulting from the creation of the VPPs was removed from its balance sheet. Such SPEs were an extension of practices involving partnerships and other entities that had long been common in the energy business (Fox, 2003, pp. 31–2, 63–4).

JEDI and Chewco

Another SPE, which was eventually to play an important role in difficulties regarding Enron's financial reporting in 2001, was the partnership called Joint Energy Development Investors (JEDI), formed between Enron and the California Public Employees Retirement System (CalPERS) in the early 1990s. This committed Enron and CalPERS to each invest US$250 million in natural gas projects during a three-year period. In late 1997, Enron sought a new partner for JEDI since it wished to engage in a new and larger partnership with CalPERS. For this purpose, in accord with a plan drawn up by its future chief financial officer, Andrew Fastow, Enron established a new partnership to buy CalPERS' stake in JEDI with an arrangement designed to ensure that JEDI remained an independent entity that would not have to be consolidated with Enron itself in its financial statements. If this condition was to be fulfilled, the new partnership, Chewco,[43] had to meet a number of requirements: 3 per cent of its equity had to be invested by a third party unrelated to Enron; the investment had to be genuinely at risk; and, finally, the entity had to be controlled by a party other than Enron. The approach to solving the last problem chosen by Enron was to place some restrictions on the Enron employee, Michael Kopper, selected to manage Chewco and to establish a new outside limited partner for Chewco, William Dodson (Michael Kopper's domestic partner), an arrangement eventually replaced by a set of entities controlled by Kopper and Dodson. The equity investment of Chewco's partners was financed with bank loans whose conditions included a requirement for the maintenance of cash collateral, which was met by a special distribution from JEDI to Chewco.

This arrangement was subsequently to be criticised on various grounds: for example, that the investment financed with a bank loan had only a doubtful status as equity; that part of the 3 per cent equity consisted of an investment by Kopper, an Enron employee; and that the equity did not consist of an investment at risk, since the loan backing it was secured by cash collateral provided by JEDI itself, to invest in which Chewco was established in the first place. Further questions over Chewco's independence were raised by fees it paid Enron for the provision of guarantees for its bank financing and for management.[44]

In early 2001, Enron bought out Chewco in a transaction that generated handsome returns for Kopper and Dodson. However, this step did not end the story of Chewco's relations with Enron. In the autumn of 2001, Enron's accountants, Arthur Andersen, reviewed the accounting treatment of Chewco, concluding, on the basis of information available to them concerning the bank financing of the supposedly outside equity investment in Chewco and the associated cash collateral, that the SPE had not been independent of Enron. As a consequence, JEDI was consolidated into Enron's financial statements from 1997 onwards, contributing to sharp downward revisions of reported income in 1997–2000 and increases in the firm's debt during these years in the range of US$561 million to US$711 million. These restatements played a major role in the loss of creditworthiness that preceded Enron's filing for bankruptcy at the beginning of December.

Rhythms

SPEs were also employed by Enron as part of hedges of exposures linked to its assets. A major instance, which served as a model in certain respects for subsequent hedging operations, involved Enron's investment in the stock of Rhythms Netconnections ('Rhythms'), an internet service provider.[45] This investment, bought in March 1998 for US$10 million while Rhythms was still a privately held company, had appreciated in value to about US$300 million after the public issuance of its stock in Spring 1999. The problem for Enron was that, in consequence, fluctuations in the value of the Rhythms investment were capable of imparting volatility to its reported income, but that gains could not be realised quickly or easily hedged: short-term realisation was impossible because investors in a privately held company are barred from selling shares for six months after the date of the initial public offering (IPO), and effective hedging was impeded by the absence of options on the stock (because of its illiquidity and thus its potentially extreme volatility) and by the lack of comparable stock whose correlation with that of Rhythms would have made them suitable hedges.

Enron's response to this problem was a series of transactions carried out through two SPEs: LJM1 and LJM Swap Sub L.P. (Swap Sub), created for the purpose of enabling the firm to hedge its exposure to fluctuations in its Rhythms investment. The hedge took the form of a put option sold to Enron by Swap Sub, whose assets consisted principally of Enron shares.[46] This hedge was potentially unstable, since Swap Sub's ability to meet its obligations under the put option depended on the value of Enron's own stock and could be compromised if the Rhythms and Enron stock declined together. In the view of the Powers Committee, the transaction did not meet the conditions of 'a typical economic hedge, which is obtained by paying a market price to a creditworthy counterparty who will take on the economic risk of a loss' (Powers *et al.*, 2002, pp. 82–3). The arrangement was also vulnerable to the charge of involving conflicts of interest, since LJM was managed by Fastow, and since Fastow and other employees of Enron were investors in LJM through a partnership called Southampton Place L.P.

The restriction on Enron's ability to sell its Rhythms stock expired in October 1999, but only in early 2000, after limits to the hedge's affectiveness in reducing earnings volatility had become evident and when the price of the Rhythms stock began to decline, thus meaning that its puts were in the money,[47] did Enron decide to unwind the positions related to its Rhythms exposure. Several features of the unwinding were questioned by the Powers Committee, including the lower than appropriate value of the assets received by Enron when it exercised the put on its Rhythms shares; a lucrative put option provided by Enron itself to Swap Sub during the negotiations on unwinding the Rhythms hedge in order to stabilise the latter's position as its obligations to Enron under the put began to mount; and large windfall gains to the investors in LJM.[48] Moreover, as in the case of Chewco, questions were raised concerning the level of Swap Sub's independent capitalisation, and eventual consolidation into Enron's financial statements in November 2001 led to downward revisions of the firm's income in 1999 and 2000.

Raptors

Another example of Enron's recourse to SPEs to hedge equity exposures, which incorporated mechanisms similar to those used for Rhythms and led to eventual downward revisions in the firm's consolidated earnings, involved a set of entities called Raptors.[49] The financial capacity of each of the Raptors for meeting obligations under hedges consisted of Enron's own stock (or stock owned by Enron), arrangements once again rendering the hedges questionable, since Enron's stock and the SPEs' financial capacity would decline in step, with the result that in the event of a sufficiently large decline in the price of Enron shares, the latter would have to be replenished with additional Enron stock or by other means. Additional questions raised about the Raptors concerned the extent of their independence from Enron, conflicts of interest owing to Enron employees' involvement in their management and to their investments in the controlling partnership (LJM2),[50] the size of payments between Enron and the SPEs (which on occasion made possible increases in Enron's reported earnings) and the valuation of the services or asset transfers which were the reason for these payments, and other accounting issues.

Raptor I was established in the spring of 2000 with financial capacity of which by far the largest part consisted of Enron's own stock and stock contracts,[51] and sold a put option (effective as of October) to Enron on 7.2 million Enron shares. This arrangement was replaced in the autumn by derivative transactions mainly taking the form of total return swaps on Enron investments, which served as a form of insurance to Enron, since Raptor I compensated it for losses on these investments in return for receiving the gains on them.[52]

The establishment of Raptor II and Raptor IV followed similar lines: put options on its stock were sold to Enron by entities, a large part of whose financial capacity consisted of contingent forwards contracts on Enron shares.[53] In the case of Raptor I the stock and stock contracts provided by Enron were subject to restrictions on selling or hedging for three years, which led to their being valued for the purpose of the transaction at a substantial discount from their market prices, and similar restrictions applied to the stock contracts provided to Raptors II and IV. However, later in the year, some of the Enron investments hedged through the Raptors began to decline in value, raising the question of whether the commitments under the hedges could be met. Enron's solution to this problem took the form of a costless collar, a structure based on options under which a floor was placed under the value of the Raptors' financial capacity: if the price of Enron's stock fell below a specified figure, Enron would pay the Raptor the difference in cash; and in exchange, if the price rose above a specified ceiling, the Raptor would pay Enron the difference. The costless collar was established in violation of the agreement originally transferring the Enron stock to the Raptors at a particular discount, since the discount reflected the restrictive effect of the provision that the stock would not be hedged for a three-year period. Thus Enron's hedging of the restricted stock transferred to the Raptors represented a transfer of value to them in return for which it should arguably have received additional consideration. It should also be noted that the costless collar did nothing to deal with the fundamental flaw of the hedging operations; that Enron was in effect engaging in a hedge with itself.

Raptor III was established to hedge a particular Enron investment in The New Power Company (TNPC). Wishing to realise a portion of the gains on its holding in TNPC, Enron formed an SPE called Hawaii 125-0 (Hawaii) with an outside institutional investor to which it sold part of its interest in TNPC. Enron then entered into a total return swap with Hawaii under which it retained most of the risks as well as the rewards of this interest, and would thus have to reflect in its earnings statements resulting gains and losses on a mark-to-market basis. Raptor III was set up to hedge this accounting exposure: once again there was an investment by LJM2, but the greater part of Raptor III's financial capacity was based on warrants on TNPC stock (which were the economic equivalent of TNPC stock) transferred to it a price approximately 50 per cent of that reached at the time shortly afterwards when the stock was publicly issued. The resulting capital gain to Raptor III provided it with the capacity to engage in hedging transactions with Enron in the form of a total return swap under which Raptor III received the gains on the TNPC stock in return for insuring Enron against losses on the same stock. Here too, an SPE was being used to hedge an Enron invest-ment with financial capacity that depended on the value of the asset being hedged.

Declines in stock prices putting the Raptor structures at risk soon followed – that of TNPC, for example, falling 50 per cent in comparison with its level at the time of its IPO by the late autumn of 2000. In consequence, by the end of 2000 Enron had a gain on its hedges, which it estimated at more than US$500 million, but one that it could only use to offset corresponding losses on the investments being hedged if the Raptors still had the capacity to meet their obligations.[54] Various approaches to solving the resulting problems were tried. For example, since the financial capacity problems were located initially in Raptors I and III, the capacity of Raptors II and IV was deployed to shore up that of those under pressure through devices such as a temporary cross-guarantee agreement that effectively merged the credit capacity of all four Raptors. Also through the infusion into them of additional Enron stock, subject to restrictions as to selling and hedging similar to those of the initial transfers, but on which Enron itself none the less again provided hedges to the Raptors in the form of costless collars, thus increasing its own liability even as it attempted to prevent the collapse of the hedges of the value of its assets. However, such solutions were capable of providing only a temporary respite, and in September 2001 a decision was taken to terminate the Raptors, the accounting treatment for the transaction chosen for this purpose resulting in a charge of US$544 million to Enron's after-tax earnings for the third quarter of 2001.[55]

Other SPEs

Many of Enron's other arrangements designed to keep debt off its balance sheet or adjust its reported earnings, which involved SPEs, were variants of more commonly used transactions. For example, sale and leaseback deals used to supply equipment for energy projects were placed in joint ventures with the equipment manufacturer, thus removing the associated debt from Enron's balance sheet. The LJM partnerships described above served as counter-parties in a number of transactions involving sales of assets that enabled Enron to record gains in its financial statements or to avoid consolidation (or both). However, the Powers Committee questioned the legitimacy of the presentation of these asset sales as involving third parties independent of Enron as well as their accounting treatment. The Committee noted that Enron frequently bought back the assets in question after the close of the relevant financial reporting period, and that the LJM partnerships always recorded profits on these transactions; but that the same transactions also generated earnings for Enron. This could be explained in some cases by undocumented side deals insuring the LJM partnerships against losses. The general conclusion of the Powers Committee concerning such trans-actions was that 'Enron sold assets to the LJM partnerships that it could not, or did not wish to, sell to other buyers' (Powers *et al.*, 2002, p. 135).[56]

Another SPE, which facilitated manipulation of Enron's financial statements, was Whitewing Associates, formed in December 1997 with funding of US$579 million pro-vided by Enron and US$500 million by an outside investor. In March 1999, this arrangement was changed so that control was shared between Enron and the outside investor, thus allowing Whitewing to be deconsolidated from Enron. Whitewing was to be the purchaser of Enron assets, including stakes in power plants, pipelines, stocks and other investments (Fox, 2003, p. 157).

Annex 2   A look at some of Enron's financial reports

The 1998 report contains description of Enron's risk management, largely at a general level. The note to its consolidated financial statement on accounting for price risk management gives an idea of the contents and the limits of this description:

> Enron engages in price risk management activities for both trading and non-trading purposes. Financial instruments utilized in connection with trading activities are accounted for using the mark-to-market method ... Financial instruments are also utilized for non-trading purposes to hedge the impact of market fluctuations on assets, liabilities, production and other contractual commitments. Hedge accounting is utilized in non-trading activities when there is a high degree of correlation between price movements in the derivative and the item designated as being hedged. In instances where the anticipated correlation of price movements does not occur, hedge accounting is terminated and future changes in the value of the financial instruments are recognized as gains or losses. If the hedged item is sold, the value of the financial instrument is recognized in income.[57]

A little later, the Report goes into a bit more detail (but still at a general level) concerning the firm's exposures and instruments for hedging and risk management:

> The investments made by Enron include public and private equity, debt, production payments and interests in limited partnerships. These investments are managed as a group, by disaggregating the market risks embedded in the individual investments and managing them on a portfolio basis, utilizing public equities, equity indices and commodities as hedges of specific industry groups and interest rate swaps as hedges of interest rate exposure, to reduce Enron's exposure to overall market volatility. The specific investment or idiosyncratic risks which remain are then managed and monitored within the Enron risk management policies.

In the section of the financial review dealing with financial risk management, Enron does discuss its use of value-at-risk (VAR) analysis in the management of its exposure to market risks,[58] but there is no mention of the role of SPEs in its management of price risk. In the note to the consolidated financial statements on minority interests there is a reference to the formation of Whitewing Associates, but its role in Enron's management of assets on and off the firm's balance sheet is not described.[59]

In the 1999 annual report, in the note on minority interests, Enron mentions its recourse to limited partnerships as follows: 'Enron has formed separate limited partnerships with third-party investors for various purposes',[60] but these purposes are not described more specifically. In the note on unconsolidated equity affiliates there is a reference to the accounting deconsolidation of Whitewing Associates following a change allowing the equal sharing of control between Enron and the third-party investor,[61] and in the note on related party transactions mention is made of the acquisition by Whitewing of US$192 million of Enron's assets at prices leading Enron to recognise neither gains nor losses on the transactions.[62] The same note also includes a description of the establishment of the LJM partnerships which deserves to be quoted at some length in view of the role played by these partnerships in the above account:

> In June 1999, Enron entered into a series of transactions involving a third party and LJM Cayman, L.P. (LJM). LJM is a private investment company which engages in acquiring or investing in primarily energy-related investments. A senior officer of Enron is the managing member of LJM's general partner. The effect of the transactions was (i) Enron and the third party amended certain forward contracts to purchase shares of Enron common stock, resulting in Enron having forward contracts to purchase Enron common shares at the market price on that day, (ii) LJM received 6.8 million shares of Enron common stock subject to certain restrictions and (iii) Enron received a note receivable and certain financial instruments hedging an investment held by Enron. Enron recorded the assets received and equity issued at estimated fair value. In connection with the transactions, LJM agreed that the Enron officer would have no pecuniary interest in such Enron common shares and would be restricted from voting on matters related to such shares ... LJM2 Co-Investment, L.P. (LJM2) was formed in December 1999 as a private investment company which engages in acquiring or investing in primarily energy-related or communications-related businesses. In the fourth quarter of 1999, LJM2, which has the same general partner as LJM, acquired, directly or indirectly, approximately $360 million of merchant assets and investments from Enron, on which Enron recognized pre-tax gains of approximately $16 million. In December 1999, LJM2 entered into an agreement to acquire Enron's interests in an unconsolidated equity affiliate for approximately $34 million. Additionally, LJM acquired other assets from Enron for $11 million.

The first paragraph describes the infusions of Enron stock into LJMI which provided the financial capacity that made possible the put option purchased on its Rhythms stock. But the hedging operation itself is not described. The second paragraph exemplifies the asset transactions in which Enron engaged with the LJM partnerships.

The 2000 annual report is a little more revealing, but still falls far short of providing the information required for a reasonable picture of the risks associated with Enron's operations and structure.[63] Under the note on minority interests there is a further reference to the separate limited partnerships formed by Enron, this time also mentioning a limited liability company formed for similar purposes. In the note on unconsolidated equity affiliates there is a reference to sales to Whitewing of Enron investments and assets amounting to US$192 million in 1999 (already mentioned above) and US$632 million in 2000 – sales on which Enron recognised neither gains nor losses. The same note also includes a further description of the shifting of assets around the network of Enron and related parties, which is worth quoting at length:

> Additionally, in 2000, ECT Merchant Investments Corp., a wholly-owned Enron subsidiary, contributed two pools of merchant investments to a limited partnership that is a subsidiary of Enron. Subsequent to the contributions, the partnership issued partnership interests representing 100 per cent of the beneficial, economic interests in the two asset pools, and such interests were sold for a total of $545 million to a limited liability company that is a subsidiary of Whitewing. These entities are separate legal entities from Enron and have separate assets and liabilities.

Note 16 on related party transactions is more forthcoming about Enron's use of SPEs for the purpose of hedging, and the information provided is such that it should have raised questions in the mind of a financial analyst as to the source of these entities' financial capacity and its relation to the value of Enron's own assets – the very assets the arrangements were being used to hedge. Key parts of the note merit quotation at length and commentary, covering as they do transactions also discussed in Annex 1:

> In 2000 and 1999, Enron entered into transactions with limited partnerships (the Related Party) whose general partner's managing member is a senior officer of Enron. The limited partners of the Related Party are unrelated to Enron. Management believes that the terms of the transactions with the Related Party were reasonable compared to those which could have been negotiated with unrelated third parties.

This would appear to be a further description of Enron's relationship to the LJM partnerships ('the Related Party'):

> In 2000, Enron entered into transactions with the Related Party to hedge certain merchant investments and other assets. As part of the transactions, Enron (i) contributed to newly-formed entities (the Entities) assets value at approximately $1.2 billion, including $150 million in Enron notes payable, 3.7 million restricted shares of outstanding Enron common stock and the right to receive up to 18.0 million shares of outstanding Enron common stock in March 2003 (subject to certain conditions) and (ii) transferred to the Entities assets valued at approximately $309 million, including a $50 million note payable and an investment in an entity that indirectly holds warrants convertible into common stock of an Enron equity method investee. In return, Enron received economic interests in the Entities, $309 million in notes receivable, of which $259 million is recorded at Enron's carryover basis of zero, and a special distribution from the Entities in the form of $1.2 billion in notes receivable, subject to changes in the principal for amounts payable by Enron in connection with the execution of additional derivative instruments. Cash in these Entities of $172.6 million is invested in Enron demand notes. In addition, Enron paid $123 million to purchase share-settled options from the Entities on 21.7 million shares of Enron common stock.

Here Enron is describing its provision of financial capacity to the Raptors. Matching the figures in the note with those in the account of the Powers Committee is not always possible. However, according to the Powers Committee, the three identical put options on its own shares purchased from Raptors I, II and IV by Enron involved payments totalling US$123 million on 21.7 million shares – the figures also specified in the note. There is also a reference here to the restrictions on the Enron shares (though the nature of the restrictions is not specified), and to the contingent right to receive up to 18 million additional shares in March 2003, subject to certain conditions (which, thanks to the Powers Report, are known to have referred to their price level).

And there is a mention of the note worth US$259 million received by Enron in connection with the establishment of Raptor III, recorded by Enron at zero:[64]

> In late 2000, Enron entered into share-settled collar arrangements with the Entities on 15.4 million shares of Enron common stock. Such arrangements will be accounted for as equity transactions when settled.

This passage clearly refers to the costless collars into which Enron entered with the Raptors but without mentioning the inconsistency of this arrangement with the restrictions on selling, pledging or hedging these shares:

> In 2000, Enron entered into derivative transactions with the Entities with a combined notional amount of approximately $2.1 billion to hedge certain merchant investments and other assets. Enron's notes receivable balance was reduced by $36 million as a result of premiums owed on derivative transactions. Enron recognized revenues of approximately $500 million related to the subsequent change in the market value of these derivatives, which offset market value changes of certain merchant investments and price risk management activities.

This passage concerns the gains of Enron on its derivative transactions with Raptors I, II and III (mentioned in Annex 1). However, realisation of the gains depended on the financial capacity of the Raptors and, as would be indicated by a careful reading of the note on related party transactions, this capacity depended heavily on the value of the very stock being hedged. The remainder of the note contains description of other transactions involving transfers of assets and liabilities between Enron and the LJM partnerships as well as of the termination of a put option on Enron shares sold by Enron to the partnerships.

Notes

1 Reprinted by permission from *G24 Discussion Paper Series*, under the auspices of the Intergovernmental Group of Twenty-four on International Monetary Affairs, UNCTAD, no. 30 (2004).
2 The author is grateful for the comments of Stewart Hamilton, Anthony Travis and members of UNCTAD's Investment and Enterprise Competitiveness Branch. However, the views expressed are his own, as is the responsibility for remaining errors.
3 The descriptions here rely largely on those in United States Bankruptcy Court Southern District of New York, January 2003, sections IV–VIII and X–XI.
4 For a narrative account illustrating Enron's use of the accounting and transactional techniques described, see Annex 1.
5 See United States Bankruptcy Court Southern District of New York, June 2003, pp. 9–10.
6 For illustrations of the treatment accorded to the firm's hedging practices and SPEs in Enron's annual reports of 1998, 1999 and 2000, see Annex 2.
7 The rules of the Independent System Operator (ISO) for California's electricity market define gaming as follows: ' "Gaming" or taking unfair advantage of the rules and procedures set forth in the FX or ISO tariffs, Protocols or Activity Rules, or of transmission constraints in period in which exist substantial Congestion, to the detriment of efficiency of, and of consumers in, the ISO markets. "Gaming" may also include taking undue advantage of other conditions that may affect the availability of transmission and generation capacity, such as loop flow, facility outages, level of hydropower output or seasonal limits on energy imports from out-of-state, or actions or behaviours that may otherwise render the system and the ISO markets vulnerable to price manipulation to the detriment of their efficiency' (*ISO Market Monitoring and Information Protocol*, section 2.1.3).
8 Enron's trading profits during the California energy crisis were large, though the proportion resulting from its gaming of the state's electricity market is for understandable reasons unidentifiable. A large part of these profits – a sum probably well

in excess of US$1 billion – was placed in undisclosed reserves (Fox, 2003, p. 220).

9 The memorandum is reprinted in Fusaro and Miller, 2002, pp. 209–16.

10 The term 'stakeholder' is unavoidably imprecise. It includes not only those most directly involved in a firm's process of wealth creation but also other parties as long as they are sufficiently strongly or directly affected by this process.

11 See Chapter 12 in this volume: John Dobson, 'Enron: The Collapse of Corporate Culture'.

12 There is a graphic description of the working of the PRC in the book co-authored by the Enron 'whistle-blower', Sherron Watkins (Schwartz and Watkins, 2003, pp. 59–62).

13 See, for example, Fox (2003), pp. 259–60, 289–90; Schwartz and Watkins (2003), pp. 257–9.

14 Enron's Audit and Compliance Committee thus fulfilled the requirement of a recommendation of a United States Blue Ribbon Commission on Improving the Effectiveness of Corporate Audit Committees in 2000 that audit committees should consist of 'financially literate' members, of whom at least one has accounting or financial management expertise (p. 6).

15 For example, in March 2001 a senior Andersen partner, Carl Bass, was removed from functions involving oversight of Enron (United States Senate, 2002, p. 58). Bass was the primary contact between Enron and Andersen's Professional Standards Group, accounting experts whose task was to make sure that Andersen's accountants observed accounting rules in their work for clients. Bass had expressed reservations concerning Enron's methods for bolstering the Raptors when they ran into difficulties, hedging connected to investments of the LJM partnerships, and other Enron transactions with the effect of boosting the firm's reported income for 2000. See Fox (2003), pp. 211–12, 228–30.

16 Staff, *Financial Oversight of Enron: The SEC and Private-Sector Watchdogs*, Report to the United States Senate Committee on Governmental Affairs, 8 October 2002, p. 28. See also Travis, Anthony, 'Enron *et al.* and Implications for the Auditing Profession', Chapter 9 in this volume; Interview by Claude Baumann, 'Qui a tué Andersen?', *Finance & the Common Good/Bien Commun*, no. 18–19 (Spring–Summer 2004), pp. 32–5.

17 See, for example, United States Bankruptcy Court Southern District of New York, June 2003, p. 54.

18 See Staff, *op.cit.*, p. 70.

19 Ibid., pp. 81–90.

20 Ibid., pp. 11, 31–40.

21 Ibid., Part Two, section II.D.

22 See Majority Staff (United States Senate Committee on Governmental Affairs), 'Committee Staff Investigation of the Federal Energy Regulatory Commission's Oversight of Enron Corp.', *Staff Memorandum*, 12 November 2002, pp. 2–3, 19–23.

23 See OECD Ad Hoc Task Force on Corporate Governance, *OECD Principles of Corporate Governance* (Paris: OECD, 1999).

24 A recent World Bank paper on corporate governance (Iskander and Chamlou, 2000, pp. 22–3) provides the following particularly fulsome account of this model:

THE DISCIPLINE OF COMPETITIVE FINANCIAL MARKETS ... Equity markets continuously monitor and place an objective value on corporations and, by extension, on their management. The day-to-day performance of a company's shares on a stock exchange is a transparent reminder to managers and owners of the company's perceived viability and value ... An active market for corporate control, fluctuations in stock prices, and the influence of shareholders keep managers focused on efficiency and commercial success ... Debt markets impose additional and often more stringent and direct discipline through threats of bankruptcy or an end to a poorly performing firm's access to capital. Transparent and properly regulated markets for debt finance prod corporations to employ debt profitably by servicing it or by covering creditor losses if the debt cannot be repaid.

The same study acknowledges that 'share prices can be an effective measure of performance only if equity markets are deep and well regulated to ensure fairness, efficiency, liquidity and transparency', and that other factors also play a role in 'external discipline for good corporate governance'. These include 'reputational agents' such as lawyers, investment bankers, investment analysts, credit rating agencies, consumer activists, environmentalists, and accounting and auditing professionals, who 'exert enormous pressure on companies to disclose accurate information to the market, to improve human capital, and to align the interests of managers, shareholders, and other stakeholders'. The paper was written before the proliferation of recent disclosures concerning corporate scandals and its consequent irony will not be lost on students of the Enron case.

25 See *OECD Principles of Corporate Governance 2004* (Paris: OECD, 2004).

26 'OECD launches drive to strengthen corporate governance', 15 November 2002, available at http://www.oecd.org.

27 See Basel Committee on Banking Supervision, *International Convergence of Capital Measurement and Capital Standards: A Revised Framework* (Basel: Bank for International Settlements, June 2004), Part 2: iv.C.

28 Ibid., Part 2: vi.

29 The Joint Forum was established in 1996 under the aegis of the Basel Committee, IOSCO and the IAIS to take forward the work of an earlier entity, the Tripartite Group, established in 1993 to address issues related to the supervision of financial conglomerates. See Basel Committee on Banking Supervision, *Compendium of Documents Produced by the Joint Forum* (Basel: Bank for International Settlements, July 2001), p. 5. For an extensive review of the work of the Joint Forum, and before it of the Tripartite Group, see Walker, 2001, Part ii, ch. 3.

30 Problems arising in the supervision of mixed conglomerates (firms including substantial non-financial activities) have been addressed by the Basel-based bodies, the Tripartite Group in a 1995 report recommending some form of supervisory ring-fencing of such activities. But the principal focus of the bodies' work were the conglomerates' financial activities. See, for example, ibid., pp. 190, 203.

31 Concerning this initiative, see Boxes 2.1 and 2.2.

32 The consequences of the differences between these two approaches can be illustrated for leases where the treatment under the IFRS is less than one-tenth as long as that of the US FASB. See J. Dini, 'Can one honest man save accounting?', *Institutional Investor*, July 2002, p. 42.

33 FASB, 'FASB Interpretation no. 46. Consolidation of Variable Interest Entities: an Interpretation of ARB no. 51', *Financial Accounting Series*, no. 240-A, January 2003.

34 See United States Bankruptcy Southern District of New York, January 2003, Appendix B (Accounting Standards), pp. 25–9.

35 The discussion that follows makes extensive use of the review of Simpson Thacher and Bartlett, *Sarbanes-Oxley Act of 2002: CEO/CFO Certifications, Corporate Responsibility and Accounting Reform*, 31 July 2002.

36 On 'blackout periods', see the section in this chapter entitled 'Enron's system of incentives and sanctions'.

37 The code of ethics is to cover standards necessary to promote honest and ethical conduct (including the ethical handling of conflicts of interest), adequate disclosure in periodic financial reports, and compliance with official rules and regulations. If such a code of ethics does not exist, the firm is to disclose the reason.

38 See, for example, the summary in Scott (2004), pp. 30–3.

39 See J. Authers and S. Silver, 'Comment and Analysis', *Financial Times*, 20 January 2005, which discusses the SEC's case against the Mexican television firm, Azteca, for breaches of Sarbanes-Oxley requirements on certification of accounts.

40 See D. C. Johnston, 'US tax report is "eye-popping" ', *International Herald Tribune*, 14 February 2003; J. Chaffee, 'Enron tax shelters bring calls for reform', *Financial Times*, 14 February 2003. The report to the Senate Finance Committee is 2,700 pages in length.

41 For the role envisaged for these key financial standards and commentary, see UNCTAD, *Trade and Development Report 2001*, Part Two, ch. IV, reprinted as A. Cornford, 'Standards and regulation', ch. 2 of Akyüz (2002); and Schneider (2003).

42 The ROSCs are the result of a joint programme of the IMF and the World Bank to assess progress in the implementation of key financial standards. Each assessment of a standard results in a ROSC module, only those standards believed by a country to be most relevant to its circumstances being covered. Although the exercise is a voluntary one, the subjects of the financial standards will still be included in IMF Article IV surveillance for countries not volunteering but on the basis of other sources of information.

43 On the history of Chewco, see Powers *et al.* (2002), ch. II; Fox (2003), pp. 123–7, 232, 275–6. The resemblance between the names of some Enron partnerships (such as JEDI and Chewco) and characters figuring in the film, *Star Wars*, is not coincidental. Chewco was named after the character, Chewbacca.

44 See Powers *et al.* (2002), pp. 49–58, which comments that its authors were unable to decide 'whether Chewco's failure to qualify [as having sufficient outside equity] resulted from bad judgement or carelessness on the part of Enron employees or Andersen, or whether it was caused by Kopper and other Enron employees putting their own interests ahead of their obligations to Enron' (p. 54).

45 On the hedging of Enron's exposure to Rhythms, see Powers *et al.* (2002), ch. IV; Fox (2003), pp. 148–54, 159–62.

46 To strengthen the hedge, Enron subsequently entered into further derivative transactions (in the form of put and call options) with Swap Sub (Powers *et al.*, 2002, p. 85).

47 A put option is in the money when its exercise price exceeds that of the asset on which it is written (in this case the Rhythms stock).

48 The Fastow Family Foundation received US$4.5 million on an investment of US$25,000, and two other Enron employees received approximately US$1 million on investments of US$5,800 (Powers *et al.*, 2002, pp. 92–6).

49 In this case the eponymous characters were the dinosaurs in the film, *Jurassic Park*. The story of the Raptors is covered in ibid., ch. V, which notes that the transactions and structured finance vehicles involved were extremely complex, so that

'although we describe these transactions in some depth, even the detail here is only a summary' (p. 99).

50 LJM2 was managed by Enron employees (Fastow, Kopper and Ben Glisan) and made an investment in each of the Raptors on which it was to receive an initial guaranteed return before any hedging or derivative transactions with Enron could take effect. The results were extremely favourable to LJM2: Fastow reported to investors in October 2000 that the internal rates of return on their investments in the four Raptors were 193 per cent, 278 per cent, 2500 per cent and 125 per cent (in the last case a projection) (ibid., p. 128).

51 The stock contracts were in the form of a contingent forward contract under which Raptor I had a contingent right to receive Enron stock at a future date as long as its price exceeded a certain level (ibid., p. 100). The contingent character of these contracts increased the risks to the financial capacity of the Raptor.

52 The description of these contracts in ibid., pp. 107–8 is a little vague, in that it fails to specify the way in which losses and gains would be calculated.

53 Concerning such contracts, see note 51 above.

54 The availability of Enron stock to the Raptors could be compromised by falls in its share price, since under the stock contracts provided to them by Enron, delivery was contingent on the condition that the share price exceed a certain level at a specified future date.

55 As the Raptors came under pressure, a separate accounting problem emerged caused by the hedges but this time involving Enron's balance sheet. When the Raptors were established, the promissory notes received from them in return for Enron shares and share contracts received accounting treatment leading to an increase in shareholders' equity. In September 2001, Andersen and Enron concluded that this had been incorrect, and that there should have been no net effect on Enron's equity. The result of this correction was a downward revision of US$1 billion in Enron's equity in its financial statement for the third quarter of the year (ibid., pp. 125–6).

56 Chapter VI of the Powers Report exemplified its conclusion with details of six transactions.

57 Enron, *Annual Report 1998*, p. 50.

58 VAR is the worst-case loss expected during a period at a specified level of probability. Larger losses are possible, but only at lower levels of probability.

59 Enron, *Annual Report 1998*, p. 56.

60 Enron, *Annual Report 1999*, p. 52.

61 Ibid., p. 53.

62 Ibid., p. 59.

63 Enron, *Annual Report 2000*.

64 According to the Powers *et al.* (2002), p. 117, the note was recorded at zero 'because it had essentially no basis in the TNPC stock' made available to provide the financial capacity of Raptor III.

References

Akyüz, Y. (ed.) (2002) *Reforming the Global Financial Architecture: Issues and Proposals* (London: Zed Books for UNCTAD and Third World Network).

Fox, L. (2003) *Enron: The Rise and Fall* (Hoboken, NJ: John Wiley).

Fusaro, P. C. and R. M. Miller (2002) *What Went Wrong at Enron: Everyone's Guide to the Largest Bankruptcy in US History* (Hoboken, NJ: John Wiley).

Henderson, S. K. (2003) *Henderson on Derivatives* (London: LexisNexis).

Iskander, M. R. and M. Chamlou (2000) *Corporate Governance: A Framework for Implementation* (Washington, DC: The World Bank).

Powers, W. C. Jr., R. S. Troubh and H. S. Winokur (2002) *Report of Investigation by the Special Investigative Committee of the Board of Directors of Enron Corp.* (known as 'The Powers Report') (1 February).

Scott, H. (2004) *International Finance: Law and Regulation* (London: Sweet & Maxwell).

Schneider, B. (ed.) (2003) *The Road to International Financial Stability: Are Key Financial Standards the Answer?* (Basingstoke: Palgrave Macmillan).

Schwartz, M. and S. Watkins (2003) *Power Failure: The Inside Story of the Collapse of Enron* (New York: Doubleday).

United States Bankruptcy Court Southern District of New York (2003) *Second Interim Report of Neal Batson, Court-Appointed Examiner*, 'In re: Enron Corp. *et al.*, Debtors', 21 January.

United States Bankruptcy Court Southern District of New York (2003) *Third Interim Report of Neal Batson, Court-Appointed Examiner*, 'In re: Enron Corp. *et al.*, Debtors', 30 June.

United States Senate (2002) *The Role of the Board of Directors in Enron's Collapse*, Report prepared by the Permanent Subcommittee on Investigations of the Committee on Governmental Affairs, 8 July.

Walker, G. A. (2001) *International Banking Regulation, Law Policy and Practice* (New York: Kluwer Law International).

3

A Revisionist View of Enron and the Sudden Death of 'May'[1]

Frank Partnoy[2]

Introduction

This chapter makes two points about the academic and regulatory reaction to Enron's collapse. First, it argues that what emerged as the 'conventional story' of Enron, involving alleged fraud related to special purpose entities (SPEs), was incorrect. Instead, this chapter makes the revisionist claim that Enron was largely a story about derivatives – financial instruments such as options, futures and other contracts whose value is linked to some underlying financial instrument or index (see Box 3.1). A close analysis of the facts shows that the most prominent SPE transactions were largely irrelevant to Enron's collapse, and that most of Enron's deals with SPEs were arguably legal, even though disclosure of those deals was not compatible with economic reality (Partnoy, 2002).[3] To the extent SPEs are relevant to understanding Enron, it is the derivatives transactions between Enron and the SPEs – not the SPEs themselves – that matter. Even more important were Enron's derivatives trades and transactions other than those involving the SPEs. This first point about derivatives is important to the literature studying the relationship between finance and law: legal rules create incentives for parties to engage in economically equivalent unregulated transactions, and financial innovation creates incentives for parties to increase risks (to increase expected return) outside the scope of legal rules requiring disclosure.[4]

Second, this chapter argues that the regulatory response to Enron was in large part misguided because it focused too much on the conventional story. If the conventional story about Enron is incorrect – and Enron is largely a story about derivatives – then the prescriptions that follow from Enron's collapse, if any, should relate to the regulation and disclosure of derivatives. Interestingly, Congress – in a little-noticed provision of the Sarbanes-Oxley Act of 2002, Section 401(a) – sought to implement precisely such an approach, directing the Securities and Exchange Commission (SEC) to adopt new regulations requiring that annual and quarterly financial reports filed with the SEC disclose 'all material off-balance sheet transactions … that *may* have a material current or future effect on financial condition [of the company filing]'.[5] The SEC originally proposed disclosure regulations based on this heightened 'may' standard, but in its final release reverted to a lower 'reasonably likely' standard, with specific rules governing tabular disclosure of particular transactions.[6] Surprisingly, the SEC promulgated these 'reasonably likely' regulations even though Congress, in debating Sarbanes-Oxley, already had considered – and rejected – the 'reasonably likely' approach. This second point about regulatory response is important to the literatures studying both mandatory disclosure and the relationship between Congress and administrative agencies: not only did interested private actors quickly capture the agency rule-making process (Stigler 1971; Wilson, 1980, p. 369), but they were able to persuade the agency to revive an interpretation the legislature already had considered and rejected.

Scholarship addressing the collapse of Enron should incorporate these two points. To date, the debate among legal academics[7] has been framed by the 200-plus pages of the report by the Special Committee of Enron's Board of Directors, which was commissioned to study Enron's SPE transactions,[8] and by the related congressional hearings and proposals, which culminated in Sarbanes-Oxley. The essential facts from these sources are well known.[9]

In the first law review article addressing the collapse of Enron, William Bratton assessed four possible 'causation stories' about Enron's collapse (Bratton, 2002, pp. 1299–333). One of those stories was 'Enron as Derivatives Speculation Gone Wrong', and Bratton cautioned scholars not to draw too many conclusions about Enron until more facts were known about the firm's

---

Box 3.1   Derivatives markets

The two basic categories of derivatives are options and futures, although these instruments can be combined to create more complex financial instruments, including swaps and other structured derivatives. Derivatives can be traded in two ways: on regulated exchanges or in unregulated over-the-counter (OTC) markets. The size of derivatives markets is measured typically in terms of the notional values of contracts. Recent estimates of the size of the exchange-traded derivatives market, which includes all contracts traded on the major options and futures exchanges, are in the range of US$13 to US$14 trillion in notional amount (Steinherr, 2000, p. 153). By contrast, the estimated notional amount of outstanding OTC derivatives as of June 2002 was US$128 trillion. In other words, OTC derivatives markets, which for the most part did not exist twenty (or, in some cases, even ten) years ago, now comprise about 90 per cent of the aggregate derivatives market, with trillions of dollars at risk. Measured by notional amount, value at risk, or any other measure, OTC derivatives markets are bigger than the markets for US stocks. See Bank for International Settlements, *Acceleration of OTC Derivatives Market Activity in the First Half of 2002*, Press release, 8 November 2002 (http://www.bis.org/publ/otc_hy0211.pdf).

trading in derivatives. Since then, most commentators on Enron have focused primarily on a handful of people and transactions – the company's senior executives (Lay, Skilling, and in particular, Fastow) and a small number of SPEs (Joint Energy Development Investments Limited Partnership (JEDI), Chewco, the LJM partnerships, and the Raptors) – concluding that these SPEs were designed to inflate Enron's income and hide its debt, and that the unravelling of these deals led Enron to restate its financial statements during 2001, and then to its collapse.[10] Scholars have also focused primarily on regulatory changes directed at these issues: increased penalties for fraud; new requirements for independent corporate directors, audit committees, and accountants; and new disclosure requirements.

The two points in this chapter suggest that the key to understanding Enron's collapse is to reframe this discussion in terms of the complexity of the financial instruments – derivatives and off-balance-sheet transactions – that drove Enron's major businesses.[11] Unfortunately, even after intense media scrutiny, congressional hearings, and other government investigations, most of the firm's derivatives dealings remain unpenetrated. Even after Enron's bankruptcy, the firm's own officials were unable to grasp enough detail to issue an annual report in 2002; even with the help of a new team of accountants from PricewaterhouseCoopers, they simply could not calculate the firm's assets and liabilities.[12] This chapter's claim is that those details are central. If scholars are to understand the implications of Enron's collapse, they must begin by revisiting the conventional story about Enron.

The next section of this chapter describes how Enron used and disclosed derivatives. Much of the relevant information about Enron's derivatives transactions was disclosed in Enron's financial reports, albeit in an unclear manner. Other derivatives were disclosed in summary form, based on SEC rules suggesting tabular presentation. Enron's risk exposure to derivatives was disclosed in limited ways, but arguably was consistent with prevailing standards of practice, which required disclosure of only 'reasonably likely' contingencies. Overall, Enron's disclosure practices were driven by accounting rules and were not necessarily compatible with economic reality.[13]

Finally, the last section of this chapter analyses the regulatory approach to derivatives disclosure. Enron's trading businesses and financial innovations were driven by a rules-based regulatory system in which derivatives were largely unregulated, even when they were economically equivalent to regulated financial instruments. The SEC's 'reasonably likely' standard did not require the disclosure of financial contingencies that are important to the assessment of derivatives-related risks. Moreover, the SEC's rules-based tabular disclosure regulations create perverse disclosure incentives. Congress recognised the limitations of such a system, and proposed a lower-threshold 'may' standard, but the SEC reverted to 'reasonably likely', supplemented by rules-based tabular disclosure. This disclosure regime has two flaws: it sets the bar too low for derivatives disclosure and creates unwarranted incentives for parties to make tabular disclosure (and not other disclosure) even if it is not useful. In general terms, efficient and fair financial regulation should treat derivatives as it treats economically equivalent financial instruments (including equivalent regulated securities). Accordingly, this chapter suggests in this context that standards based on economic reality generally are preferable to rules based on accounting reality, and that the standards for derivatives disclosure should be higher than that for other Management Discussion and Analysis (MD&A) disclosure, as Congress originally intended in enacting Section 401(a).

A revisionist view of Enron

This section assesses the importance of derivatives in understanding Enron. Enron used derivatives in transactions with other corporations and partnerships to borrow money 'off-balance-sheet' and to fund various SPEs. Derivatives were central to the SPE transactions; without derivatives, Enron could not have achieved the purposes it intended: inflating profits and hiding debt. Moreover, other derivatives deals – with outside parties other than the well-known SPEs – were even more important to Enron's collapse.

The collapse of Enron does not necessarily lead to a conclusion that *equity* capital markets were inefficient, or that high *equity* valuations were unwarranted.[14] Instead, Enron's high equity valuations through 2000 might rationally have been based, at least in part, on Enron's ability to exploit the rules-based regulatory environment applicable to debt and derivatives,[15] thereby securing an unusually low cost of capital, given Enron's risks. Enron used financial innovation to reduce a range of direct regulatory costs: it reduced reported taxable income, it issued preferred and other hybrid securities in place of equity (and debt); and it engaged in financial innovation to avoid specific rules in the natural gas and electricity markets. It also used derivatives to satisfy the rules-based regulatory regime associated with credit ratings,[16] thereby reducing its cost of capital. In other words, Enron's collapse is evidence of inefficiencies in the rules-laden debt and derivatives markets more than it is evidence of inefficiencies in equity markets. As Enron lost the ability to exploit the relevant rules during 2001, the value of its residual equity claims collapsed.

The key factor sustaining Enron's ability to secure a low cost of capital was an investment grade credit rating (for example, BBB+ from Standard & Poor's), which the major credit rating agencies gave to Enron's debt from 1995 until November 2001.[17] The rating agencies received information during this period indicating that Enron was engaging in substantial derivatives and off-balance sheet transactions (including both non-public information and information disclosed in Enron's annual reports), but they maintained an investment grade rating based in part on the assumption that Enron's off-balance sheet transactions were appropriately excluded from

Enron's debt and should not matter in calculating related financial ratios, because they were non-recourse to Enron.[18] In reality, Enron's derivatives converted its off-balance sheet debt into billions of dollars of recourse debt, depending – among other things – on Enron's stock price. If Enron's credit rating had reflected the company's actual debt levels during this period – had been sub-investment grade – its cost of capital would have been much higher, and its equity valuations would have been much lower. In sum, derivatives enabled Enron to exploit inefficiencies in debt and derivatives rules, thereby artificially (if only temporarily) inflating the value of its residual equity claims.

Derivatives and the SPEs

A complete description of Enron's use of derivatives transactions with SPEs is well beyond the scope of this chapter (or any article – the bankruptcy examiner's report detailing such transactions already runs to several thousand pages[19]). Instead, this section will briefly analyse the role of derivatives in a few of Enron's most prominent SPEs.[20] First, Enron used derivatives with the LJM1 and Raptor SPEs to hide losses suffered on technology stocks. Second, Enron used derivatives with the JEDI and Chewco SPEs to hide debt incurred to finance new businesses. The common theme in these transactions was that, without these derivatives,[21] Enron's SPE 'schemes' would not have worked.

Using derivatives to hide losses on technology stocks

First, Enron used derivatives to hide hundreds of millions of dollars of losses on its speculative investments in various technology-orientated firms, such as Rhythms Net Connections, Inc., a start-up telecommunications company. Through a subsidiary, Enron invested US$10 million in Rhythms NetConnections, an Internet service provider and potential competitor of Netscape, the company whose initial public offering had marked the beginning of the Internet boom in 1995.[22] Enron bought shares in Rhythms NetConnections at less than US$2 per share.

Rhythms NetConnections issued stock to the public in an initial public offering on 6 April 1999, during the heyday of the Internet boom, at US$21 per share; by the end of the day, the shares were trading at US$69 per share. Enron suddenly had a US$300 million gain. Enron's other venture capital investments in technology companies also increased in value at first, alongside the widespread run-up in the value of dot.com stocks. As was typical in initial public offerings (IPO), Enron was prohibited from selling its stock for six months.[23] Because these stocks were carried in Enron's 'merchant portfolio', changes in the value of the positions resulted in volatility on its balance sheet.

Enron engaged in a series of derivatives transactions designed to reduce this volatility and lock-in its profits, as well as to capture the value of futures contracts on its own stock. Specifically, Enron entered into a series of transactions with an SPE, LJM Swap Sub L.P., which was owned by another SPE, LJM1, in which Enron essentially exchanged its shares in Rhythms NetConnections for a loan, ultimately, from LJM1.[24] These deals were structured as derivatives rather than as loans or sales, because Enron would have been required to record a loan as a debt, and would have been required to pay tax on a sale (and prior to six months from the IPO date, would not have had the right to sell, because of the lock-in provision). A derivatives deal did not incur such regulatory consequences.

Enron's transactions with the Raptors worked in a similar fashion. Enron attempted to minimise the appearance of losses in its investments in technology companies by creating SPEs as 'accounting hedges'.[25] The critical element in this strategy was a series of derivatives transactions between Enron and the Raptors.

In three of the Raptors, Enron funded the SPE by giving it contingent derivatives based on restricted stock and stock contracts at below market value, in exchange for a promissory note. Most of the derivatives transactions that followed – essentially put options on Enron's stock – allowed the Raptors to keep any increases in value of the technology stocks, but required them to pay Enron the amount of any future losses. Because the Raptors' assets consisted almost entirely of Enron stock, the more the value of the technology stocks declined, the more of Enron stock would need to be sold to meet their obligations. As more Enron stock was sold to meet the obligations related to the derivatives contracts, the Raptors would have less money available to repay the promissory note to Enron.[26]

As a result, Enron continued to bear the economic risk in the transactions. The performance of the underlying technology investments was irrelevant to the other investors in the Raptors, because they were guaranteed a return. Enron recognised a gain on the technology stocks by recognising the value of the Raptor loans right away, and it avoided recognising on an interim basis any future losses on the technology stocks, were such losses to occur (which, of course, they did).[27]

In all, Enron had derivative instruments on 54.8 million shares of Enron common stock at an average price of US$67.92 per share, or US$3.7 billion total – all publicly disclosed in Enron's 2000 annual report.[28] In other words, at the start of these deals, Enron's derivatives obligations amounted to 7 per cent of all of its outstanding shares. As Enron's share price declined, that obligation increased, and Enron's shareholders were substantially diluted. Yet even as the Raptors' assets and Enron's shares declined in value, Enron did not reflect those declines in its financial statements, because its derivatives transactions fell outside rules that required Enron to record such losses.

Using derivatives to hide debt

A second example involved Enron using derivatives with SPEs to hide debt incurred to finance new businesses. Essentially, some very complicated and unclear accounting rules allowed Enron to avoid disclosing certain assets and liabilities.

Two of these SPEs were JEDI and Chewco Investments, L.P. (Chewco). Enron owned only 50 per cent of JEDI, and therefore – under applicable accounting rules – could (and did) report JEDI as an unconsolidated equity affiliate. If Enron had owned 51 per cent of JEDI, accounting rules would have required Enron to consolidate all of JEDI's financial results in its financial statements.[29]

One way to minimise the applicability of this rule would be for Enron to create an SPE with mainly debt and only a tiny sliver of equity, say US$1 worth, for which the company could easily find an outside investor. One might expect to find a pronouncement by accounting regulators that such a transaction would not conform to Generally Accepted Accounting Principles (GAAP). However, there was no such pronouncement. The Financial Accounting Standards Board (FASB), the private entity that sets most accounting rules and advises the SEC, had not answered the accounting question of what would constitute sufficient capital from an independent source, so that an SPE would not need to be consolidated.[30]

Instead, beginning in 1982, Financial Accounting Standard (FAS) No. 57, Related Party Disclosures, contained a general requirement that companies disclose the nature of relationships they had with related parties, and describe transactions with them.[31] In 1991, the Acting Chief Accountant of the SEC attempted to clarify this requirement in a guidance letter issued in the context of leases.[32]

Based on this letter, and on opinions from auditors and lawyers, companies began incurring off-balance sheet debt through unconsolidated SPEs where (i) the company did not have more than 50 per cent of the equity of the SPE; and (ii) the equity of the SPE was at least 3 per cent of the total capital (this provision was generally referred to as the '3 per cent rule'). Under these rules, Enron would have been able to borrow 97 per cent of the capital of its SPEs without consolidating that debt on its balance sheet.

Because Enron could not find a truly independent investor to provide 3 per cent equity, it entered into a derivatives transaction with Chewco similar to the one it entered into with the Raptors, but structured as a swap, effectively guaranteeing repayment to Chewco's outside investor (consequently, the investor's sliver of equity ownership in Chewco was not really equity from an economic perspective, because the investor had nothing – other than Enron's credit – at risk). In its financial statements, Enron took the position that, while it provided guarantees to unconsolidated subsidiaries, those guarantees did not have a readily determinable fair value, and management did not consider it reasonably likely that Enron would be required to perform or otherwise incur losses associated with these guarantees. That position enabled Enron to avoid recording the guarantees (even the guarantees listed in the footnotes to Enron's financial statements were recorded at only 10 per cent of their nominal value).[33]

The effect of the derivatives transaction was that Enron – not the 'investor' in Chewco – had the economic exposure to Chewco's assets. Ultimately, the ownership daisy chain unravelled once Enron was deemed to own Chewco. Then JEDI was forced to consolidate Chewco, and Enron was forced to consolidate both limited partnerships – and all of their losses – in its financial statements.[34]

Nearly a year before this unravelling, Enron disclosed some of the information related to these transactions in its public filings. In its 2000 annual report, Enron disclosed about US$2.1 billion of such derivatives transactions with related entities, and recognised gains of about US$500 million related to those transactions.[35] A few sophisticated analysts seemed to understand Enron's transactions based on that disclosure, and they bet against Enron's stock.[36] Other securities analysts either did not understand (or did not read) the disclosures, or chose not to speak, perhaps because of conflicts of interest related to Enron's substantial banking business.

In sum, Enron did numerous derivatives deals with its SPEs, thereby enabling it to inflate income, avoid losses and hide debt. Enron disclosed, at least partially, many of the relevant material facts about these deals. To the extent that these SPEs are relevant to the debate about Enron, it is the derivatives deals with the SPEs – the put options and contingent contracts with the Raptors and the swaps related to JEDI and Chewco – that are of the greatest importance.

Other derivatives use

Not only is the 'conventional story' about Enron and the SPEs suspect – in that derivatives were the key to the SPEs – but the SPEs were not especially important to Enron's collapse. Instead, it was derivatives and off-balance-sheet transactions *other* than those involved in the SPEs that were of primary importance; issues related to *those* deals should be the focus of academic and regulatory inquiry into Enron's collapse.

If the SPEs, even with the derivatives deals, were not significant to Enron's publicly reported financial statements, then why did Enron collapse? One possible explanation is that investors simply lost confidence in the company, and rushed to sell their shares, no longer trusting Enron's financial statements. However, this explanation ignores the role of sophisticated investors, who followed Enron closely and were willing to buy the company's stock when they perceived it to be undervalued. Enron's officers had several months after analysts began questioning the firm's SPEs in which to disclose additional information showing that the company was in reasonable financial condition. Yet Enron's stock price declined steadily throughout 2001, and the most significant short-term declines were not based on new negative information (Partnoy, 2003, pp. 330–41).

Instead, a more plausible reason for the decline in the value of Enron's stock was that Enron had engaged in numerous other derivatives deals to inflate reported profits, to reduce reported debt, and to make it appear that Enron was sufficiently creditworthy to justify the investment grade credit rating necessary to sustain its derivatives trading business. As it became more likely that the credit rating agencies would downgrade Enron to sub-investment grade, Enron's stock price fell. The largest single-day decline was the day the credit rating agencies finally confirmed the downgrade, when shareholders learned that Enron's access to capital would become too limited and costly to sustain its derivatives trading operation.

As with the SPE transactions, a complete description of Enron's other derivatives is well beyond the scope of this chapter.[37] Instead, this section will analyse briefly Enron's use of derivatives other than in transactions with SPEs. First, Enron's financial statements disclosed extensive use of derivatives, although the disclosures were not especially useful because they did not go beyond disclosures required by the rules. Second, there is evidence that Enron's profits arose primarily from derivatives trading. Enron did not disclose the contingent risks associated with its trading businesses, but SEC disclosure rules arguably did not require such disclosure. Even accounting for the effect of the previously discussed SPEs, as reflected in Enron's restated financials in November 2001, Enron was in strong financial condition. Its net income, even as restated, had been positive and increasing since 1993.[38] Enron's last years were especially profitable, and the company's net income for 2000, even as restated, was nearly a billion dollars.[39]

Similarly, the balance sheet value of Enron's equity was positive and increasing throughout this period. In 2000, even as restated, Enron's equity was recorded at more than US$10 billion. Compared to its reported equity, Enron's reported debt was at reasonable levels; even as restated, Enron's debt–equity ratio was roughly 1.0 during 1999 and 2000, and had declined substantially since 1997.[40]

Enron's bankruptcy examiner concluded that Enron's actual debt was more than double the amount reported in its financial statements.[41] Such high debt levels would probably not have warranted an investment grade rating, given Enron's capital structure and financial performance. But neither should such high debt levels have been a surprise to anyone who closely examined Enron's financial statements. Enron's 2000 annual report alone makes it clear that Enron had incurred substantial additional leverage and had increased significantly its risk exposure in various derivatives markets.

First, even a cursory examination of Enron's balance sheet reveals remarkable disclosures of Enron's new derivatives deals, cleverly labelled 'price risk management activities'.[42] For 2000, Enron reported price risk management activities as its most significant asset (US$12.0 billion, up from US$2.2 billion in 1999). Enron also reported price risk management activities as its most significant liability (US$10.5 billion, up from US$1.8 billion in 1999).[43] Since the previous year, derivatives assets and liabilities had increased more than fivefold.

The same conclusions are apparent from Enron's income statement, which reports US$7.2 billion of 'other revenues',[44] and explains, in a footnote, that 'other revenues' consist of unrealised ('mark-to-market') gains on price risk management activities (derivatives trading).[45] In aggregate, Enron's revenues and expenses each tripled from 1998 to 2000.[46] But Enron's net income increased only marginally during the same period; by 2000, net income was less than 1 per cent of total revenues.[47] Enron's non-derivatives businesses were not performing well in 1998 and were deteriorating through 2000. Enron's non-derivatives businesses made some money in 1998, broke even in 1999, and lost money in 2000 (Partnoy, 2002). Enron officials stated that it was not a trading firm, and that derivatives were used primarily for hedging purposes, and Enron's stock traded at much higher multiples of earnings than other trading-orientated firms. But Enron's financial statements did not support such representations.

Accounting regulations did not require additional disclosure related to derivatives in Enron's financial statements. Instead, specific rules suggested tabular disclosure of various types in footnotes to financial statements. Enron included tabular disclosure of its price risk management activities in terms of notional amount, fair value and counter-party risk.[48] But Enron did not include in the footnotes to its financial statements a description of possible contingencies related to its price risk management activities.

Instead, Enron included some information about such contingencies in the MD&A section of its annual report, where it disclosed in tabular form – as suggested by SEC rules – a range of 'value at risk' (VAR) estimates related to its derivatives risk exposure. Enron's VAR methodologies captured a 95 per cent confidence interval for a one-day holding period, and therefore did not cover worst-case scenarios for Enron's trading operations.[49] Nevertheless, Enron's disclosure arguably satisfied SEC rules, which permitted companies to comply with existing risk disclosure requirements by reporting such VAR estimates.

Enron reported high and low monthend values for its trading, but not interim values or averages, and therefore had incentives to smooth its profits and losses at month-end.[50] Enron did not report its maximum VAR during the year, or give qualitative information about worst-case scenarios, and therefore did not report how much risk its traders were taking.

Even so, Enron's reported VAR figures were remarkable. In 2000, Enron reported VAR for what it called 'commodity price' risk – which included natural gas derivatives trading – of US$66 million, more than triple its 1999 value. Enron reported VAR for equity trading of US$59 million, more than double the 1999 value. A VAR of US$66 million meant that Enron expected, based on historical averages, that on 5 per cent of all trading days (on average, 12 business days during the year) its commodity derivatives trading operations would gain or lose US$66 million. Enron's highest end-of-month commodity price risk VAR estimate was US$81 million (almost 10 per cent of Enron's reported net income for 2000).[51] These VAR estimates were higher than virtually any other company, including other trading firms.

Because Enron's derivatives frequently had long maturities – maximum terms ranged from six to twenty-nine years[52] – there were often no prices from liquid markets to use as benchmarks in valuing and assessing the derivatives. For these long-dated derivatives, professional judgement was important to valuation. For a simple instrument, Enron might calculate the discounted present value of cash flows using Enron's borrowing rates, but more complex instruments required more complex methodologies. For example, Enron completed over 5,000 weather derivatives deals, with a notional value of more than US$4.5 billion, and many of these deals could not be valued without professional judgement. Enron disclosed that it relied on 'the professional judgement of experienced business and risk managers' in assessing worst-case scenarios not covered by its VAR methodologies. But Enron did not report any qualitative information about worst-case scenarios, nor did regulations require that it do so.

Moreover, there is substantial evidence that Enron's VAR disclosures underestimated the firm's derivatives risks because they were based on inaccurate internal estimates of the variables used to value its derivatives.[53] Enron's derivatives traders faced intense pressure to meet quarterly earnings targets imposed directly by management and indirectly by securities analysts who covered Enron. To ensure that Enron met these estimates, some traders manipulated the reporting of their 'real' economic profits and losses in an attempt to fit the 'imagined' accounting profits and losses reflected in Enron's financial statements. First, traders smoothed income using 'prudency' reserves – dummy accounts that led to false profit and loss entries for the derivatives Enron traded (see Box 3.2).[54] Second, traders mismarked the forward curves used to determine the current value of derivatives trades (see Box 3.3).[55] Both methods reduced the apparent volatility of Enron's trading businesses, making Enron's derivatives trading appear less risky.

If Enron had been making money in what it represented as its core businesses, its substantial derivatives risks would not have mattered much. Even after Enron restated its financial statements on 8 November 2001, it could have clarified its accounting treatment, consolidated its debt, and assured analysts and investors that it was a viable ongoing concern. But it could not. Why not?

The answer requires a revision of the conventional view of Enron's collapse. What Enron represented as its core business was not making money, even as Enron's stock price was rising during the late 1990s. Recall that Enron began as an energy firm. Over time, Enron shifted its focus from the bricks-and-mortar energy business to the trading of derivatives. As this shift occurred, some of Enron's employees began misrepresenting the profits and losses of Enron's derivatives trading operations. Enron's derivatives trading was profitable, but it was much more volatile than it appeared, based on Enron's financial reports. Although Enron was a 'bricks-and-mortar' company when it was created in 1985, by the end it had become primarily a derivatives

Box 3.2 The concept of a 'prudency' reserve

Enron's derivatives traders kept records of their profits and losses. For each trade, a trader would report either a profit or a loss, typically in spreadsheet format. Instead of recording the entire profit for a trade in one column, some traders split the profit from a trade into two columns. The first column reflected the portion of the actual profits the trader intended to add to Enron's current financial statements. The second column, labelled the 'prudency' reserve, included the remainder.

To understand this concept of a 'prudency' reserve, suppose a derivatives trader earned a profit of US$10 million. Of that US$10 million, the trader might record US$9 million as profit today, and enter US$1 million into 'prudency'. An average deal would have 'prudency' of up to US$1 million, and all the 'prudency' entries might add up to US$10 to US$15 million. The portion of profits recorded as 'prudency' could be used to offset any future losses. 'Prudency' reserves were especially effective for long-maturity derivatives contracts, because it was more difficult to determine a precise valuation as of a particular date for those contracts, and any 'prudency' cushion would have protected the traders from future losses for several years ahead. In sum, 'prudency' reserves smoothed Enron's trading profits and losses, thereby reducing apparent volatility.

Box 3.3 Forward curves

A forward curve is a list of 'forward rates' for a range of maturities. In simple terms, a forward rate is the rate at which a person can buy something in the future. For example, natural gas forward contracts trade on the New York Mercantile Exchange (NYMEX). A trader can commit to buy a particular type of natural gas to be delivered in a few weeks, months, or even years. The rate at which a trader can buy natural gas in one year is the one-year forward rate. The rate at which a trader can buy natural gas in ten years is the ten-year forward rate. The forward curve for a particular natural gas contract is simply the list of forward rates for all maturities.

Forward curves are used to determine the value of a derivatives contract today. As with any firm involved in trading derivatives, Enron had risk management and valuation systems that used forward curves to generate profit and loss statements. However, some Enron traders selectively mismarked their forward curves, typically in order to hide losses (traders are compensated based on their profits, so if a trader can hide losses by mismarking forward curves, he or she is likely to receive a larger bonus). These losses ranged in the tens of millions of dollars for certain markets. For more complex deals, a trader would use a spreadsheet model of the trade for valuation purposes, and tweak the assumptions in the model to make a transaction appear more, or less, valuable.

Certain derivatives contracts were more susceptible to mismarking than others. Traders typically would not mismark contracts that were publicly traded – such as the natural gas contracts traded on NYMEX – because quotations of the values of those contracts would be available publicly. However, because the NYMEX forward curve has a maturity of only six years, a trader would be more likely to mismark a ten-year natural gas forward rate. At Enron, forward curves remained mismarked for as long as three years. From a disclosure perspective, such a strategy would have had a similar effect to the use of prudency reserves.

trading firm, dependent on access to low-cost capital (and, therefore, on its own investment grade credit rating).

Enron's trading operations were not regulated by US securities or commodities regulators, and the OTC derivatives it traded fell outside the scope of US securities law. OTC derivatives trading also was beyond the reach of organised, regulated exchanges. Thus, Enron – like many firms that trade OTC derivatives – fell into a regulatory black hole.[56] The absence of regulation might not have mattered if investors had been aware of the firm's risks. But Enron's key gatekeepers (Coffee, 2002)[57] – including the major credit rating agencies – either failed to spot the numerous risk disclosures related to Enron's derivatives trading, or spotted the disclosures but did not respond.

In sum, the story of Enron's collapse is not what it appears to be at first. The firm was a highly-leveraged derivatives trading firm and it collapsed when its credit rating finally reflected that fact. The scholarly and regulatory response to Enron's collapse should reflect this understanding. Given this revised view, the next section assesses the specific regulatory response to Enron's failure to disclose more information about its use of derivatives.

The regulatory response to Enron's use of derivatives

What lessons can be drawn from Enron's collapse about the type of regulation that should govern derivatives disclosure? Specifically, should regulation be weighted toward rules or standards,[58] and at what level of required disclosure should any rules or standards be aimed?

Securities regulation – like most regulation – is generally a combination of blended rules/standards with some 'rules' (for example, various types of tabular form disclosure) and some 'standards' (for example, the 'reasonably likely' threshold for MD&A), with varying levels of required disclosure, depending on the type of information. Congress, the SEC, and international regulators have suggested that the weighting should be towards standards, yet disclosure regulation in practice – particular as it relates to derivatives – has been highly rules-based. Recently, Congress and the SEC have disagreed about the appropriate level of disclosure.

This section concludes that Enron's collapse was strong evidence of the substantial inefficiencies associated with a rules-based disclosure regime, specifically rules based on accounting reality rather than economic reality, and suggests that the SEC should move – as Congress expressly intended in passing Section 401(a) of Sarbanes-Oxley – towards a standard-based regime designed to capture more disclosure of financial contingencies related to derivatives.

Market-based responses

The analysis of derivatives disclosure in MD&A raises, in a specific context, the question scholars have asked for decades about whether regulators should mandate disclosure at all. Enron's derivatives disclosure practices are a challenging example for the theoretical literature on mandatory disclosure.[59]

One possible regulatory response to Enron's collapse is no response at all. According to the argument supporting this approach, market participants, post-Enron, will put pressure on companies to disclose relevant facts about their financial contingencies, including derivatives risks, and companies that do not make the demanded disclosures will suffer a higher cost of capital and lower share valuation. For example, Larry Ribstein has argued that the markets will correct Enron-related problems, because investors and analysts will now understand where and how to look for the relevant information, and companies will have a model to follow in deciding how much to disclose (Ribstein, 2002, pp. 43–53).

However, if the argument in the previous section of this chapter is correct – and many market participants have a fundamental misunderstanding of Enron's collapse, more (at the time of writing) than a year after the company's bankruptcy – it seems unlikely that the same people will have the ability to assess, and therefore have the incentives to demand, appropriate and relevant information. Moreover, given the pace of financial innovation, even sophisticated financial analysts are unlikely to know precisely which questions to ask, or to be able to determine whether an answer is accurate or complete.[60] Perhaps most importantly, restrictions on shorting stock create asymmetric incentives, because sophisticated investors can easily buy shares to profit from positive information not reflected in market prices, but find it more difficult and costly to sell shares to profit from negative information (Shleifer and Vishny, 1997; Jones and Lamont, 2001).

Moreover, pre-Enron market failures are likely to continue if certain structural conditions in the market persist. First, disclosure related to derivatives positions is costly, and those costs are not reduced by the collapse of Enron; indeed, the cost of derivatives disclosure is greater if market participants are more concerned about such disclosures. Second, it is not necessarily easier for market participants to assess derivatives disclosure (or non-disclosure) post-Enron; they have similar technological capacity and access to information.[61] Moreover, the gap between what managers know and what shareholders understand[62] could persist if both issuers and investors become more sophisticated. Third, the collective action problems associated with a diffuse investor base have not changed. Any individual investor, even a large, sophisticated one (such as a hedge fund) will not be able to appropriate much of the gains from investigating a firm's derivatives risks. Fourth, the regulatory exemptions applicable to certain types of derivatives (for example, the Commodity Futures Modernization Act – CFMA[63]) and the limited disclosure requirements associated with accounting pronouncements related to derivatives (for example, FAS 133) will continue to permit companies to avoid disclosure even in the face of market pressure.

There has not been much pressure since Enron's collapse to reverse the CFMA exemptions for OTC derivatives, or otherwise to create regulations with incentives for companies to disclose more information about their use of complex financial instruments (indeed, the pressure from various market participants has been in the opposite direction).

In sum, if the benefits and costs of disclosure pre- and post-Enron's collapse are similar, disclosure practices – and the effects of those practices – are likely to be similar. Consider the question of whether Enron's managers would make different disclosure decisions regarding derivatives today. According to SEC rules, Enron's managers were required to decide whether it was 'reasonably likely' that a particular contingency would occur. Given the volatility in the markets where Enron participated, would managers choose to disclose the potential losses associated with a particular market change? Under a rules-based system, where the SEC specifically provides guidance regarding the kind of tabular disclosure that will satisfy its disclosure requirements, managers would be likely to make precisely those disclosures. If other companies were making such disclosures – and only such disclosures – managers of any given company would have a disincentive to make additional disclosures. Moreover, the most important contingencies would not be described definitively as 'reasonably likely'.

Tabular disclosure of the type suggested by SEC rules is unlikely to be useful, either to individual investors or securities analysts, and is therefore unlikely to promote price transparency and accuracy. Tabular disclosure is both complex and inevitably outdated, given the rapid pace of financial innovation.

Rules-based tabular disclosure would improve market efficiency if analysts found the information useful in evaluating companies. Unfortunately, rules-based tabular disclosure is quickly outdated and does not include enough information to enable even the most sophisticated securities analysts to assess the risks associated with a company's complex financial contingencies. The evidence supporting this conclusion is merely anecdotal, but is consistent with the well-established theory that financial market innovation is designed to avoid legal rules and outpace regulation (Miller, 1986, p. 460).

Congress recognised the potential for market failure in this area and provided accordingly, in Section 401(a) of Sarbanes-Oxley, that a broad-based standard would apply to issuer disclosures related to off-balance-sheet transactions, derivatives and other contingent financial contracts. Specifically, Section 401(a) provided that the SEC must promulgate rules requiring issuers to file quarterly and annual reports disclosing

> all material off-balance sheet transactions, arrangement, obligations (including contingent obligations), and other relationships of the issuer with unconsolidated entities or other persons, that *may* have a material current or future effect on financial condition, changes in financial

condition, results of operations, liquidity, capital expenditures, capital resources, or significant components of revenues or expenses.[64]

Before assessing the regulations promulgated by the SEC pursuant to Section 401(a), it is useful to place this legislation in context, among the regulatory apparatus governing disclosure of financial contingencies. The theory supporting these regulations is inconsistent with the notion that market pressure alone will create incentives for companies to make adequate disclosures, and that market participants will be able to decipher those disclosures. Instead, Item 303(a) of Regulation S–K identifies a basic and overriding requirement of MD&A to 'provide such other information that the registrant believes to be necessary to an understanding of its financial condition, changes in financial condition and results of operations'.[65]

The SEC has long recognised the importance of a narrative discussion in MD&A, and prior to Sarbanes-Oxley, MD&A regulations reflected a standard of 'reasonably likely to have a material effect'.[66] In 1987, the SEC noted that

> Numerical presentations and brief accompanying footnotes alone may be insufficient for an investor to judge the quality of earnings and the likelihood that past performance is indicative of future performance. MD&A is intended to give the investor an opportunity to look at the company through the eyes of management by providing both a short and long-term analysis of the business of the company.[67]

In other words, the SEC recognised the power and importance of narrative in supplying investors and analysts with information and analysis they otherwise might not receive, and the SEC endorsed the benefits of a disclosure regime that was weighted more to standards than to rules. The theory was that narrative disclosure would be important and useful, because it is more accessible to both investors and analysts, and therefore more likely to be reflected in market prices. The theory also suggested that narrative disclosure would be more likely to reflect accurately management's assessment of a company's future earnings – the key information in most financial valuation models – than numerical or tabular information.

In 1989, the SEC began requiring that managers make specific disclosures of financial contingencies and off-balance-sheet arrangements when a particular 'trend, demand, commitment, event or uncertainty' was 'reasonably likely'.[68] If management determined that the contingency was not reasonably likely to occur, no disclosure was required.[69]

As a separate component of the discussion of results of operations, management was required to discuss 'any known trends or uncertainties that have had or that the registrant reasonably expects will have a material favorable or unfavorable impact on net sales or revenues or income from continuing operations'.[70] These disclosure requirements were more like standards than rules. For example, the SEC noted that: 'The discussion and analysis shall focus specifically on material events and uncertainties known to management that would cause reported financial information not to be necessarily indicative of future operating results.'[71] Management was to discuss both new matters that will have an impact on future results, and matters that previously had had an impact on reported operations but were not expected to have an impact on future operations.

The key question relevant to such MD&A disclosure is whether the 'reasonably likely' standard is optimal in terms of expected costs and benefits. 'Reasonably likely' is an ambiguous term, and necessarily is subject to a range of interpretations and actions by managers. Economically rational managers will assess the expected benefits and costs of making a particular disclosure. If managers are acting exclusively in the shareholders' interests, they will disclose all financial contingencies, even without the disclosure requirement, where the benefits of doing so (to the shareholders) outweigh the costs. Accordingly, a disclosure requirement would matter only if managers either (i) misperceive how the disclosure would affect shareholder value, or (ii) are not acting in the shareholders' interests. With respect to item (i), managers might be risk averse with respect to financial disclosures.

With respect to item (ii),[72] economically rational managers would only disclose if the personal benefit was greater than the personal cost. Given the low starting point of disclosure of financial contingencies, most disclosure would probably have a negative price effect in the short run, unless the market was already discounting the uncertainty associated with potential undisclosed financial contingencies. Conversely, not disclosing financial contingencies in such an environment would lead to a higher share valuation. Accordingly, managers operating in such an environment would have an incentive to decide that contingencies were not 'reasonably likely' if their direct compensation would increase by more than the expected penalty associated with making such a disclosure. Given the standards-based nature of the regulation, the probability of a criminal prosecution for a decision about 'reasonably likely' would be an event of low probability. Similarly, the probability of personal liability would be low for such a decision, given insurance coverage and the high expected costs to plaintiffs of litigating such a suit (compared to a suit alleging more serious non-disclosure or fraud). Under such circumstances, management's disclosure might be suboptimal. Although the MD&A contingent disclosure standards arguably require a level of disclosure beyond GAAP, the penalties for failing to make such disclosures are not high, even if the most significant cases hold defendants in violation of securities law. For example, in 'In the Matter of Caterpillar, Inc.', the SEC found that Caterpillar had violated Section 13(a) of the Exchange Act by failing to disclose the importance of its Brazilian subsidiary to Caterpillar's earnings.[73] Caterpillar had argued that disclosure was not required under GAAP, but the SEC found that the MD&A rules required disclosure, even if GAAP did not. The question did not involve OTC derivatives or complex off-balance sheet transactions, but the principles were the same, and managers did not suffer any serious consequences.

Similarly, in '*United States* v. *Simon*' (*Simon*), Judge Henry Friendly found that accountants who had complied technically with Generally Accepted Accounting Principles could nevertheless be held to be criminally liable if the disclosures created a fraudulent or misleading impression among shareholders. In *Simon*, a footnote in Continental Vending's annual report had resembled the opaque disclosures in footnote 16 of Enron's 2000 annual report. As Judge Friendly put it, 'The jury could reasonably have wondered how accountants who were really seeking to tell the truth could have constructed a footnote so well designed to conceal the shocking facts.'[74] But the principles articulated in *Simon* did not increase expected costs much, because few prosecutions for similar conduct followed that case (moreover, the defendants paid small fines and were later pardoned by President Richard Nixon).[75]

Although the regulations requiring 'reasonably likely' disclosures are drafted using standards-like language, the SEC also has provided rules-based guidance by suggesting specific ways of disclosing various contingencies using tabular forms of presentation. With respect to complex financial contingencies, the SEC has even recommended particular methodologies (for example, VAR). By suggesting tabular forms of presentation, the SEC has effectively converted the standards into rules. Tabular forms of presentation discourage managers from providing other information, because non-standard disclosures are not comparable across companies. Analysts examining disclosure of financial contingencies can compare notional values and at-risk statistical measurements from dozens of companies with relative ease. But as the methods of disclosure specified in rules inevitably become less relevant because of financial innovation, and as registrants seek ways of minimising the costs of disclosure, those disclosures become less useful. Tabular presentation rules are likely to lead to lock-in, creating incentives for managers to avoid disclosing information about contingencies in addition to that required in tabular form.

In such circumstances, one would predict that companies such as Enron would increase their off-balance sheet transactions substantially, as well as their exposure to financial contingencies, without making additional disclosures. For example, given the choice between debt, which must be disclosed in the balance sheet, and an economically equivalent financial derivative such as a prepaid swap, which needs to be disclosed only in summary tabular form, rational managers would choose the disclosure with the lower regulatory cost. More importantly, managers would have an incentive to shift to complex financial contracting to the extent that these contracts were economically equivalent to other contracts, but were governed only by a 'reasonably likely' standard. In such instances, managers would not have an incentive to disclose more than the tabular disclosure suggested by the SEC. Enron's disclosures described in the previous section of this chapter are consistent with such incentives.

In sum, a relatively low standard, such as 'reasonably likely', is not likely to cover the financial contingencies most relevant to assessing a company involved in derivatives trading or complex risk-management activities. The SEC has converted even this relatively low-level standard into a set of less useful rules by providing guidance regarding tabular disclosure. Even if market incentives alone would lead managers to make adequate disclosures of complex financial contingencies, the presence of tabular disclosure rules will pervert this incentive. In such an environment, the regulatory incentives overwhelm market incentives, the level of disclosure will be suboptimal, and market prices will not reflect the risks associated with a firm's complex financial contingencies.

'May' or 'reasonably likely': the SEC's response

In a January 2002 release, the SEC restated its position on the 'reasonably likely' standard:

> Registrants are reminded that identification of circumstances that could materially affect liquidity is necessary if they are 'reasonably likely' to occur. This disclosure threshold is lower than 'more likely than not'. Market price changes, economic downturns, defaults on guarantees, or contractions of operations that have material consequences for the registrant's financial position or operating results can be reasonably likely to occur under some conditions.[76]

The SEC focused on the need for improved MD&A disclosure in three specific areas of concern: (i) liquidity and capital resources, including off-balance sheet arrangements; (ii) certain trading activities involving non-exchange traded contracts accounted for at fair value; and (iii) relationships and transactions with persons or entities that derive benefits from their non-independent relationships with the registrant or the registrant's related parties. The implication was that the SEC believed there were problems with this standard, as applied, but that these problems could be resolved with a simple warning.

Market participants, legislators and their staffs were well aware that the SEC was attempting to improve the level of disclosure by 'reminding' registrants of their previously-existing obligations under the 'reasonably likely' standard. With this SEC release as a backdrop, Congress held numerous hearings on Enron, and began debating the provisions that would become Sarbanes-Oxley.

In early 2002, Congress explicitly considered continuing to apply the extant 'reasonably likely' standard for disclosure of off-balance-sheet transactions, but rejected this standard after months of deliberations. The legislative history on this point is clear. The bill that became Sarbanes-Oxley was introduced in the House of Representatives on 14 February 2002; on 24 April 2002, the House considered and passed proposed legislation that included a 'reasonably likely' standard for off-balance-sheet transactions.[77] But on 15 July 2002, the Senate amended that proposal to add the wording in Section 401(a), changing 'reasonably likely' to 'may'.[78]

Several Senate committees held hearings on the issue of off-balance-sheet transactions, including derivatives, during the months before both houses passed the final legislation in July 2002, and the legislative history is replete with references to problems associated with the disclosures related to Enron's off-balance-sheet transactions and derivatives.[79] Indeed, the Senate Committee on Governmental Affairs, and its Permanent Subcommittee on Investigations, conducted a detailed investigation of such transactions and the disclosures related to these transactions from January 2002 until the July 2002 vote on Sarbanes-Oxley, and various Senators expressed serious concerns about these issues during this period.[80] In sum, Congress had the opportunity to weigh the costs and benefits of both the 'reasonably likely' and 'may' standards, and opted for the latter after months of hearings, debate and opportunity for public and private comment.

The legislative history does not make it clear what Congress intended specifically by the use of 'may'. Reference to the ordinary meaning of the term 'may' is not especially useful; a typical dictionary definition states that 'may' is 'used to indicate a certain measure of likelihood or probability'.[81] There are two possible interpretive approaches. First, Congress might have used 'may' to indicate that it was implementing a new standard to be used in assessing whether particular contingency disclosures were required. Second, Congress might have used 'may' to indicate that it was importing whatever appropriate measure of likelihood or probability the SEC would later deem appropriate, thereby delegating to the SEC the authority to articulate the precise contours of the standard. Under either possibility, it is clear that Congress had already considered – and rejected – the 'reasonably likely' standard and instead used 'may' in Section 401(a) to describe a different standard applicable to the disclosure of complex financial contingencies.

In proposing new rules in response to Section 401(a), the SEC indicated its belief that, in using the word 'may', Congress intended to work a dramatic change in the disclosure standard applicable to financial contingencies. The proposed rules state:

> We read the legislative mandate in the Sarbanes-Oxley Act as suggesting a lower disclosure threshold for prospectively material information related to off-balance sheet arrangements. Instead of adopting the 'reasonably likely' standard, it directs us to adopt a rule to require disclosure of items that 'may' have a material current or future effect. We believe that an

appropriate interpretation of the disclosure threshold is best captured by the concept of 'remoteness'. Accordingly, the proposals would require disclosure of off-balance sheet arrangements under circumstances where management concludes that the likelihood of the occurrence of a future event and its material effect is higher than remote. In other words, an off-balance sheet arrangement 'may' have a current or future material effect, and disclosure would be required, unless management determines that the occurrence of an event and the materiality of its effect is outside of the realm of reasonable possibility.[82]

The SEC proposed 'not remote' and 'reasonably possible' as standards consistent with Congress's intent in using 'may'. 'Not remote' and 'reasonably possible' (like 'reasonably likely') are ambiguous terms, and are long-standing probability thresholds used in financial disclosure.[83] By using a 'not remote' (or 'reasonably possible') standard, the SEC indicated in its proposed rules that managers should increase the quantity and quality of disclosures with respect to financial derivatives and off-balance-sheet transactions.[84] These comments were consistent with the legislative history of Sarbanes-Oxley and the numerous Congressional hearings related to Enron's use of derivatives.

The SEC received approximately four dozen comment letters in response to the proposed release, most of which arrived on 9 December 2002, the deadline for comments (several letters arrived after this deadline). The vast majority of the comment letters – including letters from several associations of accountants and lawyers, as well as the 'Big Four' accounting firms and several prominent law firms – argued that the SEC should replace the word 'may' in Section 401(a) with 'reasonably likely'.[85]

The 'Big Four' accounting firms argued in separate letters that the proposed 'not remote' standard would confuse investors and create inconsistencies in financial statement disclosures.[86] For example, Ernst & Young argued that: 'In our view, "reasonably likely" is a more appropriate interpretation of "may" than is "not remote" as the SEC has proposed.'[87] Several associations of lawyers argued – sometimes quite creatively – that the SEC could appropriately implement a 'reasonably likely' standard as a response to the wording in Sarbanes-Oxley,[88] and that such a standard would be preferable.[89] Various associations of financial executives, investment advisers and analysts also argued that the proposed standard would confuse and overwhelm investors by requiring companies to deliver too much information.[90]

The Financial Accounting Policy Committee of the Association for Investment Management and Research – an association of 61,000 financial analysts, portfolio managers and other investment professionals – submitted comments opposing a 'reasonably likely' standard,[91] as did a few individuals.[92] But the vast majority of the comments specifically endorsed reversion to a 'reasonably likely' standard. The SEC responded in its final rules by abandoning the 'not remote' standard in favour of 'reasonably likely'. The SEC stated a belief that the 'reasonably likely' threshold 'best promotes the utility of the disclosure requirements by reducing the possibility that investors will be overwhelmed by voluminous disclosure of insignificant and possibly unnecessarily speculative information'.[93] The SEC did not describe which investors it believed would be overwhelmed, and it did not conclude that securities prices would not reflect this information because some investors would be overwhelmed.[94]

The SEC also noted: 'We are mindful of the potential difficulty that registrants would have faced in attempting to comply with the "remote" disclosure threshold set forth in the Proposing Release. We also believe that our use of a consistent disclosure threshold throughout MD&A will preclude the potential confusion that could result from disparate thresholds.'[95] However, the SEC did not weigh these costs against the expected benefits associated with a more inclusive disclosure standard. The SEC concluded that: 'We have found no express reference in the legislative history conclusively demonstrating Congress' intent in using the word "may".' However, the SEC did not mention the numerous references in the legislative history to the problems associated with derivatives and disclosure of derivatives, nor did it mention the Senate's rejection of the 'reasonably likely' standard.

The SEC's final regulations also included a rules-based provision that management make tabular disclosure regarding (i) long-term debt obligations; (ii) capital lease obligations; (iii) operating lease obligations; (iv) purchase obligations; and (v) other long-term liabilities reflected in the registrant's balance sheet under GAAP.[96] However, tabular disclosure was not explicitly required or suggested for derivatives or contingent contracts in other categories.[97] Thus the SEC shifted the regulatory regime towards rules-based tabular disclosure.

To apply the 'reasonably likely' test, management must first 'identify and critically analyse' the company's off-balance-sheet arrangements. Then management must assess the likelihood of the occurrence of 'any known trend, demand, commitment, event or uncertainty that could affect an off-balance sheet arrangement'. If management concludes that the known trend, demand, commitment, event or uncertainty is 'not reasonably likely to occur', then no disclosure is required. If management cannot make that determination, it must make disclosure unless it determines that even if the contingency were to occur, a material change in the company financial condition was 'not reasonably likely to occur'.[98] In other words, management has two bites at the 'reasonably likely' apple: one when determining whether the contingency would be 'reasonably likely', and another when determining whether a material effect of any contingency that did occur would be 'reasonably likely'.

Even those groups advocating a 'reasonably likely' standard have suggested that specific rules-based requirements are inappropriate. For example, Sullivan & Cromwell, a law firm representing several derivatives dealers, noted that 'we believe the Commission should adopt a more flexible and less proscriptive approach, requiring companies to discuss in general terms the level and significance of off-balance sheet arrangements as well as the Company's reasons for pursuing such arrangements and specific disclosure in reasonable detail on those significant off-balance sheet arrangements according to current standards of MD&A disclosure'.[99] Similarly, the European Commission stated: 'Accordingly, there is a primordial need for an appropriate accounting treatment of arrangements and transactions whose (whole or partial) purpose is to remove from an entity's balance sheet liabilities or assets. Such accounting must reflect the economic substance of the transactions and arrangements. This should follow a principles-based approach.'[100]

The tabular disclosure rules do not cover many important financial contingencies. For example, consider the class of instruments known as credit derivatives, whose value is based on credit ratings. Many of Enron's off-balance-sheet contracts depended, explicitly or implicitly, on the level of its credit rating. Enron did not disclose relevant and material information about these contracts, except to note in its 2000 annual report that its 'continued investment grade status is critical to the success of its wholesale business as well as its ability to maintain adequate liquidity'.[101] Presumably, Congress and the SEC would want to encourage or require such disclosure, but the application of the new rules to such disclosures remains unclear.

Disclosure of 'reasonably likely' contingencies would probably not have prevented the problems associated with Enron. Indeed, Enron arguably was in compliance with the newly-enacted SEC regulations. In assessing the firm's financial contingencies at the end of 2000, management would not have considered a scenario in which Enron's stock price would decline by more than half to be 'reasonably likely'. Accordingly, management would not have needed to disclose details about Enron's derivatives contracts with the SPEs. Nor would it have been 'reasonably likely' that the volatility of commodity prices in 2000 would continue. Moreover, management's assessment is required to be objectively 'reasonable' only as at the time the assessment is made.[102] As of any particular time, the reasonableness of a decision about whether a particular contingency is 'reasonably likely' will be based on the relevant price histories for the relevant variables and predictions about how those variables are likely to change in the future. Such disclosures will necessarily exclude 'worst case' scenarios. To the extent that traders are not reporting accurately the volatility of their portfolios, they can provide managers with excuses to make more limited disclosures. In other words, a 'reasonably likely' standard creates incentives to report profits and losses that are relatively smooth, so that 'reasonably likely' disclosures will be relatively limited. In such an environment, systemic risks will increase, because investors will not have accurate information about the risk distributions of a company's derivatives trading, and companies will not disclose much useful information about their derivatives' risk exposure.

Is 'reasonably likely' a permissible construction of 'may'?

Finally, whatever the wisdom of the SEC's 'reasonably likely' standard, it is unclear whether it will survive judicial review. In the event of a challenge to the regulations promulgated pursuant to Section 401(a), a court would perform the established two-step analysis governed by *'Chevron USA Inc.* v. *NRDC' (Chevron)* in evaluating the SEC's interpretation of Sarbanes-Oxley.[103] First, the court would consider whether the statute resolves the issue clearly. If the court determined that Congress has spoken clearly in Section 401(a), then the court (and the SEC) must 'give effect to the unambiguously expressed intent of Congress'. Second, if the statute does not resolve the issue, the court would accept the SEC's interpretation so long as it reflects a 'permissible construction of the statute'.[104]

Would the SEC's interpretation withstand this analysis? There are persuasive arguments that the answer is likely to be negative. Courts applying *Chevron* analysis typically assess the comparative expertise of legislatures and agencies (and courts).[105] But arguments about deference and comparative expertise matter less where Congress has considered explicitly and rejected the *exact* wording of the interpretation the agency ultimately adopts. Even if the wording of Section 401(a) is ambiguous, so that Congress has not spoken clearly, the SEC's interpretation is unlikely to be a 'permissible construction' if it simply reverts to wording already considered and rejected by Congress.[106]

Courts generally interpret 'may' in a permissive way, as in 'maybe'.[107] A few courts have construed 'may' as 'shall', but only when the context or subject matter of the legislation made it clear that such a meaning was intended.[108] Of course, Congress might clarify the issue through new legislation, but the failure of Congress to reject expressly the SEC's final regulations need not indicate congressional acquiescence in the SEC's interpretation.[109]

The weeks between November 2002 (when the SEC, following Congress's directive in using 'may', proposed rules requiring disclosure unless a contingency was 'remote') and January 2003 (when the SEC adopted final rules requiring disclosure only if a contingency was 'reasonably likely') were an active time for financial lobbyists. The evidence that formed the basis for the SEC changing its view is scant, but the weight of opinion favouring the change was heavy. Public choice scholars looking for recent examples of agency capture will feast on the SEC's final response to Section 401(a) of Sarbanes-Oxley.

Conclusion

The reasons for Enron's collapse should affect the normative conclusions of scholars, and the standard account of these reasons is incomplete. At its core,

Enron was a derivatives trading firm; it made billions trading derivatives, but it lost billions on virtually everything else it did. Enron used its expertise in derivatives to hide these losses. For most people, the fact that Enron had transformed itself from an energy company into a derivatives trading firm is a surprise, although there were many clues buried in its financial statements.

The collapse of Enron suggests that regulations applicable to derivatives disclosure should change, in two ways. First, regulations should treat derivatives in the same way as economically equivalent financial instruments. In other words, they should become more standard-like, and create incentives for corporate managers to make disclosures consistent with economic reality, not accounting reality. Second, the SEC should follow Congress's intent in Section 401(a) of Sarbanes-Oxley and encourage additional disclosure of contingencies related to derivatives. At the minimum, courts should prevent the SEC from reverting to a disclosure standard Congress has explicitly rejected.

Notes

1 Reprinted by permission from *Villanova Law Review*, vol. 48, no. 4 (2003).
2 I am grateful to George Benston, Bill Bratton, Bill Carney, Jeannette Filippone, Peter H. Huang, Don Langevoort, Shaun Martin, Steven Schwarcz and John Tishler for comments on a draft of this chapter, and to Carole Lager for help during the editorial process.
3 See also Second Interim Report of Neal Batson, Court-Appointed Examiner, 'In re Enron', 5 March 2003 (docket no. 9551, available at http://www.elaw4enron.com).
4 Merton H. Miller began arguing during the 1980s that financial innovation was driven by regulatory changes (1986, pp. 459–60; 1997, pp. 1–14, 52–3). More recently, scholars have been citing 'regulatory arbitrage' as a significant force in international regulatory competition. See Huang and Knoll, 2000; Romano, 2001; Licht, 1998.
5 Sarbanes-Oxley Act of 2002, Pub. L. no. 107-204, 116 Stat. 745§ 401(a) (2002) (emphasis added). Section 401(a) became the new Section 13(j) of the Securities Exchange Act. This 'may' provision covered disclosure of the type related to Enron's derivatives deals with the SPEs, but also included disclosure related more generally to Enron's trading of derivatives to the extent the fair value of its derivatives was not fully reflected as an asset or liability in a company's financial statements. See *Disclosure in Management Discussion and Analysis (MD&A) about Off-Balance Sheet Arrangements and Aggregate Contractual Obligations*, Release No. 33-8182, 34-47264, 2003 SEC LEXIS 227 (28 January 2003).
6 'Reasonably likely' is the standard generally applicable to contingent disclosure in MD&A of Results and Operations.
7 See, for example, Baird and Rasmussen, 2002; Bratton, 2002; Coffee, 2002 and 2003; Gordon, 2002; Langevoort, 2002; Ribstein, 2002; Schwarcz, 2002a and 2002b.
8 See Enron Corp., 7 February 2002 Form 8-K, Exhibit 99.2, *Report of Investigation by the Special Investigative Committee of the Board of Directors of Enron Corp.*, p. 77 (hereafter 'Special Report'); see also Gordon, 2002, p. 1240 (assessing Enron's use of SPEs).
9 In a nutshell, three radically different characters – the professorial founder, Kenneth Lay, the free-market consultant, Jeffrey Skilling, and the brash financial whiz, Andrew Fastow – converted a small natural gas producer into the seventh

largest company in the USA, and on the way generated fabulous wealth for Enron shareholders, employees, and especially insiders, who cashed in to the tune of more than US$1.2 billion before the company fell spectacularly into bankruptcy. The thousands of layoffs, the imploded retirement plans, the controversy surrounding political contributions, the details of Enron executives' personal lives, and the role of now-infamous SPEs have been part of public debate since 2001.

10 See Enron Corp., 8 November 2001, Form 8-K.

11 Financial economist Myron Scholes (1998, p. 360) described Enron as one of the few non-financial services companies that was sufficiently sophisticated in such financial instruments to compete with banks and securities firms ('Product standardization will erode profits more quickly than in the past because more diverse entities, such as General Electric, Enron, or accounting firms, can compete in providing financial services using financial technology').

12 Other firms, such as Dynegy, encountered similar problems, particularly with respect to the valuation of derivatives using methodology based on forward curves. See Dynegy Inc., 14 February 2003, Form 10-K; see also 'What Worries Warren', *Fortune*, 3 March 2003, pp. 1–3.

13 *Enron's Risk Management Manual* explicitly stated a preference for accounting reality: 'Reported earnings follow the rules and principles of accounting. The results do not always create measures consistent with underlying economics. However, corporate management's performance is generally measured by accounting income, not underlying economics. Risk management strategies are therefore directed at accounting rather than economic performance.'

14 See Gordon, 2002, p. 1240 (noting that 'Enron disturbs the efficient market hypothesis').

15 The OTC derivatives markets are subject to limited disclosure requirements based on particularised rules. For example, companies are generally not required to include swap transactions as assets or liabilities on their balance sheets. Before Sarbanes-Oxley, the rules applicable to OTC derivatives required only that companies disclose summary details, in tabular form, about their derivatives transactions in the footnotes to their financial statements (Partnoy, 2001). The standard for disclosing contingencies related to derivatives in MD&A was relatively high ('reasonably likely'). In addition, other regulatory exceptions applied to the disclosure of derivatives, including exceptions based on the nature and purpose of particular instruments, such hedging with OTC derivatives. See *Accounting for Derivatives Instruments and Hedging Activities*, Statement of Financial Accounting Standards No. 133 (Financial Accounting Standards Board, 1998).

16 For a description of this regulatory regime, see Partnoy, 1999.

17 Testimony of Ronald M. Barone, Managing Director, 'Standard & Poor's', Before the Committee on Governmental Affairs, United States Senate, 20 March 2002, p. 10.

18 Enron listed billions of dollars of off-balance sheet debt in its informal non-public presentations to the rating agencies (note 17 above, p. 13). In describing these additional obligations to the credit rating agencies, Enron included what it called a 'Kitchen Sink Disclaimer', stating that 'Enron does not recommend using this analysis for anything other than illustrative purposes and for the purpose of concluding that the off-balance sheet obligations are not material to Enron's consolidated credit analysis. Cigarette smoking may be harmful to your health.' See McMahon, Jeffrey, *Enron Corp. Credit Conference Credit Profile*, 29 January 2000, p. 12.

19 See Second Interim Report of Neal Batson (note 3 above).

20   SPEs do not necessarily touch the OTC derivatives markets, and SPEs need not enter into derivatives deals with related (or non-related) entities. SPEs and SPE transactions are common in modern financial markets, and offer numerous economic benefits, including non-recourse financing, separation of financial risks, and creation of new markets. For example, credit card and mortgage payments frequently flow through SPEs, and financial services firms typically use such entities as well. See, generally, Schwarcz, 2002c.

21   These derivatives included price swap derivatives, as well as call and put options.

22   Special Report, note 8 above, p. 77.

23   See note 22. This provision was known as a 'lock-up'.

24   Special Report, note 8 above, pp. 8–9.

25   Special Report, note 8 above, p. 97.

26   Special Report, note 8 above, pp. 96–8 and 107–11.

27   Special Report, note 8 above, pp. 96–7 and 103–4.

28   Enron 2000 Annual Report, p. 44, no. 11 (hereafter 'Annual Report').

29   JEDI, in turn, was subject to the same rules. JEDI could issue equity and debt securities, and as long as there was an outside investor with at least 50 per cent of the equity – in other words, with real economic exposure to the risks of Chewco – JEDI would not need to consolidate Chewco.

30   Nor are other derivatives-related accounting rules very helpful. In 1998, FASB adopted FAS No. 133, which included new accounting rules for derivatives. *Accounting for Derivatives Instruments and Hedging Activities*, Statement of Financial Accounting Standard (SFAS) No. 133 (FASB 1998). Now at 800-plus pages, FAS 133's instructions are an incredibly detailed set of rules, describing particularised instances when derivatives need not be disclosed, but it did not answer the question of what would constitute sufficient outside capital.

31   'Related Party Disclosures', SFAS No. 57 (FASB 1982). Enron's footnote disclosure arguably satisfied the letter of FAS 57, although the disclosures were neither clear nor forthcoming.

32   This letter stated: 'The initial substantive residual equity investment should be comparable to that expected for a substantive business involved in similar [leasing] transactions with similar risks and rewards. The SEC staff understands from discussions with Working Group members that those members believe that 3 per cent is the minimum acceptable investment. The SEC staff believes a greater investment may be necessary depending on the facts and circumstances, including the credit risk associated with the lessee and the market risk factors associated with the leased property.' See Partnoy, 2002; see also Bratton, 2002, no. 118 (describing GAAP authorities for the letter).

33   Annual Report, note 28 above, p. 39, no. 3 and p. 48, no. 15.

34   See Special Report, note 8 above, pp. 2–3 and 42 (describing circumstances surrounding the consolidation of Chewco, and the subsequent financial impact on Enron's financial statements).

35   Annual Report, note 28 above, p. 48, no. 16.

36   See Richard W. Stevenson and Jeff Gerth, 'Enron's Collapse: The System; Web of Safeguards Failed as Enron Fell', *New York Times*, 19 January 2002, p. A1.

37   Enron's bankruptcy examiner has written hundreds of pages detailing how Enron used derivatives to borrow money without recording debt on its balance sheet. Enron used two strategies – end-of-year deals and prepaid swaps – to inflate reported profits and reduce reported debt, again within the parameters of a rules-based regulatory approach to accounting and disclosure. For example, in

December 1999, Enron 'sold' an interest in some Nigerian barges mounted with electricity generators to Merrill Lynch, which agreed to 'buy' Enron's interest in the barges after Enron CFO Andy Fastow promised orally that by June 2000 Enron would 'make sure Merrill Lynch was relieved of its interest'. This year-end deal was designed to enable Enron to recognise a profit during 1999. Enron also did US$8 billion of 'prepaid swaps' with J.P. Morgan Chase and Citigroup. These prepaid swaps were loans from an economic perspective, but Enron recorded the loan proceeds as cash flow from operations, based on accounting rules. See Second Interim Report of Neal Batson (see Nt 3); Richard A. Oppel, Jr., 'US Studying Merrill Lynch in Enron Deal', *New York Times*, 27 July 2002, p. C1; Richard A., Jr. Oppel. and Kurt Eichenwald, 'Citigroup Said to Mold Deal to Help Enron Skirt Rules', *New York Times*, 23 July 2002, p. A1.

38 See Enron Corp., Form 10-Ks, 1993–2001.

39 See Enron Corp., 8 November 2001, Form 8-K.

40 See Enron Corp., 8 November 2001, Form 8-K.

41 See Second Interim Report of Neal Batson, note 3 above.

42 See Annual Report, note 28 above, p. 36 (describing accounting for 'price risk management activities' as including forwards, swaps, options and energy transportation contracts).

43 Annual Report, note 28 above, pp. 32–3. Much of the growth in both assets and liabilities was created increased trading through Enron Online, Enron's Internet-based trading platform. Enron Online's assets and revenues were qualitatively different from Enron's other derivatives trading. Whereas Enron's derivatives operations included speculative positions in various contracts, much of Enron Online's operations purported to match buyers and sellers. Accordingly, a portion of the 'revenues' associated with Enron Online arguably did not belong in Enron's financial statements. But even without these additions, Enron's liabilities from derivatives trading were substantial and increasing.

44 Annual Report, note 28 above, p. 31 ('Revenues, other' category). Interestingly, Enron reported notional amounts of derivatives contracts as of 31 December 2000, of US$21.6 billion. Annual Report, note 28 above, p. 38 (total of columns 'Fixed Price Payor, Notional Amounts' and 'Terms'). Either Enron was generating 33 per cent annual returns from derivatives (indicating that the underlying contracts were very risky), or Enron in fact had much larger positions and in some way reduced the notional values of its outstanding derivatives contracts at year-end for reporting purposes. Enron's financial statements do not explain this issue.

45 Annual Report, note 28 above, p. 36 ('Unrealized gains and losses from newly originated contracts, contract restructurings and the impact of price movements are recognized as "other revenues" '); see also Baird and Rasmussen, 2002, pp. 1801–2 (describing Enron's substantial trading activities).

46 See Annual Report, note 28 above, p. 31. Enron's gains from price risk management activities from 1998 to 2000 (US$16 billion) were roughly comparable to the annual net revenue for all trading activities (including stocks, bonds and derivatives) at the investment firm, Goldman, Sachs & Co., during the same periods, a time in which Goldman, Sachs first issued shares to the public. See Partnoy, 2002.

47 See Annual Report, note 28 above. Enron's consolidated statement of cash flows similarly reflected the importance of price risk management activities (p. 34).

48 Annual Report, note 28 above, pp. 38–9.

49 Annual Report, note 28 above, p. 28.

50 See note 49.

51 See note 49.

52 Annual Report, note 28 above, p. 38.

53 Consider the following statement in Enron's 2000 annual report: 'In 2000, the value at risk model utilized for equity trading market risk was refined to more closely correlate with the valuation methodologies used for merchant activities' (p. 28). Enron's financial statements do not describe these refinements, or their effects, but given the recent failure of the risk and valuation models at other firms, including Long-Term Capital Management, there should have been reason for concern when Enron referred to 'refining' its own models.

54 See generally Partnoy, 2003, ch. 10; see also Partnoy, 2002 (describing the use of prudency reserves).

55 See note 54.

56 The Commodity Futures Trading Commission began considering whether to regulate OTC derivatives in 1997, but its proposals were rejected, and in December 2000 Congress made the deregulated status of derivatives clear when it passed the Commodity Futures Modernization Act. As a result, during its final year, Enron operated in a largely unregulated market. (Commodity Futures Modernization Act, S.2697, 106th Cong. (2000); H.R. 4541, 106th Cong. (2000)). See also Michael Schroeder, 'Lugar in Senate Charges CFTC, SEC Impede Bill to Deregulate Derivatives', *Wall Street Journal*, 22 June 2000, p. C26 (describing legal and regulatory uncertainty and the legislation proposed to reduce it).

57 Commentators have also blamed Arthur Andersen, Enron's auditor, although they have not directly addressed the accountants' role in disclosures related to Enron's derivatives. Arthur Andersen's was responsible not only for auditing Enron's financial statements, but also for assessing Enron management's internal controls on derivatives trading. When Arthur Andersen signed Enron's 2000 annual report, it expressed approval in general terms of Enron's system of internal controls from 1998 to 2000 (Annual Report, note 28 above). Yet it does not appear that Arthur Andersen systematically and independently verified Enron's valuations of certain complex trades, or even of its forward curves. Arthur Andersen apparently examined day-to-day changes in these values, as reported by traders, and checked to see if each daily change was recorded accurately. But Andersen checked only sporadically Enron's forward curves, and did not confirm that the values Enron had recorded reflected fair market values (Partnoy, 2003, ch. 10).

58 As a general matter, rules are formal or mechanical and depend on uncontested facts, whereas standards are flexible and depend on context.

59 The early assessments of the effects of mandatory disclosure did not consider the disclosure of complex financial contingencies. See Stigler, 1964, pp. 120–4; Benston, 1973, pp. 144–5; Friend and Westerfield, 1975; Jarrell, 1981; Seligman, 1983.

60 For example, analysts have admitted that they are incapable of deciphering derivatives disclosures. In response to a question raised at an International Swaps and Derivatives Association conference, Ethan M. Heisler, a Vice President at Salomon Brothers, expressed scepticism that even sophisticated securities analysts could draw anything of value out of financial disclosures about derivatives: 'Show me an equity analyst who has taken the disclosures that you currently have on derivatives and made any kind of meaningful use out of those disclosures. I would challenge you to find it. I have never seen it.' (*Derivatives Accounting Disclosure and Market Surveillance*, International Swaps and Derivatives Association Conference, 25 September 1996, p. 7). Steven Schwarcz has suggested a related point: that some transactions may be so complex that they simply cannot be disclosed (2002b, pp. 9–11).

61 For example, Regulation Fair Disclosure ('Reg FD') – which requires managers to disclose non-public information publicly (and simultaneously) – remains in effect. See 17 C.F.R. § 243 (2001).

62 Much of this information was publicly available in early 2001. See, for example, Bethany McLean, 'Is Enron Overpriced?', *Fortune*, 5 March 2001, p. 122 (questioning Enron's high stock valuation based on public disclosures).

63 Commodity Futures Modernization Act of 2000, Pub. L. No. 106-554, 114 Stat. 2763 (21 December 2000).

64 Pub. L. 107–204, 116 Stat. 745 § 401(a) (2002).

65 Regulation S-K, Item 303(a).

66 See, for example, Release No. 33-5433 (12 December 1973).

67 Concept Release on *MD&A of Financial Condition and Results of Operations*, Securities Act Release No. 6711 (17 April 1987).

68 *MD&A of Financial Condition and Results of Operations*, 'Certain Investment Company Disclosures', Securities Act Release No. 6835 (18 May 1989).

69 If management could not make a determination about whether the contingency was 'reasonably likely', then management needed to make an 'objective' evaluation of the consequences of the contingency. Under this second prong, management was required to disclose the contingency, unless they determined that the consequences were 'not reasonably likely' to occur (see note 68). See also *In the Matter of Bank of Boston Corp.*, Admin. Proc. File No. 3-8270, 1995 SEC LEXIS 3456, 22 December 1995 (applying 'reasonably likely' standard).

70 Regulation S-K, Item 303(a)(3)(ii).

71 Regulation S-K, Item 303(a), Instruction 3.

72 A complete analysis of the second instance is beyond the scope of this chapter, but the behavioural economics literature suggests that the interests of managers and shareholders might diverge under such circumstances (Langevoort, 1996).

73 'In the Matter of Caterpillar, Inc.', Release No. 34-30532 (31 March 1992).

74 *'United States v. Simon'*, 425 F.2d 796 (2d Cir. 1969).

75 Norris, Floyd, 'An Old Case Is Returning to Haunt Auditors', *New York Times*, 1 March 2002.

76 See Release No. 33-8056 (22 January 2002).

77 'SEC. 6. Improved Transparency of Corporate Disclosures. (a) Modification of Regulations Required. The Commission shall revise its regulations under the securities laws pertaining to the disclosures required in periodic financial reports and registration statements to require such reports to include adequate and appropriate disclosure of (1) the issuer's off-balance sheet transactions and relationships with unconsolidated entities or other persons, to the extent they are not disclosed in the financial statements and are *reasonably likely* to materially affect the liquidity or the availability of, or requirements for, capital resources, or the financial condition or results of operations of the issuer' 148 Cong. Rec. H. 1544, 107th Cong., 2nd Sess., 24 April 2002 (emphasis added).

78 'SEC. 401. Disclosures in Periodic Reports. (a) Disclosures Required. Section 13 of the Securities Exchange Act of 1934 (15 USC 78 m) is amended by adding at the end the following: (j) Off-Balance Sheet Transactions. Not later than 180 days after the date of enactment of the Public Company Accounting Reform and Investor Protection Act of 2002, the Commission shall issue final rules providing that each annual and quarterly financial report required to be filed with the Commission shall disclose all material off-balance sheet transactions, arrangements, obligations (including contingent obligations), and other relationships of

the issuer with unconsolidated entities or other persons, that *may* have a material current or future effect on financial condition, changes in financial condition, results of operations, liquidity, capital expenditures, capital resources, or significant components of revenues or expenses' 148 Cong. Rec. 6734, 107th Cong., 2nd Sess, 15 July 2002 (emphasis added).

79 See, for example, http://govt-aff.senate.gov/hearings02.htm (listing hearings in the US Senate Committee on Governmental Affairs).

80 See *Financial Oversight of Enron: The SEC and Private-Sector Watchdogs*, Report of the Staff to the Senate Committee on Governmental Affairs, 8 October 2002, p. 1, no. 2 (http://govt-aff.senate.gov/100702watchdogsreport.pdf).

81 *Webster's II New Riverside Dictionary*, p. 734 (1984).

82 Disclosure in *MD&A about Off-Balance Sheet Arrangements*, 'Contractual Obligations and Contingent Liabilities and Commitments', Release No. 33-8144, 34-46767, 2002 SEC LEXIS 2810 (4 November 2002).

83 See FASB SFAS No. 5, Accounting for Contingencies (March 1975).

84 In supporting its proposed rules, the SEC concluded that:

> The proposed disclosure would be required if management determines either that an off-balance sheet arrangement is material in the current period or that it may become material in the future. Disclosure would not be required for off-balance sheet arrangements where the likelihood of either the occurrence of an event, or the materiality of its effect, is remote.

The SEC further stated that:

> Under the proposed disclosure threshold, management first must identify and carefully review the registrant's direct or indirect guarantees, retained interests, equity-linked or indexed derivatives and obligations (including contingent obligations) that are not fully reflected on the face of the financial statements. Second, management must assess the likelihood of the occurrence of any known trend, demand, commitment, event or uncertainty that could either require performance of a guarantee or other obligation, or require the registrant to recognize an impairment. If management concludes that the likelihood of occurrence is remote, then no disclosure would be required under the proposed rules. If management cannot make that determination, it would have to evaluate objectively the consequences of the known trend, demand, commitment, event or uncertainty on the assumption that it will come to fruition. Disclosure then would be required unless management concludes that likelihood of the event having a material effect is remote.

Release No. 33-8144, 34-46767, 2002 SEC LEXIS 2810 (4 November 2002).

85 Indeed, one commenter explicitly suggested that the SEC 'replace' the word 'may' in the statute, asserting that the drafting process had been rushed. See Comments of Jerry W. Powell, General Counsel and Secretary, Compass Bancshares, Inc., 9 December 2002 ('We encourage the Commission to replace the word "may" as it appears in the sixth line of paragraph (a)(4)(i)(C) of proposed Item 303 of Regulation S-K with the words "is reasonably likely to" in order to align the disclosure threshold of other similar information.').

86 See, for example, Comments of KPMG LLP, 9 December 2002. KPMG argued that the standard would

> confuse investors and other financial statement users who are unlikely to understand that different probability thresholds attach to different disclosures

within the same item, imply that off-balance sheet arrangements are inherently more significant and vulnerable than on-balance sheet items (an inference that we believe may be misleading since risk of loss applies equally to on- and off-balance sheet items); and create inconsistency with the historical purpose of MD&A to discuss the business through the eyes of management, which may consider remote outcomes, but which is more likely to manage based on reasonably likely outcomes.

See also Comments of PricewaterhouseCoopers LLP, 9 December 2002 ('While we note the use of the word "may" in the Sarbanes-Oxley Act, we do not believe that the intent was to further lower the threshold and thereby overwhelm the reader with information that may not be useful to an understanding of the issuer's operations if it is not at least reasonably likely that there will be an impact on the registrant'); Comments of Deloitte & Touche LLP, 9 December 2002 ('We believe the proposed disclosure threshold would require highly speculative judgments and would be burdensome to issuers and investors because it would result in overly voluminous disclosure of information that is of questionable relevance to investors'); Comments of Ernst & Young LLP, 9 December 2002 (making similar arguments in favour of 'reasonably likely' instead of 'may'); Comments of William F. Ezzell, CPA, Chairman, Board of Directors; Barry C. Melancon, CPA President and CEO, American Institute of Certified Public Accountants, 9 December 2002.

87 Comments of Ernst & Young LLP, 9 December 2002.
88 File No. S7-42-02, Comments of Stanley Keller, Chair, Committee on Federal Regulation of Securities, Business Law Section, American Bar Association, 31 December 2002 ('We do not believe that the statute's use of the term "may" requires a departure from current MD&A standard of "reasonably likely" particularly as construed by the Commission, and we are concerned that such a low standard will undermine the usefulness of the disclosure for investors while greatly increasing the cost of compliance'); Comments of Gerald S. Backman, Chairman, Committee on Securities Regulation, Business Law Section, New York State Bar Association, December 13, 2002 ('We urge the Commission to change the proposed "remoteness" disclosure threshold for off-balance sheet arrangements and transactions to the existing "reasonably likely" threshold applicable to other MD&A disclosures. Sarbanes-Oxley Section 401(a) does not use, and we do not believe it requires, a remoteness standard'; 'If the statute intended possibility, it would have used the word "could" which indicates possibility, in the place of "may" which is "[u]sed to indicate a certain measure of likelihood or possibility" ' (citation omitted); Comments of Charles M. Nathan, Jr., Chair, Committee on Securities Regulation; Steven J. Slutzky, Ad Hoc Subcommittee, Committee on Securities Regulation, Association of the Bar of the City of New York, 9 December 2002:

> The word 'may' in the Sarbanes-Oxley Act allows for a broad range of meanings in the context of the threshold for disclosure. This range certainly includes the 'reasonably likely' disclosure threshold currently applicable throughout MD&A, and, absent a legislative history requiring otherwise, 'may' should be presumed to have a meaning consistent with the existing disclosure threshold throughout MD&A. Furthermore, while the legislative history of the Sarbanes-Oxley Act does refer to the fact that there was testimony that enhanced disclosures concerning off-balance sheet arrangements are necessary to prevent future Enron-type problems, there is no suggestion that manipulation of the

MD&A disclosure threshold itself led to any of the well-publicized accounting failures of recent history or that it creates loopholes that undercut clear disclosure.

89 File No. S7-42-02, Comments of Stanley Keller, Chair-Committee on Federal Regulation of Securities, Business Law Section, American Bar Association, 31 December 2002. See also No. 6 ('By placing the burden on management to determine that a contingent event is not reasonably likely to have a material effect, the current MD&A standard of probability already provides an appropriate standard of probability for disclosure'); Comments of Gerald S. Backman, Chairman, Committee on Securities Regulation, Business Law Section, New York State Bar Association, 13 December 2002:

> In addition, we are not aware of any problem with the reasonably likely standard, and there has been no showing of any basis to justify a change in that standard. It would not be sound disclosure policy to introduce a different standard into MD&A, which could mislead investors. Finally, the lower threshold could result in information overload, and the additional disclosures would not provide investors with information management uses to manage the company; there should be one standard for everything in MD&A.

90 Comments of Karen L. Barr, General Counsel, Investment Counsel Association of America, 10 December 2002 ('Moreover, we are concerned that the use of the "remote" standard could result in voluminous information and overwhelm the reader.'); Comments of Frank H. Brod, Chair, Committee on Corporate Reporting, and David H. Sidwell, Chair, SEC Subcommittee, Committee on Corporate Reporting, Financial Executives International, 20 December 2002 ('We believe lowering the threshold for MD&A disclosure from "reasonably likely" to "more than remote" will result in less meaningful disclosures because there will be a vast increase in the quantity of disclosures, the very extent of which will outweigh meaningful disclosures about higher probability matters'); Comments of Karen Doggett and Broc Romanek, Co-Chair, Subcommittee on Off-Balance Sheet Arrangements, American Society of Corporate Secretaries, 18 December 2002 ('To summarize, the application of a "higher than remote" standard could have several unintended results, including a disproportionate emphasis on off-balance arrangements over other portions of MD&A that are more material to a particular issuer, and too much information about off-balance sheet obligations so that an investor would struggle to determine which are most likely to have negative impact'); Comments of Sullivan & Cromwell, 9 December 2002 (arguing that the proposed rules 'will result in voluminous disclosures that are more likely to confuse and overwhelm investors than provide important information that will enable investors to make informed investment decisions').

91 File No. S7-42-02, Comments of Jane Adams, Chair, Financial Accounting Policy Committee; Rebecca McEnally, PhD, CFA, Vice-President, Advocacy, Association for Investment Management and Research, 31 December 2002.

92 See, for example, Comments of Robert G. Beard, 25 November 2002:

> The 'remote' disclosure threshold appears to be most consistent with Sarbanes-Oxley. Off-balance sheet transactions are permitted under relatively aggressive accounting standards in that accounting recognition is not required by the obligor or guarantor even if such obligor/guarantor may be ultimately liable for a significant portion of the indebtedness of the special purpose entity. For

that reason, a stricter disclosure threshold is warranted. Also, given the complex nature of these transactions, the unsophisticated investor deserves an explanation of the potential risks even if such risks appear remote at the time. The remote standard allows investors to make judgments on potentially material adverse consequences to the registrant that are not required to be recognized or possibly even disclosed in the financial statements.

93 See note 92. Sophisticated analysis, not individual investors, are the target audience for these kinds of disclosures. According to a survey by Ernst & Young, the length of an average annual report had increased from 35 pages, when FASB first began setting accounting rules, to 64 pages in the early 1990s; and the number of footnotes increased from four to seventeen. Few individual investors can read or understand the basics of an average annual report, much less the complexities of contingent disclosures related to derivatives. Ray J. Groves, 'Here's the Annual Report. Got a Few Hours?', *Wall Street Journal*, 4 August 1994.

94 In fact, such information is precisely the type of information that would be most useful to sophisticated investors and analysts, whose activities are reflected in securities prices.

95 Disclosure in *MD&A about Off-Balance Sheet*, 'Arrangement and Aggregate Contractual Obligations', Release No. 3-8182, 34-47264, 27 January 2003.

96 See note 95.

97 The SEC included a standards-based requirement stating that management must provide other information that it believes to be necessary for investors to understand both the company's off-balance sheet arrangements and the material effects of these arrangements on its financial condition. This 'catch all' standard is intended to capture any 'reasonably likely' events that otherwise would not fall into a particular category covered by the regulation. Whether this standard is effective depends on the extent to which the SEC enforces it. This catch-all provision is consistent with the SEC's more general approach to MD&A disclosure, requiring that companies disclose facts even if accounting rules do not require disclosure. See Sec. Act. Rel. No. 33-8040 and No. 33-8056.

98 See note 97.

99 Comments of Sullivan & Cromwell, 9 December 2002.

100 Comments of Alexander Schaub, Director-General, European Commission, 9 December 2002.

101 Annual Report, note 28 above, p. 27.

102 See Release No. 3-6835 (18 May 1989).

103 See '*Chevron, USA, Inc.* v. *NRDC*' (*Chevron*), 467 US 837 (1984); see also '*FDA* v. *Brown & Williamson Tobacco Corp.*', 529 US 120 (2000) (applying *Chevron* analysis in assessing whether Congress granted the Federal Food and Drug Administration jurisdiction to regulate tobacco products).

104 *Chevron*, 467 US at 842–43.

105 See, for example, Rodriguez, 1994, pp. 133–8 (assessing arguments regarding relevant expertise of legislatures, agencies and the judiciary).

106 The issue is conflated by two unique problems. First, 'may' includes within its definition the meaning specifically encompassed by the term ultimately used in the regulation. Second, the standard for judging the agency interpretation – whether it was reasonable – is also subsumed within the text of the regulation.

107 See, for example, '*La Bove* v. *Employers Ins. Co.*', 189 So. 2d 315, 317 (La. Ct. App. 1966); '*People* v. *Hoehl*', 193 Colo. 557, 568 P. 2d 484 (Colo. 1977). For example, consider '*People* v. *Hoehl*', in which a court rejecting the dictionary definition

of 'may' in favour of a definition similar to the one adopted by the SEC. The relevant statute provided that 'a person commits child abuse if he knowingly, intentionally, or negligently, and without justifiable excuse, causes or permits a child to be placed in a situation that may endanger the child's life or health'. The court indicated that if the word 'may' in the clause 'may endanger the child's life or health' were strictly construed according to the dictionary definition (in that case, 'be in some degree likely'), the statute would be unconstitutional taken at face value, because 'virtually any conduct directed toward a child has the possibility, however slim, of endangering a child's health'. To preserve the constitutionality of the statute, the court rejected the dictionary definition and created its own definition of 'may' as meaning a 'reasonable probability' (Hoehl, 568 P.2d at 485).

108 '*US* v. *Lexington Mill & Elevator Co.*', 232 US 399, 411 (1914) (considering meaning of 'may' as mandatory); '*Bloom* v. *Texas State Bd. Of Examiners of Psychologists*', 475 S.W.2d 374, 377 (Tex Civ. App. 1972) (same).

109 '*Sierra Club* v. *EPA*', 540 F.2d 1114, 1126 (D.C. Cir. 1976).

References

Baird, D. G. and R. K. Rasmussen (2002) 'Four (or Five) Easy Lessons from Enron', *Vanderbilt Law Review*, vol. 55, pp. 1787–812.

Benston, G. J. (1973) 'Required Disclosure and the Stock Market: An Evaluation of the Securities Exchange Act of 1934', *American Economic Review*, vol. 63, no. 1 (March), pp. 132–55.

Bratton, W. W. (2002) 'Enron and the Dark Side of Shareholder Value', *Tulane Law Review*, vol. 76, no. 5-6 (June), pp. 1275–362.

Coffee, J. C., Jr. (2002) 'Understanding Enron: It's about the Gatekeepers, Stupid', Columbia Law and Economics Working Paper, Columbia Law School, The Center for Law and Economic Studies, no. 207.

Coffee, J. C., Jr. (2003) 'What Caused Enron? A Capsule Social and Economic History of the 1990s', Columbia Law and Economics Working Paper, Columbia Law School, The Center for Law and Economic Studies, no. 214.

Friend, I. and R. Westerfield (1975) 'Required Disclosure and the Stock Market: Comment', *American Economic Review*, vol. 65, no. 3, pp. 467–72.

Gordon, J. N. (2002) 'What Enron Means for the Management and Control of the Modern Business Corporation. Some Initial Reflections', *Chicago Law Review*, vol. 69 (Summer), pp. 1233–9.

Huang, P. H. and M. S. Knoll (2000) 'Corporate Finance, Corporate Law and Finance Theory', *South California Law Review*, vol. 74, no. 1 (November), pp. 175–92.

Jarrell, G. A. (1981) 'The Economic Effects of Federal Regulation of the Market for New Securities Issues', *Journal of Law & Economics*, vol. 24, no. 3 (December), pp. 613–75.

Jones, C. M. and O. A. Lamont (2001) 'Short Sale Constraints and Stock Returns', CRSP Working Paper, No. 533.

Langevoort, D. C. (1996) 'Selling Hope, Selling Risk, Some Lessons for Law from Behavioral Economics about Stockbrokers and Sophisticated Customers', *California Law Review*, vol. 83, no. 3, pp. 627–701.

Langevoort, D. C. (2003) 'Managing the "Expectations Gap" in Investor Protection: The SEC and the Post-Enron Reform Agenda', *Villanova Law Review*, vol. 48, no. 4, pp. 1139–65.

Licht, A. N. (1998) 'Regulatory Arbitrage for Real: International Securities Regulation in a World of Interacting Securities Markets', *Virginia Journal of International Law*, vol. 38 (Summer), pp. 563–638.

Miller, M. H. (1986) 'Financial Innovation: The Last Twenty Years and the Next', *Journal of Financial and Quantitative Analysis*, vol. 21, no. 4 (December), pp. 459–71.

Miller, M. H. (1997) *Merton Miller on Derivatives* (Chichester: John Wiley).

Partnoy, F. (1999) 'The Siskel and Ebert of Financial Markets: Two Thumbs Down for the Credit Rating Agencies', *Washington University Law Quarterly*, vol. 77, pp. 619–712.

Partnoy, F. (2001) 'The Shifting Contours of Global Derivatives Regulation', *Pennsylvania Journal of International Economic Law*, vol. 22, pp. 421–95.

Partnoy, F. (2002) 'Testimony before the US Senate Committee on Governmental Affairs', 24 January 2002; available at http://govt-aff.senate.gov/012402partnoy.htm.

Partnoy, F. (2003) *Infectious Greed: How Deceit and Risk Corrupted the Financial Markets* (New York: Times Books).

Ribstein, L. E. (2002) 'Market vs. Regulatory Responses to Corporate Fraud: A Critique of the Sarbanes-Oxley Act of 2002', *Journal of Corporate Law*, vol. 28, no. 1, pp. 1–67.

Rodriguez, D. B. (1994) 'The Positive Political Dimensions of Regulatory Reform', *Washington University Law Quarterly*, vol. 72, no. 1, pp. 133–8.

Romano, R. (2001) 'The Need for Competition in International Securities Regulation', *Theoretical Inquiries in Law*, vol. 2, no. 2 (July), pp. 387–401.

Scholes, M. (1998) 'Derivatives in a Dynamic Environment', *The American Economic Review*, vol. 88, no. 3 (June), pp. 350–70.

Schwarcz, S. L. (2002a) 'Enron, and the Use and Abuse of Special Purpose Entities in Corporate Structures', *University of Cincinnati Law Review*, Symposium Issue.

Schwarcz, S. L. (2002b) 'Rethinking the Disclosure Paradigm in a World of Complexity', Duke Law School Public Law Research Paper, No. 34.

Schwarcz, S. L. (2002c) *Structured Finance. A Guide to the Principles of Asset Securitization* (New York: Practising Law Institute).

Seligman, J. (1983) 'The Historical Need for a Mandatory Corporate Disclosure System', *Journal of Corporate Law*, no. 9, pp. 1–61.

Shleifer, A. and R. Vishny (1997) 'The Limits of Arbitrage', *Journal of Finance*, vol. 52, no. 1, pp. 35–55.

Steinherr, A. (2000) *Derivatives. The Wild Beast of Finance* (Chichester: John Wiley).

Stigler, G. J. (1964) 'Public Regulation of Securities Markets', *Journal of Business*, vol. 37 (April), pp. 117–42.

Stigler, G. J. (1971) 'The Theory of Economic Regulation', *Bell Journal of Economics and Management Science*, no. 2, pp. 3–21.

Wilson, J. Q. (1980) 'The Politics of Regulation', in J. Q. Wilson (ed.), *The Politics of Regulation* (New York: Basic Books), pp. 357–94.

4

Who Is Who in the World of Financial 'Swaps' and Special Purpose Entities

François-Marie Monnet

The title of a German war novel – rather a magazine series – did encapsulate the arch-ethical distinction between the means and the end as it emerged from the debacle of the Third Reich: 'Und keiner wusste warum' ('And nobody knew why'). The Enron financial rout, although different in magnitude – only the French would dare comment that no loss of money is lethal – will fascinate scholars because it has revealed that the 'invisible hand', which is meant to bring rationality into the market forces, may have no shadow, like the character of another German novel who had sold his own shadow to the devil – thinking it was of little value until it made him a monster banned from any human society.

Only literary references provide an adequate opening to the mystery of a series of events which proved, as they came to be known, to contain no other mystery than their linkage: each piece of the puzzle (of non-viable financial entities) was perfectly legal, balanced, certified, rubber-stamped. Even the grandiose Enron strategy covering the impressive set of industrial, commercial and financial entities, all flying the colours of the liberalisation of trading practices in an area hitherto encumbered by dusty regulations, was so obviously in perfect synchrony with the prevailing definition of progress, that the word 'transparency' came first to mind, to describe the process started by a courageous and determined management: 'Let there be light!' And yet, it was no 'revolution' in the sense of a dangerous change of order that would deprive the wealthy of their wealth, or give for free what the 'deserving poor' should earn. There was a Chairman, a CEO and a CFO, and they gave interviews; they mingled with the successful, but they seemed to be just the high priests of something better: a 'story', which eventually almost reached the stage where it would become *the* story. If Einstein was right, everything is energy: Prometheus reportedly once stole fire from the gods; Enron would prevail over the new order of *the matter* itself. The Enron 'success story' was widely advertised by US and international media as a cultural development that verged on the religious: negative comments or even lack of enthusiasm would have been 'un-American!'. Enron employees and business partners were to march as the initial 144,000 promised salvation in the Book of Revelations, immediately followed by the innumerable crowd of all the American citizens of all the American states ... and then the world, because energy knows no borders, and the regulations of all countries had little choice but to extend their necks for a swift beheading that would liberate them towards the Way ... this final analogy being borrowed from Hergé's comics strips character Tintin, whose (mad) Chinese friend is convinced that the best way to help his fellow men is to chop off their heads.

But in the Enron 'story', nobody ever seemed to lose his head, either in the figurative or in the proper sense. They may not all have been 'honourable men', but they were sensible from start to finish, and once their enterprise was emptied of substance, other sensible bankers and managers came in to 'pick up the pieces' and ensure that 'the show would go on', albeit with less panache and fanfare. Trading has continued without *the* Trader. Rather than belittling the role of individual persons whom justice will try in due course, it may be that the heart of the matter is the emergence of a confusion about the economic subject, the conditions for which have been brought together since decades. Confusion at the level of the subject naturally increases the probability of mishaps, and disarms any ethical, albeit legal assessment of particular situations. Should this intuition be correct, Enron's experience, if understood from the confusion that allowed it to happen, may help to avoid other 'Enrons'.

The secret of 'white' magicians, beautifully illustrated in Jérôme Bosch sober (for once!) painting commonly entitled '*L'escamoteur*' is deliberately to divert the attention of the audience from their hands, or the place where the trick is performed, and draw the maximum benefit from the inclination to laziness or intellectual arrogance that characterises our faculty of paying attention. Instead of remaining vigilant and open to each of the numerous perceptions combined in the overall view, most of us prefer to focus on the easiest feature, on what is thought to be well understood – or the most attractive. Meanwhile, the horse gets out of the barn! All features, however, are not of equal importance and the point raised by the Enron 'trickery' is nothing less than the identity of the subject – which opens the way to investigate its ethical dimension. The long and short of the Enron story is about trading. Indeed, innovation in trading consists less in defining new trading methods, than in finding ways to trade in what had hitherto been considered as non-tradeable.

For many decades, energy had been delivered in a physical form that did not seem to lend itself to trade: instead, long-term agreements were the norm, to organise production and distribution. Enron's success can be summarised as the transformation of a commercial company dedicated to the production and distribution of energy, into a major 'trader' in energy, an activity that it was not the first to practice, but that had undeniably remained at the experimental level (the first electricity futures contracts had first been traded at the London International Financial Futures Exchange (LIFFE) in the late 1980s). The demise of Enron cannot be understood without recognising the drastic change in the relationship between two economic subjects when they move from the realm of long-term agreements to a trading mode. The continuity of contacts between two parties to an agreement can be compared to walking (where one foot remains in touch with the ground at all times), while the 'cut' involved in trading is closer to a running mode, where progression is achieved by jumps, one imbalance being corrected by the next.

Modern trading techniques that have been developed in the financial markets since the 1980s are based on the extension to long-term commitments of a complacency that had long been (and still is) found convenient for short-term commitments among banks. This complacency consists in accepting the superiority of form over substance, as long as the form is given a respectable social status by a broad enough segment of the business community. The 'form' is the commitment reduced to its terms; the 'substance' is the mutual trust of the parties in their respective ability, to fulfil their obligations – which implies a mutual knowledge of each other. Restricted to the world of banks and short-term financial commitments, this means that among banks, short-term loans can be made by the lender without looking in great detail at the quality of the borrower as long as both are banks: a bank is a bank is a bank. The system may suffer from temporary distortions (when Canadian or Japanese banks must pay a premium on the loans they obtain from other banks because they are deemed to be less secure) but a prompt return of the principle of 'equality among peers' is considered to be the norm.

Needless to say, this also means little profit can be made in these interbank loans. They are extremely important, however, and often referred as a market (the 'interbank' or 'money' market) and their function is to provide the 'liquidity' that is the lifeline of any trading activity. Trading, in this context, describes the process whereby long-term commitments originally made to one party can be transferred to another party without having to 'restructure' or renegotiate the original chain of obligations. Trading breaks the original relationship between the seller and the purchaser: in the case of a bond, only the holder of the bond at maturity will get back in touch with the original seller (the issuer of the bond); during the 'life' of the bond, which may extend over several decades, successive holders will effectively 'discount' the bond to its present value and allow it to change hands without affecting the business of the original seller, who has secured the long-term availability of the borrowed money. The original borrower is thus able to invest the (borrowed) money for the full duration of the loan (or 'bond'). On the other hand, the original lender (the purchaser of the bond) may get his money back, thanks to a 'trading' transaction with a third party, without forcing the original borrower to liquidate the investments he has made.

The 'primary' or traditional liquidity created by the existence of the interbank market (based on the interchangeability of short-term bank commitments and hence a sort of dilution of the economic subject in this specific
context) had long been secured by the fact that the cost of financing in
the short-term debt market was the same for all 'banks' as long as they *were*
banks (and had access to the 'interbank' or 'money' market). However, the
difference between the level of short-term rates and medium to long-term
rates (the 'term structure') does create a substantial risk for any bank that
would be lending for a period in excess of its usual (short-term) borrowing
time horizon. This risk is called the 'maturity mismatch' risk and has long
reduced the extent of the exposure that banks were prepared to take to provide 'liquidity' to any instruments extending beyond short- term maturities.

This situation was corrected during the 1970s by the emergence of 'floating-rate' loans (or bonds), which were instruments with a longer maturity
(up to ten or twelve years) but where the interest rate was re-set every three
or six months, to accommodate the lending banks that could lend for longer
maturities without incurring the maturity mismatch risk. However, floating-
rate loans or bonds left the borrower exposed to the volatility of short-term
interest rates and made it impossible to calculate at the start of a ten- or
twelve-year period, what the 'cost of borrowing' would be. Fixed rate bonds –
the bulk of long-term financing instruments because borrowers demand to
know their 'cost of borrowing' in order to assess the profitability of their
investments, remained outside the area where banks could provide 'liquidity'
without incurring the maturity mismatch risk.

Radical modernity in trading emerged with a twist brought to the traditional
short-term interbank market during the 1980s, in the form of the long-term
'Interest Rate Swap' (hereafter 'Swap') transactions. At the risk of using a
technical legal term that might alienate certain readers, the real nature of the
Swap cannot be captured without referring to the 'novation' process,
whereby a party ('the new obligor') who is not involved in a primary agreement, undertakes (through a secondary 'Swap' agreement with one of the
parties of the primary agreement) to fulfil the obligations of such a party,
without disclosing to the other party the effective substitution (of the entity
accepting responsibility for the obligations). The absence of disclosure has
historically been justified by the fact that the party who is formally involved
in the primary agreement remains liable, should the new obligor default
under the Swap agreement she has made with the initial obligor.

It is generally considered that the disclosure of the existence of the Swap
agreement – which would include the identity of the *de facto* guarantor and the
terms of his/her remuneration – would/might distract the attention of the parties to the initial agreement and might lead them not to enter into an agreement, despite the terms of which being deemed attractive 'in themselves'.

This scheme is the basis of all Interest Rate and Currency Swap agreements
that have utterly changed the face of the financial markets since the 1980s,

by establishing a rigorous anonymity between the parties to most major long-term financial commitments that used to take the form of 'face-to-face' long-term commitments. It may come as a surprise that this anonymity was accepted as easily as it was. Indeed, in spite of the fact that the primary borrower maintained the 'front' responsibility for the primary obligation, it became progressively more and more obvious, that 'somebody else' was behind the nominally obligated party (the issuer), somebody whose name would appear on the offering circular, but who had the effective capacity to satisfy the economic obligations. The initial Interest Rate Swap Agreement having often quickly become a 'Currency and Interest Rate Swap Agreement', it became usual to see a French utility such as Electricité de France (EDF) borrow in the form of a long-term, fixed-rate Japanese yen denominated bond, while everybody knew that EDF, in its usual business, had no resources in Japanese yen. The exposure to the currency risk, however, was covered by the existence of one (or several) Swap agreements whereby the Japanese yen fixed-rate obligations of EDF were in fact paid by an (undisclosed) Japanese entity, while EDF made fixed-rate FRF or EUR denominated payments to a bank which, in turn 'transformed' such payments into floating rate payments in EUR, then from floating payments in EUR into floating payments in JPY, and ultimately from floating payments in JPY into fixed rate payments in JPY.

The readiness of lenders (investors) to accept the regime of ignorance of the identity of the counter-party imposed by the generalisation of the Swaps is all the more surprising as the Swap agreements, historically, had been developed by investment banks servicing borrowers (bond issuers) in order to allow them take advantage of different 'market perceptions' and borrow more cheaply. The purpose was (and still is) to take advantage of the appetite of investors for securities issued by Company A, while other lenders (or investors) would prefer securities issued by Company B. Both financings are arranged separately, and both companies do enter one (or several) Swap Agreement(s) whereby they do effectively, either directly or through a chain of intermediaries, exchange their obligations. Investors/lenders do ignore that the money they receive from the entity to which they have given their money comes from a third party. The early interest rate swaps of the 1980s typically allowed a US utility (such as Enron before trading was even thinkable) that was almost bankrupt because of the anti-nuclear movement, to secure access to long-term financing through a public fixed-rate bond issue made by a Japanese bank enjoying, at the time, a top AAA rating. A parallel floating rate loan was arranged for the US utility – although it would not accept the uncertainty created by the re-setting of the interest rate every six months. The Swap agreement – a private agreement between the US utility and the AAA-rated bank – obligated the utility to pay the coupons on the bond issued by the Bank, while the Bank would pay the floating rate interest due by the utility to its lenders (and was able to finance such floating rate payments at a significantly lower cost through its access to the short-term interbank market). Nobody knew that the payments made to the bondhold-ers by the Japanese bank were in fact coming from a US utility, and it had been considered preferable to 'dress' the transaction in this way, rather than having a bond issued by the US utility, and formally guaranteed by the Japanese bank.

The 'cost' of the secret surrounding the involvement of the AAA-rated bank in the access to long-term finance by a discredited US utility, was the profit arising from the difference between the borrowing cost of the two entities (US utility and AAA-rated bank) – plus the not insignificant commissions paid to the industrious investment bank involved in the transaction.

The irony of the scheme is that it had taken a lot of effort to structure a 'trading' transaction based on the differing perception by investors of the credit quality of both parties. Since then, the AAA-rated Japanese bank has lost its rating and ceased to exist as such, while the US utility has recovered the 'investment grade' rating that allows it to 'tap' the long-term bond market as in past decades!

More recently, in November 2004, the European Investment Bank (EIB) launched an 'innovative' bond issue, the coupon of which is indexed on the Cumulative Survival Rate published by the UK's National Statistics Office, in order to allow pension funds to hedge against the risk that beneficiaries will live longer than expected: the coupon is reduced if the rate of deaths accel-erates (no need to pay pensions anymore!), and increases if the rate of deaths slows (pensions need to be paid for a longer period). Irrespective of the moral dimension of a scheme dealing with 'bets' on the average duration of human life, it is relevant to those who are interested in the identity of the economic subjects brought together by such a transaction (i) that it was considered more palatable to prospective investors in this bond, to have it launched by the European Investment Bank, a most 'honourable' institution; (ii) that the European Investment Bank only took on this commitment on condition that a 'swap counter-party' would immediately transform the terms of a complex set of uncertain future commitments into a 'classic' set of cash flows expressed in terms of floating interest rate at a level substantially lower than the cost of borrowing from prime-quality banks ('Libor'); and (iii) that the ultimate party responsible for fulfilling the coupon variations linked to the Cumulative Survival Rate is the counter-party to the swap agreement with the European Investment Bank, that is PartnerRE, a Bermudas-based reinsurance company set up in 1993 by Swiss Reinsurance Co., the world's second biggest reinsurer, to benefit from higher catastrophe reinsurance rates after Hurricane Andrew in 1992.

The purpose of the Swaps is therefore to keep an important element of information out of the public eye. However, in the early days of the development of this technique, it would have been easy for an inquiry to trace the chain of obligations. Subsequently, banks systematically acted as middle-persons to ensure anonymity between Company A and Company B, but at least one bank knew the identity of one of the parties. The ultimate step of the dilution of knowledge of the economic subject was reached with the development of 'credit derivatives', whereby banks are able to reinsure themselves against the risk of default of the entities to which they have extended loans, by issuing financial instruments purchased by other investors (on a completely anonymous basis), who undertake to indemnify the banks in case the borrowers do not repay them in accordance with the terms of the loan agreement.

The advent of the Interest Rate and Currency Swaps did radically change the long term debt market ('bonds'): transactions that had traditionally formed the basis of a commercial relationship between two parties (or 'subjects') trusting each other, ended by acquiring a sort of existence of their own, since the answer to the question about who would satisfy the claims became more and more difficult to obtain. The nominal obligor being only one of several obligated parties, it was enough to concentrate on the technical details of the claims (including the legal option of transferring the benefit of such claims to another party) under the assumption that whoever was 'behind' the nominal obligor would pay. But the acceptance of this new anonymity regime would have been unthinkable, if it had not been associated at the same time with a considerable improvement of 'liquidity' – that is, the availability of bank intermediaries prepared to purchase the chain of claims. The same Swaps that were hiding the true nature of the economic subject of the obligations, made it easy for banks to take the risk of holding temporarily any fixed-rate bonds denominated in any currency, because these transient financial assets could be converted into floating rate assets denominated in the currency of the money market to which the bank had access.

It is obvious, however, that the bank temporarily holding the fixed-rate bond that incorporates several obligors through one or several Swap agreements, is as ignorant about the ultimate counterpart as is the *bona fide* long-term investor holding the bonds, but the time horizon of its holding allows it to make a quasi-legal distinction between financial assets held for 'trading purposes' and financial assets held as 'investments'. This is just another example of the confusion surrounding the economic subject: does the nature of the subject change when the time during which a person's obligation is effective is shorter than, or in excess of, one year?

The acceptance of the waning of the identity of the economic subject was further institutionalised when the large rating agencies (Moody's and Standard & Poor's) accepted the granting of 'credit rating' notations to 'special purpose entities', that are not commercial or industrial corporations assessed by reference to their ability to generate the revenues necessary to pay back interest and principal (as had been the case in the past), but legal entities without any past (or future beyond a certain pre-defined time horizon) set up and endowed by other parties (again!) to possess the adequate financial resources to cover their obligations.

Special purpose entities (SPE) are precisely what Enron came to create in order to raise money and present to financial analysts its consolidated 'group' liabilities in the most favourable way. Most commentators have been looking into the question of control: whether these SPEs had been consolidated correctly, whether they were plain subsidiaries without a proper identity as economic subjects on their own. We believe that it is equally worth recognising that the 'structural' dilution of the 'subject' of financial transactions through a process that secures the anonymity of each party finds its ultimate perfection in the SPE in connection with the generalisation of the technique of the Swap system described above.

Historically, SPEs were set up on the model of the arm's-length subsidiaries created to recognise the existence of a specific business within a commercial company. The typical example of such subsidiaries is the well-known case of the finance companies created by US automobile manufacturers to extend loans to purchasers of (their) cars. GM Finance, Ford Finance, Chrysler Finance soon reached a size of operations that was comparable to their parent. In the main, their business was similar to banking, and their exposure to industrial cycles was different from that of industrial companies. Their financing needs were also different, which prompted all US automobile companies to define a legal structure that allowed them to carve out a specific niche – typically medium-term fixed-rate financing corresponding to the duration of car loans. The 'arm's-length relationship, intended to avoid consolidating the accounts of these obviously affiliated companies within the parents' accounts, was carefully documented and negotiated – for example, by authorising the finance company to extend loans for the purchase of cars other than those manufactured by the 'obvious' parent.

In the new financing world dominated by 'Swaps', the time horizon of fixed-rate financings became irrelevant – since every liability can be toggled from a fixed rate commitment to a short-term-indexed ('floating') rate regime, and back. As a result, financial analysts cannot determine the effective exposure of a company to interest rate and currency gyrations (as mentioned above, Swap agreements had quickly extended their 'transformation' ability to currency-and-interest-rate swaps). The disclosure of the existence of Swap agreements is still debated among most auditing authorities. A recent attempt to standardise the valuation methods for Swap agreements contracted by banks within the European Union by the end of 2004 came to nothing.

Without an objective reference to a specific financing pool resource (as was the case for the medium-term financing needed by automobile finance companies), or a specific business pattern (as was the case for car-purchase lending), the ability of an SPE to stand for itself, or to exist in the world of finance as a 'subject' in its own right, can only be established in practice by the opinion of a rating agency. The agency, in turn, has agreed to grant such favourable opinions in consideration of pre-defined series of cash flows that are brought to their present value through a calculation process identical to the one used in the negotiation of Swap agreements. It is therefore assumed that the economic subject of each commitment is not affected by the passage of time. A legal structure replaces a commercial and social sub-universe, which makes it both easier to analyse by an expert and easier to falsify, as turned out to be the case with Enron.

The last nail in the coffin is (again) the perfection of the 'liquidity' element brought about by the generalisation of the Swap agreements: the reason why so many market participants agreed to go ahead with long-term financial commitments to entities that either only had a legal existence and structure, or were bound by obscure side-agreements for which additional information was not requested, is that the number of potential holders of such instruments was multiplied infinitely by the ability of banks throughout the world to convert any fixed rate debt instrument (which formerly they were reluctant to hold because of the risk of maturity mismatch) into a floating-rate debt instrument for which they could immediately ascertain their profit versus their cost of borrowing in the short-term interbank market. The profit margin has become the only criterion and it is an established fact that most 'bonds' issued by the equivalent of SPEs are held by banks. Considering that banks allocate only a minimum percentage of capital to the financial assets they hold, a floating rate asset with a return of 2 per cent (above their borrowing cost) provides a return on equity of more than 30 per cent – and secures a full 'coverage' of the committed capital after a holding period of little more than three years (whoever the borrower/issuer might have been).

Beyond the complacency introduced by the broadening of liquidity (read: the ability of any investor to 'pass the buck' and let another investor worry about the nature or identity of the ultimate obligated party) the dilution of the economic subject – and therefore of any responsibility leading to a moral judgement – results from the general evolution towards anonymity that has its roots in a perverted form of intellectualism within the world of business itself. The fascination for the anonymous 'in-between' is closely related to the very nature of trading, which tends to reduce the importance of the economic reality from which it generates a profit, by confronting two different perceptions of the value of the same object (although the same object may initially be located in two different places – the cost of transport from one place to the other is usually a fraction of the perceived difference in value). This trend towards a formalist (or 'nominalist') approach can be identified in the evolution of the structure of increasing numbers of industrial and commercial companies where CEOs and CFOs are both obsessed by the financial ratios that support the price of the stock which is their main source of income, either by virtue of their employment contract or in connection with the stock options they have received. These companies tend to outsource manufacturing units or even any activity reliant on 'hard' assets, such as inventories. The importance given by financial analysts to certain criteria do influence perceptions in the same direction: drawing the attention towards the 'return on equity' eventually encourages a reduction of assets and an increase of liabilities – and would end up transforming all industrial and commercial businesses into financial holdings and banks. The reorganisation of Enron is a typical illustration of this recent trend. Internally, the hitherto 'heavy' utility company with factories built (and financed) for twenty years, exploiting a considerable distribution network with numerous personnel in charge of maintenance, underwent a caterpillar-to-butterfly metamorphosis and gloriously entered the white-collar only service sector as a 'trading' company. Seen from the outside, the infatuation of financial analysts and investors with the Enron 'model' added to the upward spiral of the share price that eventually enticed the top management to cross a few bridges that they might not have crossed without the pressure placed on them to perform miracles in the rarefied atmosphere of 'pure' profit that seemed at hand.

The ultimate confusion brought about by the generalisation of the trading mentality, and its specific techniques and tools, is the dimension of time, within which the 'subject' asserts its existence. The Swap agreements could only bridge the difference between short-term and long-term financial commitments through agreements between two parties prepared to ignore any change in their mutual perception of each other over the future. As mentioned in the case of the US utility and of the Japanese AAA-rated bank, the terms of their Swap agreement made the implicit assumption that their respective credit quality would not change over the life of the agreement – which proved to be incorrect. As the market for Swap agreements developed and turned such agreements into a 'standardized' commodity (although it never quite succeeded in transforming the Swap agreement itself into a 'tradeable' security), it has become customary to arrange transactions on the basis of the calculation of the present value of the future flows. The basic assumption of such calculations is that the relationship between short-term and long-term interest rates will not change for the duration of the agreement and – in the case of interest and currency swaps – that the relationship between long-term interest rates in the two currencies involved will remain the same for the duration of the agreement. Those assumptions are known to be incorrect from the start, but they make it possible to exchange future obligations as if the future were today.

The importance of what sounds like a pure accounting consideration may be difficult for the uninitiated person to assess: in practical terms, however, future cash-flows, brought to their 'present value', may give very different results, depending on the calculation methodology. To take a recent example, the two largest US mortgage loan agencies, known as 'Freddie Mac' and 'Fannie May', have been accused of having engaged in swap agreements, the result of which has not been reported adequately in their accounts. The adjustment imposed on Freddie Mac by the regulatory authorities was

US$5 billion (for having understated its earnings) while Fannie Mae may have to restate its earnings by recording a US$9 billion loss (*Financial Times*, 17 November 2004). It is striking that (i) both agencies appear to have been inaccurate by very similar amounts; (ii) the amounts are a 'hidden' gain for one and a 'hidden loss' for the other; and (iii) the magnitude of the adjustment can be considered to be huge. In the 1980s, the budget of a major hydroelectric project in Quebec (James Bay dams) was US$6 billion.

It is for the US courts to determine when and where members of Enron's management did or did not engage in irregular operations that led eventually to the demise of the large US corporation. The greater difficulty is to assess the extent of the responsibility of a few individuals, against a prevailing economic order in which the identity of the economic subject – defined as the place where responsibility arises – is threatened through perpetual shifting (liquidity) and a denial of exposure to the passage of time. The byzantine discussions that started in the US courts, about the nature of the co-operation between certain banks and Enron: whether they were making loans, purchasing energy futures, or holding an equity interest in some of the SPEs, will not exhaust the concern of outside observers about the conditions that made the inflation (and explosive deflation) of the 'bubble' possible. On the other hand, inquiring about the identity of the several parties involved in most 'modern' financial transactions would bring the flow of ordinary transactions to a halt. A separation between the world of finance and the world of businesses organised to satisfy 'primary' needs used to characterise the former banking regulations that separated commercial banks from investment banks, but this US law has been abolished; the temptation to turn a commercial corporation into a trading – or quasi-financial – entity is not new.

The solution to Enron's woes does exist in the capitalist system: financial conglomerates have made the deliberate choice to keep their 'ordinary' investors in the dark and making transparency a secondary objective. The well-known result is that the market value of such economic subjects is generally lower than the theoretical market value of their components. This 'cost' of the secrecy intuitively confirms the merit of other, more transparent, economic structures. The ultimate responsibility for the disastrous result of the transition of Enron from being an industrial company to become a financial conglomerate could then be attributed to the financial analyst community, which failed to identify the nature of the evolution and its likely consequences for the valuation of the company's shares. But financial analysts are also bank employees, and the banks that engineered the techniques and practices that spread confusion about the economic subject could not be expected to escape the confusion they themselves had created.

Part 2
Ethics in Thought and Action

5
An Ethical Diagnosis of the Enron Affair

Etienne Perrot

In order to conduct an ethical analysis of the Enron affair, we need a clear idea of what ethics in fact is. This is tricky, as the word 'ethics' has almost as many meanings as it has users: ethics is all about acting for good, and every-one has his or her own idea of what that means. In any case, we must start by distinguishing between principles of action and the foundation of ethics, and then focus on what is the most rousing element: the foundation.

Principles of action and the foundation of ethics: some diagnostic tools

Ethical principles are not about what induces players to act for good – their motivation – but about the rational logic behind their actions. For example: 'Do unto others as you would have them do unto you' (the 'golden rule' of ethics), Kant's injunction to treat others not merely as means but also as ends, or La Fontaine's warning: 'Beware, as long as you live, of judging people by appearances.' In our turbulent world, the most popular principle is the precautionary principle, which induces us to act without waiting for scientific proof of potential damage. At the time of writing, this principle is supplanting two other principles of government that have dominated the modern Western mind: (i) the solidarity principle, which prescribes that each member of society can be required to pay when another is unable to; and (ii) the subsidiarity principle, which prescribes that decisions should be taken at the level closest to those they will affect (the higher level being seen as 'subsidiary', both in the sense of secondary and in the sense of a provider of subsidies). Professional ethics, for its part, has traditionally invoked the responsibility principle, entirely in keeping with the instrumental ratio-nality that dominates the business world. To these can be added probity (wishing the best for one's partners) and its counterpart, honesty (refusal to lie), as well as prudence (which does not mean weakness of will, but rather a clear understanding of specific situations), and diligence (providing the expected service without delay), avoidance of conflicts of interest (so that clients do not suspect their partners' professional consciences). Other principles that are trotted out like so many clichés are: transparency (so that partners can make well-informed decisions) and fair play (respect for the rules of the social game). In short, there are countless principles of action, as numerous as the various ways of linking up ends and means.

Confusion between the principles of action and the foundation of ethics makes it virtually impossible to regenerate a corrupt system, for simply reminding people of principles has never motivated anyone. Indeed, those who wield principles may be suspected of indulgence in clerical moralising that bandies intellectual abstractions about but fails to take into account the specific circumstances in which they are applied. As the Scriptures put it, they 'load people down with burdens they can hardly carry, and … will not lift one finger to help them' (Matthew 23:4). Principles allow disputed actions to be judged after the event; they allow people to justify their decisions to themselves and to others, and to check that plans are correct before they are put into practice; they can sometimes even serve to put a stop to ongoing activities; but they are not the mainspring of action.

The mainspring of action, the foundation of ethics, is motivation. One way to approach this topic is to read the writings of philosophers. Their ethical treatises (Aristotle's *Nicomachean Ethics*, Spinoza's *Ethics*, Hans Jonas' writings on the ethics of responsibility, and Max Weber's on the ethics of conviction, for example) identify the motivations of those who act for good, and what it is that makes them do good: to Marcus Aurelius and the Stoics it was self-mastery, which ensured mastery of the world and impassiveness in the face of torments that wise men refused to deem either good or bad; to the disciples of Epicurus it was enjoyment of the present moment without fear of things to come; to Aristotle it was the πολις (*polis*), the city, designated politically organised society and with which each citizen identified; to Plato it was the 'idea of good', to which wise men could accede by making the effort to discern the internal laws behind phenomena; to Jesus it was disinterested love of one's neighbour; to Thomas Aquinas it was society as mutual recognition; to Spinoza it was perseverance in being in harmony with the laws of the cosmos; to Adam Smith it was self-love, a reflection of social approval; to Kant, Rousseau and the Enlightenment philosophers of the eighteenth century it was universal conscience; to Schopenhauer in the nineteenth century, in line with Buddha's intuitions, it was the sense of compassion; to contemporary philosophers it is the need to communicate among reasonable people (Habermas), the otherness reflected in others' faces (Levinas), the taste for freedom acquired by working for the freedom of others (Ricoeur) or the sense of responsibility towards future generations (Hans Jonas). There is thus no lack of philosophers who have attempted to identify the foundation of ethics.

The ethical basis for an analysis of the Enron affair

It is important not to confuse motivation – the foundation – with the justi-fications players provide after the event on the basis of principles. In the light of this distinction, this chapter will attempt to reveal the ethical basis for analysis of the Enron affair, that is to say, the motives involved, rather than the principles that those responsible should have espoused in order to act for good, or the justifications provided after the event. It will do this by examining various analyses and identifying the economic, professional or legal motivations they ascribe to the parties involved in the collapse. Clearly, there can be no question here of reviewing all the philosophers who, from the ancients up to Comte-Sponville, have attempted to define the foundation of ethics, in order to see whether the Enron affair is an illustration of Theory X rather than Theory Y – a job that can be done perfectly well by any handbook on the history of philosophy.[1] Nor can there be any question of selecting one philosopher whose thinking supposedly provides the most satisfactory ethical basis for analysis of the Enron affair. Instead, an attempt will be made to identify, behind the various proposals and analyses, what it was that supposedly motivated the various players involved in the affair: managers, employees, auditors, lawyers, controllers and legislators.

Perhaps it is simplest to begin by assuming that the various motivations fit into one of three categories proposed by Lawrence Kohlberg (1927–87) in his study on the stages of moral development from childhood to old age. The first level comprises two stages based on fear and enticement; the second level comprises two stages based on membership of a group and legal authority; and the third level comprises the last two stages, based on the equal value of all human beings. Kohlberg's study moves inductively from justification to motivation, assuming a one-to-one relationship between the two. He thus confuses justificatory principles with the foundation of ethics, which is the motive of action. Despite this confusion, Kohlberg's stages of development can help to clarify our discussion by dividing motivations into three cate-gories known as 'pre-conventional', 'conventional' and 'post-conventional', reflecting the three great classic motivations: utility, interest and self-esteem. Kohlberg's three levels, like three levels of a building, are a fairly accurate reflection of the structure of every social nexus and reveal a threefold foun-dation for ethics, at an ever deeper – more intimate – level.

The value of punishment, or the beginnings of wisdom

When those in charge of Enron are blamed for having set up 'special-purpose entities' to conceal the company's misfortunes and make its position appear healthier than in fact it was, the principle behind such accusations is that of transparency, which supposedly reflects the notion of respect for one's partners (suppliers, customers, shareholders, government bodies, col-leagues). Behind this principle lies a primary motivation, namely the fear of punishment. Indeed, it was the consequences – financial collapse and its legal implications – that led people to consider the moral aspects of the affair, far more than any sense that professional principles of transparency had been violated. Just as little children assess the seriousness of their actions in terms of how angry their mother is, the company in fact had to collapse before people started subjecting management and accounting practices and lax supervision procedures to closer scrutiny.

Here we are in the first 'level', the most visible frame of reference in analyses of the Enron affair, in which the law is seen not as a social nexus that transcends personal interests, but as a vehicle for punishment. The various analyses treat the law as an instrument of more or less vengeful coercion. The idea is either to penalise past illegal actions, of which there are few, and whose perpetrators are duly sentenced, or else to approach things in terms of legal obligation, supervision and punishment.

Much has been said about the Sarbanes-Oxley Act, a repercussion of affairs such as the one that concerns us here and an almost grotesque example of the basic logic of stricter supervision and harsher punishment designed to scare directors and financial managers into publishing truthful accounts, and insistence that all those who are, directly or indirectly, required to be party to financial information report any irregularities they come across, on pain of prosecution. However, American law seems to consider accountants to be above suspicion. Is this assumption of good intentions based on actual experience, or simply a sign of how strong the accountants' lobby is? The very question raises sufficient doubt to sustain the idea that no one should be exempt from supervision or punishment.

Proposals for stricter supervision and harsher punishment all approach the foundation of ethics in terms of Kohlberg's pre-conventional stage. This is not unlike the 'moral arithmetic' advocated in the nineteenth century by the champion of utilitarianism, Jeremy Bentham, who proposed that problems of government be simplified by applying a strict calculation of reward and punishment, so that everyone would be led, not by some invisible hand but by the secular arm of government, to fear punishment for acts damaging to society and to seek reward for acts favourable to it. This twofold principle of fear and enticement is clearly apparent in Enron's 'rank and yank' staffing policies: applauded as long as the company was performing well, they were dismissed just as categorically as being unethical when they proved to be counter-productive. This utilitarian outlook gives a pointer to the players' primary motivations.

Ironically, comments on the economic and practical limitations to stricter supervision point in the same direction: here, again, the idea is to base any moral assessment of the system on the likelihood of punishment. However, there is an organisational obstacle to this approach: in addition to the costs of supervision, there are the costs of supervising the supervisors, and perhaps even of supervising those who supervise the supervisors. As the old greybeard Karl Marx put it in the *Parisian Manuscripts* (1844): 'The materialist doctrine that men are products of circumstances and upbringing forgets that it is men that change circumstances and that the educator himself needs educating' (third thesis on Feuerbach).

At this first level, where the law is applied in carrot-and-stick fashion, education is seen as a sort of 'breaking-in'. Quite apart from the fact that such a motivation will no longer work for players who have passed this infantile stage of moral development, there is a second obstacle – one that is no longer organisational but truly moral, and has been very clearly formulated by classical ethics (in which the individual is seen as an autonomous, responsible human being). This considers that no one is morally obliged to tell the truth to judges or supervisors: *nemo tenetur edere contra se* (no one is required to testify against himself). On the other hand, it also considers that people do have a moral duty to tell the truth to counsellors, coaches, assistants, relatives or friends, who are assumed to wish only the best for them. The reason for this is immediately obvious: the function of judges and police officers is to defend society, and their reference value is law and order, whereas the highest value in classical ethics is the individuality of the human being. In Enron's case there was a moral contradiction in the fact that the same firm was responsible for auditing, supervision and counselling – an arrangement that has been subject to increasing criticism in the USA ever since the affair erupted.

The value of playing by the rules

The second level of the foundation of ethics involves the interplay of circumstances, education and good practice. This second 'level' is a combination of economic institutions and playing by the rules. Playing by the rules is essential: it is not without good reason that there have been calls for a complete overhaul of professional ethics, since opportunities to cheat (something supposedly regulated by the law, supervision and punishment back at the first level), take unfair advantage of privileges and indulge in other unacceptable behaviour are inherent in the game.

The institutions involved in the Enron affair – especially markets, money and law – are all rule systems that essentially have to make sense to people. All the players obey the rules of the social game because they believe they make sense, not just because they fear punishment. At this second level there is no longer any question of changing the rules, or applying stricter supervision and harsher punishment, which would compromise the efficiency of the system. As Schumpeter emphasised, markets can only be efficient if partners trust each other. If everything had to be supervised, markets would lose their intrinsic advantage of responsiveness, initiative and competition. So how can players be induced to play by the rules?

It has been said with regard to derivatives, which tend to destabilise the prices of products (especially non-storable products such as electricity, in which Enron traded), that market forces encourage short-termism. Particular criticism has been levelled at disintermediation, which initially benefits both buyers and sellers but at the same time causes prices to fluctuate wildly. The implied mutualisation of risk created not so long ago by financial intermediaries has made way for a rougher game in which markets tend to overreact, especially since the lack of transparency created by deregulation leads them to anticipate trends and act upon virtualities almost before they have taken shape. Stock options have led the main players to gamble on short-term stock-market values rather than the health of the companies concerned. Swaps altered Enron's financial structure and at the same time transferred responsibility for debts to other entities that were ultimately anonymous. Meanwhile, in a classic instance of 'patrimonial capitalism' (to borrow a term from the Régulation school), Enron was becoming an increasingly indefinable entity: having begun as an energy producer, it extended its activities to marketing and then financing, and responsibility for the insurance implications was shifted to the anonymous mass of stock-market investors.

In line with current trends in capitalism, Enron's institutional responsibility was dissipated by an evasive process which lent each part of the picture a false depth that prevented people from pinning any of them down. In this rush to anonymity, special-purpose entities played the part filled by vistas in fifteenth-century Italian paintings. Vistas were openings: through a window in the wall in the background, the viewer could see a garden in whose wall there was a door that provided a glimpse of a road; the road guided the viewer's eye to a distant hill or sea; on the hill there was an almost invisible speck which might be a tree, far out at sea was a blurred white dot which might be a sail. ... In this way, those supposedly responsible for the company's risks vanished into the background of the economic picture (financial markets), taking corporate ethics with them.

This second level, at which individuals vanish into the anonymity of commercial institutions, is referred to by Kohlberg as 'conventional'. Here ethics is based on a convention, in other words a systemic effect produces a social reality by co-ordinating supposedly independent anonymous initiatives. Conventional reality is fairly well described by John Maynard Keynes in the paradox he uses to account for the formation of certain interest rates on financial markets. Given the almost total lack of certainty as to the actual value of debts, he says, players rush to respond to the slightest rumour, and this rush leads to convergence of prices and a precarious equilibrium that creates a degree of unity between all the players. The same was true of the complex market in which Enron was operating. In a system that could operate only if the players were well-intentioned, it was in each party's interest that everyone else should play by the rules. However, those in charge of Enron soon realised they had a more immediate interest in 'jumping the gun' (as Keynes saw it) by manipulating prices and taking advantage of insider information. This callous attitude illustrates the truth of Jean-Jacques Rousseau's remark that the notion of 'rational self-interest' (which according to liberal ethicists causes the interests of the individual and those of society to converge) is a very fragile foundation for ethics – as it presupposes the harmonious co-ordination of diverging interests by means of rules that will only operate if, in addition to cheats being punished, everyone plays by those rules.

The limitations of rational self-interest

In its crudest form, the argument based on rational self-interest was summed up in Adam Smith's famous aphorism about the baker in his book *The Wealth of Nations* (1776). It is for reasons of self-interest rather than altruism that the baker endeavours to serve his customers to the best of his ability:

> Man has almost constant occasion for the help of his brethren, and it is in vain for him to expect it from their benevolence only. He will be more likely to prevail if he can interest their self-love in his favour, and show them that it is for their own advantage to do for him what he requires of them ... It is not from the benevolence of the butcher, the brewer, or the baker that we expect our dinner, but from their regard to their self-love, and never talk to them of our own necessities but of their advantages.

In *A Treatise of Human Nature* (1738), David Hume drives this point home when he remarks that passions are much more fully satisfied if contained than if given free rein.

The limitation of arguments based on rational self-interest is that they fail to take account of decision-makers' specific situations and individual interests. Above all, they overlook the contradiction inherent in all individuals and legal persons, namely that they all have interests that are mediatised by the society in which they dwell (the view taken by Smith as well as his friend Hume) but at the same time have an immediate interest in playing their own game at the other players' expense. Moreover, as Vilfredo Pareto noted in his *Treatise on General Sociology*, interests are heterogeneous and cannot be compared with one another. Clearly, then, ethics based on rational self-interest is likely to prove inadequate, as it fails to take into account the complexity of the business world.

In the case of the Enron group, however, it would be better to speak of a 'complicated' rather than a 'complex' structure. This distinction between complex and complicated structures is almost irrelevant to organisational and legal analysis of the situation: when it comes to ethical analysis, however, it is essential.

A 'complex' structure has numerous different logics that appear contradictory even to those who run the company: diverging interests, conflicting values, contradictions between the short and long term, and conflicts between immediate advantages and advantages mediatised by the various social groups. This is the essence of contemporary ethics, and it justifies an ethical analysis of the Enron affair.

A 'complicated' structure, on the other hand, has nothing to do with the human or social contradictions of the situation, but refers to the difficulty of revealing a logic that is hidden among the 'folds' of countless screens (which is why it is described as 'com-plicated', that is, folded up). Unlike complex structures, complicated ones can be 'ex-plicated': unfolded or revealed. Enron's commercial and financial situation was complicated, but patient analysis revealed what was hidden among the folds and to spread out on a single surface the logic behind the company's actions, which was in fact quite simple: to maintain the appearance of profitability in order to pocket a larger share of society's wealth. Yet this simple rationality that was hidden among the folds of a complicated legal set-up clashed with the collective interplay of market forces, with the social complexity of the market economy.

Ethical arguments based on rational self-interest behave as though everyone's space and time scale is identical with those of the group they belong to, or indeed of society as a whole – although this is contradicted by the Enron affair and by everyday business experience. In his book *Emile, or Education*, Jean-Jacques Rousseau clearly exposed the weakness of this common-sense ethics:

> Even the precept of doing unto others as we would have them do unto us has no true foundation other than conscience and sentiment [*sic*]; for where is the precise reason for me, being myself, to act as if I were another, especially when I am morally certain of never finding myself in the same situation? And who will guarantee me that in very faithfully following this maxim I will get others to follow it similarly with me? The wicked man gets advantage from the just man's probity and his own injustice. He is delighted that everyone, with the exception of himself, be just.

Strengthening people's sense of belonging and solidarity

So how can we reform practices that distort the interplay of market forces? How are we to encourage the 'conscience and sentiment' that induce people to play by the rules? Kohlberg provides a pointer when he distinguishes between two stages of this conventional level: the ties of affection between people in the same group, and the ties created by legal authority.

Clearly, people will have fewer ulterior motives if they have ties of affection with their fellow players. In order to achieve this, it is necessary to strengthen their sense of belonging, *affectio societatis*, the sense of solidarity that unites all the players in a market economy despite their diverging interests. The most direct way is to brandish the threat of regulation as a substitute for inadequate self-regulation; this takes us back to the previous level, which is based on fear and enticement. Other ways are more subtle: ritualised events that celebrate the best practitioners on the market, emphasis on the shared risks posed by foreign competitors, recognition by society through non-prohibitive taxation, all of which create a vague sense of solidarity (although this is still a far cry from what the military know as 'team spirit'). This is the affective dimension of culture.

Professional ethics could have a part to play here. Unfortunately, to the individual's delight but at the expense of society, professional ethics is increasingly confused with regulation; this takes the foundation of ethics back to the first, preconventional level, based on fear of supervision and punishment. This can be seen in the emergence of professions such as that of the 'compliance officer', with a gradual shift away from discernment (the choice of criteria for action) towards mere compliance with legal, accounting, financial and reporting standards. This shift in professional ethics has been accompanied by the increasing prevalence of purely procedural ethics well suited to a liberal ideology that treats society as a purely contractual product, with disputes always being settled by appealing to the legal authorities (the first level of ethics). In both businesses and schools, the tendency is to settle all problems by examining how the various parties played the part society expected of them and judging them on that basis, rather than by looking at the consequences (which are mere pointers).

To combat this temptation to let ethics become purely procedural, and to avoid the pitfalls of which American legal history has provided so many examples, the legal framework needs to be simplified. The accumulation of rules and regulations, the complicated wording of legislation and the resulting legal uncertainty lead to conflicting legal interpretations that gradually undermine the rule of law. The law is then taken hostage by legal experts, and managers who are supposed to abide by the law use their ignorance as a pretext for relying on conjurers who juggle with regulations so disparate that loopholes are inevitable. Some of the blame can be put on politicians. They have taken the law – supposedly a clear expression of general interest – and turned it into a mere instrument of government; they are then forced to promulgate lengthy, technocratic legislative texts which cannot be understood by those who run the businesses to which they apply; and they thus encourage unfair economic and financial practices.

Training in self-esteem

At the third, deeper level, the motivation is the ethics of conviction so beloved of Max Weber. But where is such conviction to come from? Some analysts of the Enron affair have criticised the lack of courage, character, modesty, fairness and honesty that led to the now celebrated disaster. Such virtues do not exactly grow on trees. The Enlightenment philosophers – Rousseau, Kant, Hume, Smith, Quesnay and the physiocrats – saw Nature (to which they accorded varying degrees of divinity, depending on their religious inclinations) as the source of those virtues that are so crucial to the operation of market forces. Yet they all stressed that people must make an effort – 'work on themselves', as it were – in order to discover and recognise these 'natural' virtues and model their behaviour on them. The ancient philosophers, for their part, placed the virtues in a logical order, as if to emphasise that they were interlinked, and that people could discover one only by practising another. The classic example was Aristotle's sequence of cardinal virtues. The first was prudence, the practical understanding of sin-gular situations; but prudence was nothing without justice, whose purpose was the harmonious adjustment of the elements in the world; justice pre-supposed the power that would allow it to be enforced; and power called for temperance, without which it would degenerate into injustice and violence. The Judaeo-Christian tradition also had its procession of virtues, the 'gifts of the Spirit' inspired by the prophet Isaiah in the sixth century BC: wisdom, understanding, science, counsel, power, devotion and finally fear of the Lord who, according to the Book of Proverbs, is the fount of all wisdom – bringing us full circle! (Isaiah 11:2–3).

This ordered arrangement shows that the foundation of ethics is based on a 'ratio', as used in mathematics, when an arithmetical (or geometric) progression is said to have a 'ratio' of 2, 3, etc. This points to an inner need on the part of economic players, rather than external coercion. This is why Kant called the ethic imperative 'categorical' – that is, independent of exter-nal circumstances, and born, he believed, out of 'the starry heaven above me and the moral law within me'. Schopenhauer was thus mistaken in locating this Kantian imperative at the first level of the foundation of ethics, that of punishment; he saw it simply as a piece of Judaeo-Christian moral theology, and an incoherent one at that – for what, he said, could a categorical imperative mean in the absence of supervision and punishment? In today's economic context, the ethics of conviction calls for greater self-esteem. This is the most intimate foundation, even if not always the most rousing one. If we are to do anything more than simply remind people of ethical princi-ples (which is nice, but of little help), people need to be trained in self-esteem. This could be done in three stages: (i) perceiving complexity; (ii) fostering pride; and (iii) accepting symbols.

Perceiving complexity

Perceiving complexity means being able to identify the full range of rationalities in given economic situations: short-term and longer-term ratio-nality, sociological rationality (which is often very different from economic rationality), and psychological rationality, which is often multiple and sometimes diverges from what instrumental rationality would demand – plus the host of conflicting legal references, the bane of auditors particularly when they have to deal with multinational firms. The Jesuits' centuries of experience could provide some good examples of casuistry (the ability to decide which law applies prima facie in each geographical, historical or political situation, according to the specific circumstances) that would help us to find our way through this complexity. However, if we do not want to venture into this somewhat unusual culture, it is sufficient to realise that complexity is a constant feature of the business world: dialogies (the full range of different logics which remain in 'dialogue' – provided we use this term without any false connotation of consensus); organisational recursion (feedback or circular causality, which means that a given effect cannot be ascribed to a single cause; in other words, that causes and effects are inter-linked); and a hologram structure, which implies that each component of the economic system is a reflection of the whole. Those with a naïve view of the economy see nothing more in this complexity than functioning incoherence and active disorder,[2] but a more sophisticated view identifies the vast number of interlocking rationalities as so many networks that communicate at various inconstant points.

If we do not want to confuse them with theories of complexity, it is enough to confront managers, lawyers, auditors, colleagues and politicians with the downsides of the values that dominate the business world: cost (the downside of economic value); failure (which can happen to any business that operates in an uncertain environment, however relevant it may be); and interdependence (the downside of any partnership, whether within an organisation, firm or government body or within an institution such as the market, the law or money) – for it is value that gives meaning to costs, relevance that justifies the ever-present risk of failure, and mutual recognition that makes sense of the risk of otherness. Existentially, anyone can see how real value outweighs the cost it has generated, how relevance wins from disappointment, and how gratification overcomes indifference.

Fostering pride

A second, more positive way of increasing self-esteem would be to foster pride. The most direct way is to set an example, provided this is not dressed up. We are not talking here about behavioural management, which teaches those who run businesses to adopt the attitudes expected by the people around them, but which proves counter-productive once their duplicitous attitudes (exemplary in public, cynical in private) are exposed. This reveals the ambiguous nature of role play, the mantra of psychosociological semi-nars for senior management. Although role play certainly discloses the full range of interests and logic involved, it also brings to the forefront of the stage (how apt a metaphor!) formal attitudes and ultimately compliance with the social norm, not to say the ritual of the ambient environment, whose function is to smooth the rough edges of social intercourse and so lubricate communication. Setting an example will only help colleagues or partners to behave more ethically if it arises out of real-life dilemmas. Dilemmas occur where interests fail to meet, where moral values conflict, or where the law itself is incoherent. This is where ethics truly comes into its own, for it is precisely in such back-to-the-wall situations that players can show 'who they really are' and 'what they really want' (or, to be more precise, what criteria they apply).

An even more fruitful means of encouraging people to act for good is infectious indignation. However unreasonable, indignation can challenge ethics that has become entrenched in questionable positions. Here we could mention certain corrupt practices in international trade which were an almost grotesque illustration of Pascal's aphorism: 'Truth on this side of the Pyrenees, error on the other side!' The indignation shown by Anglo-Saxon countries brought continental Europeans to their senses, and eventually a number of international bodies such as the OECD built up a pressure of opinion that was able to influence standards of conduct. However, the classic 'indignation effect' remains that of human rights in the West. The history of natural law began with the indignation caused by 'the destruction of the Indies', as it was termed by the Dominican friar Bartolomé de las Casas, who was scandalised at how Spanish colonists treated the native population of the newly conquered Americas. As he saw it, what had previously been termed the law of nations, or the law of strangers, was in fact a natural law that derived from human nature rather than culture, history, geography, religion or even legislation. People only became aware of these 'human rights' when confronted with the fact that suffering inflicted on a stranger – any stranger, irrespective of race or religion – was an injury inflicted on the entire 'human race'. Bartolomé de las Casas thus felt justified in referring to the war waged by local populations against the Spaniards – subjects of the 'most Christian king' – as something 'holy'. In defending themselves and killing Christians, he said, these pagans were acting 'in full justice and dignity'. In other words, the quality of being human transcended beliefs, even those one was trying to propagate.

Another Dominican friar, Francisco de Vitoria – an intellectual who never moved beyond the confines of his university – was to reformulate de las Casas' spluttering indignation in positive rules. His *Lesson on the Newly Discovered Indians* (1539) was a work of rationalisation which stated that the Spaniards had no right to dominate the Indians, even if they were 'unbelievers' (non-Christians). Neither the Emperor nor the Pope were masters of the world. They could not invoke 'rights of discovery' in countries that were already inhabited. Nations, in all their diversity, must live in 'friendship' in accordance with 'natural law'! As both de las Casas and Vitoria saw it, this was simply the application of the Christian religious principle that all human beings were brothers in God and were entitled to equal dignity. God was in a sense the guarantor of natural law. However, their reflections on the rights of Indians enabled Hugo Grotius, writing in the early seventeenth century, to take a further step in the direction of autonomous natural law. Universal respect for human beings and nations would remain valid, he stated, even if we held that God did not exist (*etiamsi daremus Deum non esse*): 'Natural law is so immutable that it cannot be changed by God himself.' Leibniz later cited Grotius's *etiamsi daremus* in the specific sense of God being subordinate to goodness, and stated that what was right was what would please God if he existed – whether he existed or not. This completed the shift from a personal God to a God who was identical with 'goodness'. This 'goodness', which de las Casas perceived in terms of feelings and was later formalised in the principles of natural law, would eventually be enshrined in the various 'universal' declarations of human rights, since it was based on the 'self-evident' principle that everyone was entitled to respect, irrespective of their race or religion. History has shown that this principle is by no means so 'self-evident', and that it emerges from a sense of indignation experienced in specific circumstances before being moulded into theoretical justifications and principles. If the foundation of ethics is so dependent on our experience of actual events, it loses its mythical aura and descends from the heaven of ideas, like the tongues of fire at Pentecost, to become part of a history that is never written in advance and in that everyone has his or her part to play. In short, indignation at the wrong-doings in the Enron affair, legal or otherwise, was not irrational – it was simply pre-rational. It was based on a specific experience, even if it was subsequently enshrined in a rational justification that laid claim to universality.

Accepting symbols

The ultimate, and most intimate, degree of motivation is based on the symbolic approach, from the Greek συν-βαλειν (*sun-balein*), literally 'throwing together'. This approach is based on mutual recognition by people who have never met. The classic symbol is the password, which enables members of the same clan to recognise each other even if they have never seen each other. This approach leads us to the foundation for good actions through the experience of otherness. It corresponds to Kohlberg's third level, at which we become aware that human laws, however necessary they may be in order to curb violence, fail to take proper account of the individual's singularity. Why should we respect each person's dignity, not as a human being in general but in his or her own specific circumstances? Rather than appealing to universal principles, which Kohlberg saw as the height of ethics but were in fact merely an abstract way of describing otherness, the symbolic approach tests universality through the risks of uncertain relationships between individual players who each have their own unique features and travel their own unique paths. Here we perceive the distance that is essential to all human intercourse and is experienced in the time-lag created by the interplay of institutions.

According to Robert Reich, the professional future of the world lies with the 'symbol manipulators'.[3] Here he is not talking about priests or freemasons, but counsellors, experts, financiers, advertisers and, in general, any communication professional capable of identifying problems and problematising projects in order to communicate and explain them. This potentially includes any profession that becomes distinct from the anonymous gear-wheels of the vast machine that is society. As Reich sees it, the professional quality of symbol manipulators is made up of four components, which could serve as frames of reference for training in financial ethics: (i) the capacity for abstraction, which is essential in order to be able to problematise and shift from one issue to the next; symbol manipulators use equations, formulae, analogies, models, intellectual constructions, categories and comparisons to create possible ways of reinterpreting, and hence re-ordering, the chaos of data whirling around us – in short, they are able to construct their own meanings; (ii) the ability to think in terms of systems (complex structures with their dialogies, circular causalities and hologram configurations); (iii) the ability to test and interpret phenomena – to formulate refutable hypotheses; and (iv) the ability to work in teams – to discover procedures based on mutual subsidiarity. Ethics is practised in just the same way.

Conclusion

There is little point in identifying the foundation of ethics at arm's length, in the hope that managers and companies that seek to avoid the misfortunes suffered and caused by Enron will be spurred into action. Laws that are upheld by a combination of fear and enticement, feelings that are sustained by each person's interest in the social game of commercial relationships, and the self-esteem that one acquires by showing respect for stakeholders are merely words that cannot replace the actual things they stand for – especially since the foundation of financial ethics cannot be seen in isolation from those who practise it. Spectators are not footballers, and theorists are not usually players in the field. Depending on the events that have marked their lives and the way they account for these to themselves and to others, managers can each discover the foundation of ethics in one of the three categories described above (utility, interest and self-esteem, or a mixture of the three). However, this very process is part of the practice of ethics – because the foundation of ethics cannot remain frozen in previously tested positions, however valid these may seem. Instead, it has to be reinvented in response to each new dilemma. The practice of ethics is thus rather similar to the practice of science, in which the analytical frameworks and formal models that serve as principles for ethical action are there to be challenged and stretched to breaking point on the rack of inquiry. Once we are aware of the limitations of our own ethics, we can begin to act for good – and, as we do so, discover who we really are.

Notes

1 For a clear summary of the various philosophers' views of ethics, see Jacqueline Russ, *La pensée éthique contemporaine* (Paris: PUF, 1994).
2 Paul Valéry, 'L'âme et la danse', in Paul Valéry (ed.), *Eupalinos; L'âme et la danse; Dialogue de l'arbre* (Paris: Gallimard, 1970). The expression is used by Eryximachus, a mythical physician who attempts to define life in terms of this twofold paradox.
3 R. Reich, *The Work of Nations* (New York: Knopf, 1991).

6
Anonymity: Is a Norm as Good as a Name?

Edward Dommen[1]

The sound of your hammer at five in the morning, or nine at night, heard by a creditor, makes him easy six months longer, but, if he sees you at a billiard table, or hears your voice at a tavern, when you should be at work, he sends for his money the next day, demands it, before he can receive it, in a lump.

Benjamin Franklin, *Advice to a Young Tradesman*, 1748

[In Mexico] family firms ... are all about trust – or, rather, the lack of it in any institution other than the family ... Mexican businessmen [*sic*] have become used to operating in an environment in which, at one time or another, almost every other institution, from the banks, to the regulators, to the police, to the government has proved to be corrupt, often extremely so. ... Family businesses can enjoy other innate advantages. Not having to deliver endlessly improving quarterly results, they tend to be more stable and to 'have a long-term vision'. They may grow slowly, but they grow more solidly.

The Economist, 20 March 2004, p. 70

Over the last twenty years and more, financing in public markets has been associated with ... swap agreements which in effect create effective but asymmetrical situations of novation[2] under which the debtor, while bringing in a third party to satisfy the obligations which he has contracted, does not subrogate[3] the rights of his lender in the creditor's rights for the simple reason that he becomes joined to a chain of links who are in ignorance of each other, unless they can work back up the whole series of bilateral agreements which the banking market has striven with some success to standardise without completely succeeding in getting these private agreements recognised as public titles. Such recognition would subject them to extra constraints of public information and rigour and above all thwart their economy which rests on the differences in perception

> of credit which banking intermediation masks ... *What is at stake is no less than the identity of the parties. The arrival and then the generalisation of swaps have conferred absolute priority to the commitment to pay, over the subject of that commitment ... [The end result] is to conceal the very being of the subject at the level at which the principle of responsibility is specified.*
>
> François-Marie Monnet, 'Enron: où est passée la main invisible?', *Finance & the Common Good/Bien Commun*, no. 18–19 (Spring–Summer 2004)[4]

The first and the last of the texts just quoted present two radically contrasting descriptions of the relationship between creditor and debtor. The first refers to a village economy, the last to the rarefied world of high finance. The second text describes an intermediate situation.

All three reflect the same favourable inclination towards knowing with whom one is dealing. The discussions crystallised in this volume have brought out several of the dangers that can be hidden in anonymity or veiled identity by financial operators such as Enron. It offers a mask to the complications that the clever exploit to their advantage. Yet anonymity, or at best slight acquaintance, is not only indispensable to moving around in a complex market (which is not the same thing as a complicated one). It not only has its uses, but even has virtues. Several of the issues raised by the Enron case invite a closer examination of the role that anonymity plays in finance.

Given the far-reaching moral implications of anonymity, it is surprising that not only encyclopaedias of morals, but general encyclopaedias as well are typically silent about it, beyond giving a dictionary definition of the word. A search in French computerised library catalogues in Geneva – which is, of course, an international financial centre – generally throws up references to the law of the limited liability company (*société anonyme* in French). There is literature on the protection of the personality,[5] or the private sphere so dear to Swiss bankers,[6] but it deals with only a small number of aspects of the more fundamental issue of anonymity.[7] This chapter is therefore no more than a tentative approach to the question. Although inspired by the Enron debate, it limits itself to sketching in observations about anonymity which are general rather than specific to the case at hand.

A society of the anonymous

La société anonyme in French can be understood in English as either of two quite different concepts: on the one hand the limited liability company, and on the other the anonymous society – the kind of society in which people go unrecognised both in the sense that other people do not know or care who they are, and in the sense that their particular talents and merits do not get the credit (or blame) they deserve. The two meanings of *la société anonyme* overlap in financial relations.

An association of capital

The limited liability company is called 'anonymous' in French because it is not a society of people, who have names; but of amounts of capital – and individual bank notes or sums in a bank account do not bear distinct names. Within a given currency, money has no identity, as Vespasian emphasised in his dictum 'Money has no odour'.[8] Thus, in French, the limited liability company is not merely anonymous, but also literally inhuman.

In Switzerland, the paradox of the anonymous corporation is further complicated by the existence of registered shareholders who should in principle not be anonymous at all. However, the proportion of registered shares whose owners have not registered their name is now a cause of concern to the companies in question. They account for over 40 per cent of registered shares of Swiss Life, Union des Banques Suisses (UBS), Clariant or Crédit Suisse. Firms are concerned that the anonymous shareholders might in fact be preparing a stealthy takeover.

What does anonymity convey?

It would be fastidious to try to draw up an exhaustive answer to the question. We shall confine our efforts to enumerating some aspects that are particularly relevant to financial ethics.

The anonymous act on behalf of the institution

Those who speak for a public administration or a large company are often – and used to be even more often in the past – held to anonymity. The institution exists in its own right, regardless of which individuals happen to be serving it.

Anonymity can be an expression of team spirit. UBS investment bank once offered to distinguish outstanding scorers in ice-hockey with a golden helmet, which would be highly visible. The players themselves, however, refused the proposal, arguing that every goal was the outcome of the concerted effort of the whole team.

This attitude has the merit of recognising the concept of structural violence or structural sin. Institutions have effects in their own right, beyond the control of any individuals who compose them. It contradicts the neo-liberal dictum of Margaret Thatcher's 'There is no such thing as society'. Institutions can in this perspective be regarded as proper objects of moral judgement. They can be held responsible for their actions.

On the other hand, the anonymity of agents simply shifts the issue of name along by one notch: the institution on whose behalf they are acting has an identity. Corporations on occasion, however, try to achieve anonymity by hiding behind a succession of masks, even if they bear colourful names such as Chewco, Rhythms or the remarkably explicit Raptor (be it I, II, III or IV).[9]

The anonymous are interchangeable

One anonymous agent can be replaced readily by another. Salutary modesty! One cannot make a name for oneself, one is simply a servant of the greater whole. Salutary with respect to the outside world, it can, however, be demotivating and counter-productive within the institution. If only in the interests of productivity, employers need to arrange work 'so that the employee feels significant and retains motivation and identification'.[10]

For the concept of anonymity relative to the outside world to work, however, if those who have dealings with the institution are to trust it and consequently be willing to continue to deal with it, all the anonymous agents must work to the same set of rules. The anonymity implies that the institution is in fact governed by established norms. In this perspective, anonymity is inseparable from norms, and the norms are those of a named collectivity, be it a particular firm, a trade association or a form of culture. 'Integrity: I mean by that a reflection of a Swiss culture and reputation, marked by honesty and a mountain people's common sense' (Blaise Goetschin, CEO, Banque Cantonale de Genève).[11]

The anonymous are free

People are identified by their antecedents, their relations, their history and their status. All of that hampers their social mobility, hindering their freedom to embrace initiatives that will take them out of their expected role. Against such a background, anonymity provides a foil that frees their spirit of enterprise. This argument is often heard in countries of Anglo-Saxon immigration such as the United States or Australia, where people have 'made new lives for themselves' after shedding in transit the dead weight of their earlier identity. Migration from rural villages to big cities can have similar liberating effects. In Switzerland, a person's criminal record is wiped clean after a certain period. This expresses one's right to shed one's past, to allow parts of it to fade into oblivion. Of course, an identity that evolves over time, even with a conscious helping hand, is not the same thing as anonymity.

The opposite can also hold true. People with appropriate connections or a recognised social background often find doors open to them that are closed to others. An important aspect of the microcredit movement in the Third World is to open the doors of mainstream and therefore low-cost credit to small customers hitherto unknown to the banks.

Anonymity protects the anonymous

Anonymity protects the individual from pressure, or revenge. Hence the great debate about how to identify police officers – or taxi drivers. That they can be identified is useful in case of complaints against them in their professional capacity, or simply if a passenger forgets some belongings in a taxi. The question is whether they should display their name or an identity code that the public cannot decipher. To display the name can be helpful to police officers who hope to be rewarded for favouring a person with whom they have had dealings. More generally, though, if the public knows the name, the person can be more easily traced outside his or her professional setting. In Geneva, women taxi drivers have been complaining about being harassed at home. A code shifts control from the individual to the institution in which he or she is engaged. The individual becomes directly responsible to the institution and only indirectly to the public. The debate about the means used to identify agents turns on the relative degree of trust the public feels towards the kind of individual and institution in question.

The air traffic controller in Zurich stabbed to death by a distraught father who had lost his family in a mid-air collision between two planes would have been better off if he had been anonymous. Furthermore, although he was on duty at the time, his company (Skyguide) had not provided sufficient staff on duty, and indeed the Swiss government (which owns the company) had been signally insensitive to the victims' distress. The anonymity of the controller himself would have pointed the finger at more appropriate loci of responsibility.

On the other hand, every thief knows that anonymity guarantees impunity: s/he risks no punishment as long as his/her identity is not discovered. Senders of e-mails who hide behind unusable return addresses know it too, as do firms that ask for payment in advance to be made to a post office box for goods that in the end they do not supply.

It is easy to oppress the anonymous

The anonymous may be those whose identity is unknown. They may, on the other hand, be precisely those who lack the network of relationships that are so essential to constituting an identity, and in particular relations with the powerful. Being defenceless in that regard, they are particularly exposed to oppression and exploitation: 'The undocumented, who, plunged into anonymity, have to put up with deplorable conditions of life'.[12]

The anonymous can take French leave[13]

One means of avoiding responsibility is the freedom to withdraw without being noticed when things turn sour. The anonymous shareholder enjoys that freedom. Anonymity makes it easier to turn one's back on a problem, even if one had been involved in causing it. It enables one to walk away and leave others to clean up the mess. If a shareholder sells a sizeable holding precipitately, the share price may fall, but if the market cannot identify the seller it will have difficulty in ascertaining the cause and taking action in consequence.

The anonymous lender enjoys the same freedom. If a lender whose identity is known, and who as a result is understood to be well-informed about the borrower, seeks to sell his/her title, the action may arouse doubt about the solidity of the loan and therefore spoil the terms on which s/he is able to sell.[14]

The passage of F.-M. Monnet's quoted at the start of this chapter brings out one consequence of this aspect of anonymity. Since the creditor does not know the lender and can therefore form no opinion of his/her underlying capacity to honour commitments, all the creditor has to go on is punctual payment: the commitment to pay takes priority over all other considerations (that, of course, is no guarantee: a well-known form of fraud consists of holding out the prospect of enticing returns, and indeed serving them punctiliously to the early creditors, by drawing on the contributions of latercomers – until in the end the whole empty structure collapses). That sort of case apart, even in normal business circumstances the overriding commitment to pay can easily take on an unfair or extortionate character (Dommen, 2001). Or, as the passage quoted above points out, it may interfere with a company's ability simply to get on calmly and steadily with its business as a means of producing useful goods and services.

Anonymity and compartmentalisation

Many of the foregoing illustrations concern not so much anonymity in a strict sense, but rather the compartmentalisation of identity. An identity known in a particular context is restricted to that one; in a different context, the same person or institution is protected from recognition as such. That is one result of identifying police officers by a code. It is one of the consequences of the limited liability in limited companies: the shareholders' liability is restricted to the value of their shares, and whatever other assets they may own are walled off in a separate compartment. In the image of the convivial village, people are known in their entirety. Benjamin Franklin's picturesque scenario would be impossible in a compartmented setting; conversely, the kind of mechanism F.-M. Monnet describes can only function in such a setting. There are indeed those who maintain more broadly that modern capitalism generally depends on the existence of compartments separated by firewalls.

Norms and names

The sketches presented above begin to form an overall picture. Anonymity can play a constructive role in society in general, and in the economy in particular, but it can also easily provide a cover for irresponsibility and deception. More insidiously, it can create the conditions for inhuman insistence on honouring commitments regardless of circumstances.

If anonymity is to play a constructive role, it must be confined within a rigid framework that identifies explicitly – names – the place where the buck stops. The anonymous actor points to an agent with a name. Naming is the norm; anonymity, regulated within and disciplined by the norm, is a subsidiary instrument.

Laws, rules, codes – whether moral codes or explicitly drafted or negotiated codes of conduct; and norms – whether they are technical standards set by recognised bodies or commonly accepted manners of proper conduct: all these govern behaviour and expectations. If everyone always obeyed them, there would be much less need to know with whom one was dealing, although the need would always be there to a degree: to be sure that an electrical installation is safe, it is reassuring to know that a qualified electrician is doing the work.

There are two problems, however. First, rules are often broken or ignored. Controls are necessary to ensure their observance. If the controls are external, the inspectors need to select – to name – those whom they inspect on any given occasion. If the controls are self-imposed – for example, through voluntary codes of conduct – those who are a party to the code name themselves. Indeed, naming oneself publicly in this way is one of the commercial advantages of claiming adherence to the code. For that reason, there is a temptation to put it on like a mask, presenting to the world a face that is not one's own. There are those who use this argument against the United Nations' Global Compact, since it contains no mechanism for verification.

Second, no set of rules can conceivably cover every eventuality, no matter how long and detailed they are (indeed, beyond a certain length, they increase rather than decrease the probability that they will not be implemented).

For both of these reasons it is of material importance to know what to expect of the person or institution with whom one is dealing. That information is contained in the party's identity.

Identity

Identity includes three dimensions relevant here. The first involves time: what is the history of the person or institution concerned? How has it behaved in the past? Expectations, including trust as a particular expression of them, are steadily built up with the experience that time brings. With respect to institutions, and particularly to companies, how can one ascertain whether a new hermit crab has taken possession of a familiar shell? Less individualistically, what are the traditions, what is the culture that the person or institution embodies (culture is what remains when one has forgotten everything else, someone said)? They provide a short cut to expectations, saving to some extent on the information one needs to gather about an individual.

Of course, the past is never a guarantee of future behaviour. Indeed, many kinds of misbehaviour exploit the expectation that it will be; the type of fraud described in the section 'It is easy to oppress the anonymous' above is a case in point.

The second dimension is relational and involves sanctions: into which social entity does the party fit, and what sanctions will its relations impose if it violates their rules or norms? How far can one count on the discipline this will impose on the party with which one is considering doing business?

Naming and shaming is an ancient form of social control. The Swiss Federal Banking Commission has been resorting to this technique since 2002. It is effective in so far as the institutions at risk have a sense of honour; it is furthermore effective in so far as they need to be able to continue selling their services under the name that has been named: these two conditions are essentially independent of each other. Firms on occasion change their name to shed an image that has become an embarrassment. Thus when the Windscale nuclear facility in England got a bad name for its radioactive pollution, it changed its name to Sellafield.

The third dimension of identity is self-identification: the image a person has of him/herself and the consistency with which s/he lives it. This dimension comes fully into play in situations where established rules do not provide clear directions on how to behave; it comes into operation as an ethic that casts a light on a quandary and points to an appropriate course of action. To be able to anticipate how a person is going to act in particular circumstances requires, over and above the contextual information just mentioned, an understanding of the person's character. The same applies, albeit in an attenuated and less durable way, to institutions.

The inevitable stereotype

The interactions between identity and expected behaviour are complex and flow in both directions. As a Buddhist lama, Lama Mingyour, said recently in the *Tribune de Genève* (9–10 October 2004), 'the ego creates an illusory external identity which names things instead of living them'. The interactions bring stereotypes into play. Recourse to stereotypes is indispensable if life is to be manageable – not only business but also personal life. On the other hand, to be able to put a name to something is reassuring. Indeed, 'the unnameable' refers to the particularly frightening and horrible.

However, to impose a stereotype on to a real person or firm not only does violence to its individuality; it can be misleading and result in erroneous decisions. Arthur Andersen's role in the Enron affair damaged the reputation of the whole accountancy profession, according to the principle that a cat that has once jumped on to a hot stove won't jump on to a cold one.

The Quakers and credit

The Quakers provide a convenient illustration of these ideas. Quakers are important in the history of British banking, as the Quaker family names Barclays or Lloyds still reflect. The Quakers are not an ethnic community: the

Religious Society of Friends (their official name) grew out of the politico-religious troubles of seventeenth-century Britain. Subsequently, in the eighteenth and nineteenth centuries, intermarriage did, however, give it something of a clan character that strengthened its business network, but this characteristic thereafter diluted to the point of disappearance. What is particularly relevant for the present argument is that Quakers attached great importance to scrupulous respect in their financial engagements, and this was underwritten by group discipline:

> It was not ... simply a question of 'obeying the rules', it was more a case that there was no point in remaining a Quaker if the ethics were unacceptable. Thus it was that members quite voluntarily allowed themselves to be called to account for their business affairs and have their accounts inspected for indebtedness and good practice, if either were felt to be at risk. Members knew that whilst such procedures undoubtedly helped protect the Society from the risks of external criticism it was also done out of love and concern. When, in fact, members were found to be deficient then it was the duty of other Friends to help them out of their difficulties. In this way the Society was tremendously supportive of Friends in business'. (Windsor, 1980, p. 168)

The mutual support had its boundaries: a member whose financial difficulties could be imputed to extravagance, dishonesty or other forms of misbehaviour, were disowned – that is, excluded from the Society.

There is no doubt that the quality guarantee associated with membership of the Religious Society of Friends encouraged others to do business with them, and in particular to entrust financial matters to them.[15]

Look your partner in the face

The foregoing arguments concern the means of establishing the trustworthiness of one's partners, an essential consideration in any business relationship. Beyond that, however, there is a moral requirement to value everyone as a subject, not just an object, as a person with his or her own dignity to be respected.

Not only the fight against money-laundering, but simple business prudence, would seem to encourage bankers to know their clients. However, in so far as that principle is codified into standard practices and rules that come to stand for acquaintance, there is a danger of knowing only the client's mask and missing what lies behind it. Here again, as in so many cases mentioned in this chapter, there is no choice but to find a balance between facing a real, complex and essentially elusive individual on the one hand, and resorting to classification to manage a larger number of cases on the other. Another scenario would be the banker who knows his/her client well enough to trust him/her not to harm the bank's interests while suspecting that his/her money is not all that clean. In that case the banker can be content with the mask facing him/her while covering his/her own behaviour with the screen of standard procedures.

Justice is often portrayed blindfold, dispensing her decisions impartially without considerations of person. To treat everyone equally can, however, result in having to hide useful information so that everyone operates on a footing of equal ignorance. It can be argued that rules against insider trading, under which the stock market is constrained to behave like horseracing, do little to enhance the capacity of firms to produce useful goods and services. The nineteenth-century industrial banks in the German (or Swiss-German) tradition, who knew their clients intimately and sat on their Boards, contributed incontrovertibly in an important way to the development of prosperous and creative economies.

The fair trade movement is founded on this way of looking at economic relations. The consumer wants to get behind the object traded, to know who produced it and under what conditions. According to the ideology of the World Trade Organization (WTO) on the other hand, the manner in which a product is produced is not part of it; methods of production are to be ignored in setting the rules of trade. This flies in the face of widely-held attitudes, however. A large proportion of buyers consider, consciously or subconsciously, that in buying a product they are sharing in its conditions of production. Why else would advertisements for orange juice display photographs of smiling young women picking colourful fruit in verdant orchards? It is quite normal to consider that the conditions of work, among other considerations, constitute an integral part of what one is buying, to imagine oneself looking the worker in the face.

Is communitarianism the answer to anonymity?

We are now sailing close to the rocks of communitarianism (Kymlicka, 1996):

> In the short-distance economic relations of the erstwhile craft society, the worker's individual moral worth played an important role in estimating the value of the services he rendered.[16] It was therefore within the possibilities of each person to improve their lot by the quality of their exertion, their initiative and their personal virtues ... Things no longer work that way as longer-distance relationships take hold ... The proletariat is plunged into a wretchedness escaping any ethical concern on the side of the employers, the quantitative clearly prevailing over the qualitative. Thus economic mechanisms develop in which the effect of individual ethics becomes less and less while that of decisions taken by the representatives of anonymous financial institutions grows. (Biéler, 1995, pp. 130–1)

Trading locally (*commerce de proximité*), and similar attitudes have undoubted charm and merits. They do not, however, have the capacity to overthrow the globalised economy; they do not even dent it.

Working on the basis of a clan or a closely defined group can constitute a form of guarantee (see the second quotation at the start of the chapter); certainly, it has often served as the root stock even for major transnational enterprises. However, as the example of the Quakers confirms, their expansion depended not on restricting dealings to themselves but, on the contrary, on reaching out to trade with the surrounding society. A collective as well as individual reputation for reliability can, we have seen, be an invaluable asset in that regard.

On the other hand, for outsiders to rely solely on the internal control mechanisms of the communities with whose members they are dealing has evident shortcomings, precisely because they will never be in a position to grasp fully the internal workings of a group of which they are not a part.

More fundamentally, communitarianism embodies an essential element of unfairness. If, in our economic dealings, we are called to seek out and support the weakest and most disadvantaged, it is more than likely that those people are living over the horizon, beyond our field of direct vision. Global reach is indispensable, even to the preferential option for the poor.

Decent dress: how much to reveal?

'From each according to his means, to each according to his needs' – this aphorism is generally attributed to Karl Marx (1875), although it was formulated earlier by Mikhail Bakunin (1870) in a declaration signed by forty-seven anarchists.[17] To apply it, one needs to know the means and the needs of each; they cannot be utterly anonymous.

The problem of finding the right degrees of anonymity and identity is well illustrated by medical insurance. The principles underlying such insurance are unsettled. At the simplest extreme there is pure solidarity: everyone within a defined collectivity contributes according to their means – their income or wealth; those who are in need of medical care have their costs covered. Little information is needed about participants. The administrators need to know on the one hand the extent of each contributor's means, and on the other the costs involved in providing medical care. They do not necessarily even have to know the identity of those receiving the care. The British National Health Service (NHS) at its outset came close to this model. Indeed, since it was financed through general taxation, its administrators did not even need to know the financial means of the individual contributors.

At the other extreme, medical insurance provided through private enterprise is looked upon as a provident fund, in which each individual's contributions are set in such a way as to cover over time that same individual's medical expenses. In this situation, the insurance scheme will wish to have as much information as possible about that person's propensity to need medical care so that appropriate premiums can be set; in consequence, it will seek to obtain intimate details about the individual.

In countries such as Switzerland, the situation is a muddled combination of the two types. Legally bound to a degree of solidarity, the insurance companies none the less seek to classify their clients into risk types as finely defined as they can get away with, so that the better risks contribute as little as possible to the costs of the worse (quite the opposite of the axiom quoted at the head of this section). The authorities, however, place restraints on the extent to which the insurance companies may collect information useful for this purpose, preserving a degree of anonymity in order to maintain an element of solidarity.

As that example shows, a degree of anonymity is, paradoxically, an essential bond that holds a community together. In medical insurance, less anonymity goes with greater individualism and less concern for one's neighbour.[18]

Conclusion

'Anonymity assures the passage from an individualistic ethic to a social ethic which requires an ever more attentive reflection on the complexity of the mechanisms which secretly determine the fate of individuals and especially of the least favoured social categories' (Biéler, 1995, p. 131). The least favoured constitute one class of the anonymous, as we have seen above.

The capacity to put a name to a person or an institution has three aspects relevant to the present context. The first is the most demanding: to know someone is to have an *understanding* of what makes him or her tick – of the individual's motivations, reflexes, aspirations and the culture in which s/he functions. That is the kind of familiarity that Benjamin Franklin describes, and this understanding grows with experience. Over time, the observer gets to know the other party better. Meanwhile, however, the latter is in his or her own way gaining in experience and his/her identity is evolving. The process never reaches a fixed point, and the observer will never completely catch up. Above all, it is time-consuming for the observer: no person can manage more than a small number of friends.

The second aspect focuses specifically on one portion of the culture in which the party functions: the sanctions to which he or she is liable. This is quite different from the penalties to which people might theoretically be subject, but which might not be applied.

Understanding and liability to sanctions are of instrumental interest in deciding on business relations. The third dimension goes much deeper than that. Not to know with whom one is dealing can be an expression of indifference, a denial of the relationship of love that is so essential to the viability of a truly human society, in which the economy should be a supporting element. 'Just measure does not lie ... in a rule or norm dictated from outside or coming from some general morals; it is given by the relationship of love ... between people' (Biéler, 1961, p. 452).

Some sort of systematic, rule-based, control is indispensable in virtually all circumstances. For reasons not just of cost, but also of logic, not to mention the need to provide information in a form sufficiently succinct to be absorbed by users who also have other things to worry about during their limited day, such methods cannot hope to capture the full individuality of each situation. Decision demands simplification, but what is omitted in the process needs to be kept under review in the light of its failures to reveal what is important. This has long been evident to those who audit accounts. Financial analysts are now being pressed to learn fast before firewalls within their banks isolate them from their very job.[19] Those who design and attempt to apply social and ecological norms – a field rapidly turning into a jungle – are still trying to establish paths through the luxuriant growth.

In a nutshell, anonymity has its dangers in the world of finance. More fundamentally, it makes short shrift of the regard due to each and every person as a whole human being. However, life in all its aspects is only rendered possible by simplifying it into manageable models. Anonymity can be a convenient instrument if used in a proper framework – a framework built of identities and names.

Notes

1 An earlier version of this chapter, published in *Finance & the Common Good/Bien Commun*, no. 18–19 (Spring–Summer 2004), was the object of a discussion by the Ethics group of the Swiss shareholder association Actares (http://www.actares.ch). Several of the ideas expressed on that occasion are reflected in this expanded version.

2 Novation: substitution of an earlier bond by changing the debtor, the creditor or the title.

3 Subrogate: substitute one party for another as creditor, with the transfer of rights and duties.

4 The layout of the text has been translated and modified in order to emphasise the key points.

5 Covered by Articles 28ff. of the Swiss Civil Code.

6 It is anchored in Article 13 of the Swiss federal constitution in a manner that falls within the 'compartmentalisation' discussed below.

7 These sources have more to say about antonyms of 'anonymity': 'identity' and 'recognition'. Both concepts hark back to Hegel, whose extensive analysis captures much of the moral ambiguity reflected in the discussion of anonymity presented here. In his recent book, *Parcours de la reconnaissance*, Paul Ricoeur stresses in particular the value of recognition in a passive sense for dignity (being recognised).

8 Odour can be a significant factor in identity. The Roman emperor Vespasian (AD 69–79) coined the phrase in response to someone who expressed surprise at his decision to levy a charge on the use of public urinals.

9 See Andrew Cornford's chapter in this volume.

10 *Encyclopædia Britannica CD*, 1999 Standard Edition, article 'Mass Production and Society'.

11   *BCGE Dialogue*, Spring 2004, p. 13.
12   Marco Danesi, *Domaine Public*, no. 1610, 9 July 2004.
13   *Filer à l'anglaise*, in French.
14   A different argument applies to financial institutions whose trade consists of placing loans on the market.
15   Apart from Windsor, the above section draws on Walvin (1997) and Kirby (1984).
16   As Benjamin Franklin points out in the first epigraph.
17   See the *Oxford Dictionary of Quotations* (1959), 333:12 and 29:14, respectively.
18   In Switzerland, the issue of anonymity and community is taking an even starker form. Article 12 of the Federal Constitution provides that everyone is entitled to the means needed to lead an existence in conformity with human dignity. The courts of the Canton of Berne have decided that this constitutional right includes people who insist on remaining anonymous. The courts of Soleure have, in contrast, decided that the right is restricted to those who accept to decline their identity. As of November 2004, it seems that the Federal Supreme Court will have to settle the issue.
19   *The Economist*, 20 March 2004, p. 84.

References

Biéler, A. (1961). *La pensée économique et sociale de Calvin* (Geneva: Georg).
Biéler, A. (1995). *La force cachée des protestants* (Geneva: Labor et Fides).
Dommen, E. (2001). 'Sous quelles conditions est-il légitime d'exiger le remboursement d'une dette? Une perspective éthique', in E. Dommen (ed.), *Debt Beyond Contract* (Geneva: Observatoire de la Finance).
Kirby, M.W. (1984). *Men of Business and Politics* (London: George Allen & Unwin).
Kymlicka, W. (1996). 'Communautarisme', in M. Canto-Sperber (ed.), *Dictionnaire d'éthique et de philosophie morale* (Paris: PUF).
Ricoeur, P. (2004). *Parcours de la reconnaissance* (Paris: Stock).
Walvin, J. (1997). *The Quakers: Money and Morals* (London: John Murray).
Windsor, D. B. (1980). *The Quaker Enterprise* (London: Frederick Muller).

7
Spaces for Business Ethics
Domingo Sugranyes Bickel

An analysis of the Enron story raises the question again as to whether there is room for ethics in business, given the current *modus operandi* of major corporations and financial markets. It would be easy to say that ethics has no place in decision-making, that the multifarious pressures on senior executives and managers turn them into machines programmed for a single purpose: to maximise profits over the year, and even over a quarter. But is this a realistic description? I don't think so. First, while operating in the same economic and financial environment, the majority of companies do not plan or act as did Enron. Moreover, the reasons for Enron's fall lie not in the environment but, precisely, in a profound failure in the ethical dimension, underlying a chain of erroneous decisions.

New forms, old problems

Discussions of Enron and similar cases usually try to place the blame on the current market economy: excessive short-termism, a boom in financial engineering, financial criteria taking precedence over industrial or production matters, and, above all, an economy distorted and fragmented because the players' sole motivation is personal enrichment.

Such criticism is always useful, but it merely scratches the surface, bringing to light new forms but not necessarily a substantial change. In a case like Enron's, it fails to address the underlying question. In fact, the story is timeless: we could be dealing with any company whose operations are loss-making, or which has taken on too much risk. It is the old story of the flight forward, the search for ways to conceal a company's real situation from the public (even from the company itself) in the hope that things will get better on their own, that the as-yet unreported losses will be recovered, that the risks will be dispelled, and that creditors' trust can be restored without having to maintain the cover-up. Unfortunately, that is not how things normally turn out.

Market deregulation and instant communications have led many non-financial companies to expect greater returns on their investments and to place greater emphasis on cash management. These trends have also fostered the unprecedented development of businesses that are based specifically on speculation, on tangibles or intangibles. The spread of financial activity internationally has made it even easier to take on debt and undertake increasingly leveraged operations, which increase the return on equity. As a result, international investment bankers can offer executives an ever-widening range of novel – and sometimes risky – financial and investment solutions. And sometimes there is the temptation of large short-term profits.

However, things have evolved since 'Enron and Co.' a few years ago. Partly as a result of the resulting scandal, and partly because of the markets' development, expectations have changed, laws have been strengthened, audit firms have become more demanding and, generally, the perception of risk has changed. An example from a field with which I am personally familiar – insurance: after 11 September 2001, in a context of low interest rates and a slump in many stocks, insurance and reinsurance companies have become much more cautious about underwriting, they charge adequate premiums, apply rigorous cost controls, and, in short, are now seeking operating profits in their *industrial* activity, regardless of financial performance. The companies that were reluctant to heed the siren song of financial gain and maintained greater rigour in their operations are now obtaining particularly good results. In this case, at least, 'financialisation' has receded spectacularly.

An unfinished revolution

As some analysts have observed, even within the context of the stock market and financial boom some years ago, a case like that of Enron, made possible by the situation at the time coupled with novel financial techniques, in fact hinged on an extreme and exceptional use of a number of motivational instruments and systems. The very dynamics of the business (speculative by nature), the unbridled application of short-termist motivation systems, and rash management decisions all contributed to putting the company in a situation of potential or actual losses, which management sought to conceal by various means, for image and rating reasons, when a transparent view would probably have shown that the conglomerate's continuity and equilibrium were already damaged and that they were unlikely to find an untraumatic solution. The Enron managers' attitude was undoubtedly influenced by pressure from financial analysts and by the desire to maintain the company's good image in the market.

To prevent a recurrence of 'Enron' and similar cases, is it therefore necessary to curtail the process of opening companies to the scrutiny of equity analysts? I believe that to generalise this case would be an error of method and a distortion of the facts. If we look at business activity worldwide, in developed countries (and, more particularly, in emerging countries), the priority is quite the opposite: it is necessary to continue and perfect market deregulation and extend a financial discipline that enables competition and a free market to unleash their full benefits for economic development.

Opening stock markets to investors worldwide – standardisation of reporting, external audit, governance and transparency rules – have greatly improved the way that business and the real economy work in many countries: independence from political interference, simplifying red tape, truthful information reaching the markets quickly, the possibility of comparing financial ratios of companies in a given sector, transparency in transactions between related companies, protection for minority shareholders' interests and so on. One could continue to cite basic principles of modern business that have evidently favourable effects on economic development. This is all part of an ongoing revolution in many developed and emerging economies, but the transformation is still far from complete. It is clear that Enron and its fellows breached some of these basic principles, but it would be wrong to mistake the exception for the rule and to question the progress made in liberalising and opening the business environment.

I admit that new uncertainties arise, since some of the current reforms introduce greater subjectivity, such as in the valuation of assets and liabilities. In this connection, the IFRS (International Financial Reporting Standards) are considered in certain quarters to aggravate the risk since they imply in some cases the calculation of the market value of certain liabilities by applying stochastic models where the initial assumptions can decisively shape the final result. Similarly, the new rules on bank and insurance company solvency are based on an assessment of a company's own risk map, which includes making internally generated judgements about operating risk. There is a suggestion, therefore, that these developments may increase the opportunities of the accounting abuse and arbitrariness that lay at the heart of Enron and similar affairs; it is possible that these reforms are being dogmatic as regards transparency (everything absolutely at market value where market value is available) applied indiscriminately without regard for certain real risks or, in particular, for certain players' natural tendency to exploit weaknesses in the legal system in their own interests (and to the detriment of the general interest).

This question will be answered in the coming years; at present it is shrouded in conjecture. Nevertheless, the underlying argument persists: more transparent reporting and the exposure of business to a fully competitive playing field are necessary steps to ensure we have *more* markets and *more* business – that is to say, more economic development. And that is what is needed, particularly in less developed economies, to reduce the problems of poverty and inequality.

Codes of conduct and social responsibility

Enron's executives would perhaps claim that they did not ostensibly break any law or flout any code of conduct. Nevertheless, this did not stop the company from committing serious breaches of social ethics and from collapsing, with serious consequences for its employees, customers, auditors, bankers and other stakeholders. At Enron, there was probably the intention to breach the spirit of certain laws or, at least, an implicit tolerance of actions of doubtful legality but none the less difficult to discover. Even if there had been no legal or tax irregularity, Enron's business approach and the situation of intolerable risk that it had attained involved immorality of a form that has been present time and again: diversion of funds for unjust enrichment, and criminal cowardice through lack of the nerve required to admit the problem and take timely corrective measures.

Where are we to find the strength to avoid a repetition of such highly immoral conduct? Although it may sound trite or old-fashioned, the answer lies in executives' personal ethics. An analysis of the Enron case may help to identify these problems in their current shape, since it reveals an extreme form of collective error, both in the search for fraudulent enrichment and in the concealment of actual losses. In fact, this danger of deviant conduct can be found in almost any business experience, albeit to a lesser, and less spectacular, degree.

'Corporate social responsibility', 'corporate citizen', 'codes of ethical conduct' and similar terms are now standard in corporations' annual reports. The various collectives of stakeholders believe that a company's activity should have positive spin-offs for them. Equity analysts ask about codes of governance and equal opportunity policies. This is all part of the milieu in which business currently operates. There is, inevitably, a component of political correctness in all of this, and some companies are better than others at putting a positive spin on their actions in terms of social responsibility.

It is quite discouraging to sit down and complete a questionnaire from one of the many social responsibility rating agencies (there is an entire market in external consulting and rating, paving the way for a new professional field of 'experts' in social responsibility). They usually focus on data that are relatively easy to measure, but also relatively useless in rating a company's underlying ethics. Whether it uses recycled paper is not a sufficient measure of a company's ethics – and I mean no disrespect to environmental conservation. Let's take an example: it is necessary to turn off the lights at night, but this tells us little about a company's cost-cutting efforts, which can really only be achieved through efficient organisational structures. In the same way, any change in a company's ethical profile is profound, slow and difficult, and does not lend itself to turnkey formulas. The demands of corporate citizenship are important, but they are not the in-depth answer to the problems we are discussing. The key lies in the concept of corporate culture, which is intimately linked to senior executives' moral approach, because of their importance in the hierarchical structure and their power as trend-setters.

Corporate culture as the key

One of the faults highlighted most clearly by Enron and similar cases is that remuneration systems linked directly to a company's share performance may be excessive. Such mechanisms are advantageous if used in moderation and on a broad basis, as a means of cohesion among large groups of employees, but they become morally questionable if confined to a small group of senior executives and if they involve huge sums of money. Media reports on cases of this type in recent years have probably contributed to moderation. In theory, it is perfectly acceptable that people who devote the best years of their lives to a company should share, as part-owners, in the company's appreciation in the markets. However, as always, the problem lies in the practical applications of this pretty theory in an imperfect human context: share price movements, in the short term, at least, are driven by many factors other than a company's fundamentals, and they are prone to manipulation, particularly if a company does not control insider trading effectively, or if its accounting information is not as truthful as one might wish. Even if there is no criminal conduct, it is clear that a company's management has much greater moral force if its decisions are not seen to be driven immediately and directly by the possibility of personal gain.

What we call 'corporate culture' is a phenomenon that perhaps does not lend itself to rigorous description but it is very real to anyone who has experienced it over a period of time. Remuneration is clearly the motivation for those who devote their time and, in many cases, their best energies to a company: but most behaviours and decisions are not driven by gain or greed. The main motivation is the company's success, measured simply and unequivocally by its growth and bottom line; within the company, the motivation comes from the growth and results of individual areas and departments. This is helped by the rapid, comprehensive information systems in modern companies, which can be used to set specific economic incentives. Beyond this factor, which is common to all companies, each company's culture has its own distinctive features: ways of approaching team work, the concept of quality, criteria for good service, a brand, a history, a collective ambition identified in people past and present and so on. These features and rituals are sometimes ridiculed in pictures of cohorts of employees singing the company song, but they are generally more subtle, though no less real.

I would like to distinguish what I believe to be three components in a corporate culture that are needed to foster collective ethical behaviour:

(i) exemplary behaviour by senior management; one could call this 'zero tolerance for fraud'. The dissemination of behaviour patterns via trickle-down is very powerful in any group of people, particularly one that is strongly hierarchical. Senior executives can set the standard for the entire company if they are absolutely open in rejecting any suggestion of fraud or corruption, no matter how small. Of course, conditions vary from one sector to another, and the foregoing is not always easy to apply. However, in this respect, the clarity of approach depends on it being applied across the board without exception;

(ii) constant probing analysis of internal information in search of the deviations and other factors that point to impending problems, making it impossible to conceal situations that endanger operations or results for any length of time. This should be done carefully, using teams selected specifically for each subject, and without causing alarm or creating the conditions for conflicts or internal vendettas. An internal audit department that fully understands its function while being able to assist management and denounce any loopholes or breaches is an invaluable asset in this connection; and

(iii) the formulation of business principles that clearly set out the company's ethical experience, enabling them to be handed down from one generation to the next. The idea is not to write a grand charter for the purpose of publicity or for internal image, or in the hope that simply writing and publicising it will make it a reality. There is a set of rules and punishments in every legal system, and there is only one valid approach to them: they should be obeyed! But when we talk of culture, we are dealing with something deeper and distinctive, which holds the key to a company's long-term success while also determining its moral conduct: general principles which reflect a clear and genuine rejection of any fraud, corrective measures applied whenever necessary, and a really humanistic approach rooted in the company's history.

The combination of people and capital

If we are looking for guidance in order to reflect on the sources of such a humanistic vision of the company, I suggest turning to one of the indisputable moral teachings of the modern era, that of John Paul II, who speaks to Christians and non-Christians alike on the subjects of civilisation.

It is worth quoting some paragraphs of John Paul II's 1991 encyclical, *Centesimus Annus*, which are very apt with respect to problems revealed in the Enron affair:

> It is precisely the ability to foresee both the needs of others and the combinations of productive factors most adapted to satisfying those needs that constitutes another important source of wealth in modern society ... Organizing such a productive effort, planning its duration in

time, making sure that it corresponds in a positive way to the demands which it must satisfy, and taking the necessary risks – all this too is a source of wealth in today's society. (32)

Important virtues are involved in this process, such as diligence, industriousness, prudence in undertaking reasonable risks, reliability and fidelity in interpersonal relationships, as well as courage in carrying out decisions which are difficult and painful but necessary, both for the overall working of a business and in meeting possible set-backs. (32)

The Church acknowledges the legitimate role of profit as an indication that a business is functioning well. When a firm makes a profit, this means that productive factors have been properly employed and corresponding human needs have been duly satisfied. But profitability is not the only indicator of a firm's condition. It is possible for the financial accounts to be in order, and yet for the people – who make up the firm's most valuable asset – to be humiliated and their dignity offended. Besides being morally inadmissible, this will eventually have negative repercussions on the firm's economic efficiency. (35)

The absence of stability, together with the corruption of public officials and the spread of improper sources of growing rich and of easy profits deriving from illegal or purely speculative activities, constitutes one of the chief obstacles to development and to the economic order. (48)

I could continue quoting from the encyclical; it may not serve as a treatise on business economics (and that is not its aim), but it describes succinctly some basic points on which to build an ethical corporate culture.

We should not be misled by negative headlines. Although the pundits have not paid sufficient attention to this, the fact is that many of the world's millions of companies already have a culture that recognises the combination of people and capital as an essential condition for continuity and success. And there are probably also many instances where this is not the case, where people are 'humiliated and have their dignity offended'. It would be very interesting to conduct a systematic study of the explicit and implicit content of corporate culture in the most successful companies in order to disseminate their experience through business schools and trade associations.

The bottom of the pyramid

To conclude, I would like to ask a broader question: what is the scope of senior executives' moral responsibility in the twenty-first century? Faced with the challenges of unequal economic development and immense zones of poverty in the world, it is necessary to take a broader view and consider the business opportunities that lie in responding to human needs. I shall quote John Paul II once again:

> even the decision to invest in one place rather than another, in one productive sector rather than another, is always a moral and cultural choice. (36)

> But it will be necessary above all to abandon a mentality in which the poor – as individuals and as peoples – are considered a burden, as irksome intruders trying to consume what others have produced. The poor ask for the right to share in enjoying material goods and to make good use of their capacity for work. (28)

As C. K. Prahalad (2004) stated in his book, which proposes a practical, realistic way to mobilise business in order to address 'the Bottom of the Pyramid': 'If we stop thinking of the poor as victims or as a burden and start recognizing them as resilient and creative entrepreneurs and value-conscious consumers, a whole new world of opportunity will open up' (p. 1).

There are over 4 billion people in the world who survive on less than 2 dollars per day; they are the bottom of the pyramid. Big corporations usually ignore this market: because the bottom of the pyramid presumably cannot afford their products, because that market is not vital for the company's future, and so on. As Prahalad shows, that reasoning is based on prejudice and misconceptions. For example, many poor dwellers in the large cities of the developing world already overpay for everything, from rice to credit, as a result of local monopolies, poor access, deficient distribution and high intermediation costs. The private sector has the means to remove these 'poverty penalties', lower the prices of products and services, and thus release purchasing power.

No company anywhere in the world will decide to invest in a product for poor consumers or for an underdeveloped region purely for humanitarian reasons; that would run counter to its economic nature and profit motive. But no economically-reasonable decision is bereft of a cultural context, and the latter is decisive when judging its overall consequences and ethical meaning.

Direct business investment in underdeveloped areas plays a positive part from the standpoint of social ethics as it leads a company to become involved in the country-risk of the area and to contribute some of the factors needed for development (management training, technology transfer, support for a network of local providers, competitive employment, quality products and so on). Perhaps I could mention the case of the Spanish insurance group where I had the opportunity to go through this process step by step since the early 1980s: we started looking for investment opportunities in Latin America around 1980, after our representatives had been visiting Spanish- and Portuguese-speaking countries for several years as reinsurers. The learning process was difficult and risky. Now, finally, we are showing our shareholders more or less reasonable results, and we have substantial market shares in practically all Latin-American countries. The first motivation to go to Latin America was moral and cultural, based on language, history and a sense of duty. It took many years to change these operations and bring them up to 'state of the art' technologies and management. The aim was to improve the quality of their insurance products and services, but we were always convinced that in the end it would also add value for our shareholders. A big business opportunity for a group like ours, which allowed us to become totally involved in developing a modern insurance sector in each of these countries and, at the same time, to acquire a multinational dimension. And now it is reciprocal: in Spain we are starting to use some of the imaginative, flexible IT solutions developed by our Latin-American subsidiaries; and young managers, who spent their best training years overseas, are among the brightest in the next generation of company leaders in our group.

I believe that, in the aftermath of economic and human disasters such as Enron, some executives in both large and small firms are looking for a more constructive meaning for their activities. I suggest that they seek that meaning, and an ethically-satisfactory approach, not just in a culture that includes the internal human dimension of the company as a whole, but also a new projection of business ambition, by looking more broadly to the needs and business opportunities posed by the challenges of poverty.

Reference

Prahalad, C. K. (2004) *The Fortune at the Bottom of the Pyramid. Eradicating Poverty Through Profits* (Upper Saddle River, NJ: Wharton School Publishing).

Part 3

Corporate Governance and Auditing

8
The Demise of Andersen: A Consequence of Corporate Governance Failure in the Context of Major Changes in the Accounting Profession and the Audit Market

Catherine Sauviat

The sudden collapse of Enron at the end of 2001 provoked the fall only a few months later of one of the most prestigious accounting firms in the world, the 89-year-old, Chicago-based global network, Andersen, the smallest of the accounting's Big Five. As the auditor of Enron Corporation, the US firm Arthur Andersen LLP was charged in March 2002 with obstructing justice by shredding Enron-related documents to impede a Securities and Exchange Commission (SEC) investigation. When the trial started in May 2002, the break-up of the organisation was already under way with a mass exodus of Andersen partners and staff, as well as clients all over the world. The firm had disintegrated before the verdict was handed down by a grand jury at the Federal District Court in Houston on 15 June 2002. It was the first criminal case, if not the first victim, to emerge from the December 2001 Enron collapse.[1] Although the US Supreme Court overturned the 2002 criminal conviction of Arthur Andersen three years later, on 31 May 2005, this event raised questions about failures and loopholes in the accounting firm's specific corporate governance operating process. Undoubtedly, Andersen's ability to enforce quality standards and internal procedures and to impose tougher controls to its regional offices was called into question. This deficiency in quality control was closely related to the specific organisation of the firm as a partnership and to features of the prevailing self-regulated model favoured by the accounting profession. This was not just a 'Houston' or a 'Texas' anomaly: Qwest, Global Crossing and WorldCom were also audited by Andersen, and were the subject of accounting improprieties, shareholder lawsuits and SEC investigations. During 2001, Andersen paid more than US$100 million to settle lawsuits for audit problems concerning waste management (also a Houston client) and Sunbeam, without admitting any guilt about the Enron audit, was the fourth major audit failure affecting Andersen since 1999.

But the problems encountered by Andersen were not unique within the accounting profession. Indeed, to be understood fully, the downfall of Andersen has to be put into perspective. In the USA, the end of the 1990s was characterised by a surge of accounting anomalies and fraud (inflated profit, hidden debt and omitted liabilities) that have affected investor confidence and the functioning of financial markets. Between January 1997 and June 2002, 10 per cent of publicly traded companies have been forced by the SEC to restate their accounts because of material error or fraud, whereas this phenomenon had been rather unusual over the previous decades. In 2001, restatements reached record numbers.[2] Furthermore, the largest audit firms have been involved in a growing number of visible audit failures during the 1990s to early 2000s[3] although it was not new in the profession's history (Allen and McDermott, 1993). This trend was fed by deregulation, the atmosphere of market euphoria and the stock market bubble that characterised the decade, as well as by legislation that was increasingly favourable to employers and professionals.[4]

This process of increasing failures in auditing was also the result of important transformations that took place in the auditing market, including growing global competition, concentration and diversification as well as ongoing changes within the accounting profession, leading increasingly to 'unconscious bias' (Bazerman *et al.*, 2002). All this had a negative impact on earlier standards of professionalism, notably codes of ethic and values that had been established and consolidated at different times and under different conditions. To some extent, Andersen may be seen not only as a protagonist but also as a victim. The firm was left to hang alone and used as a scapegoat. It paid for the whole auditing profession and the profession's failure to fulfil its role as an independent gatekeeper of the free market economy. If this failure was not limited to the auditing profession (Sauviat, 2003), it is worth noting that it led to the disappearing of Andersen as a firm. This was not the case with other faulty professions such as securities analysts, who were held personally accountable but did not put their entire bank at risk.

The Andersen collapse as a case of corporate governance failure

The Andersen corporate culture and its original business model

For a long time, Arthur Andersen LLP was a pioneer in innovation. The firm was created in 1913 by Arthur Andersen, the fourth child of a Norwegian immigrant family recently established in the USA. He graduated as a certified

public accountant (CPA) and worked for four years at Price Waterhouse's Chicago office. With one of his colleagues, C. M. DeLany, he bought a small audit firm in Chicago (Andersen, DeLany & Co.) that was renamed Arthur Andersen & Co. after the departure of Mr DeLany in 1918. As early as 1912, Arthur Andersen taught accounting at NorthWestern University and held the department's chair. There, he became aware of the importance of having young, well-educated and trained professionals, and of attracting the best students for his firm (Arthur Andersen and Company, 1984).

Andersen soon entered the area of new services beyond traditional audit activities (tax and financial consulting). Auditors at Arthur Andersen & Co. were the best paid employees in the profession and the time required to become partner of the firm was shorter than that among the firm's main competitors. As early as the 1920s, the company had already distinguished itself from its competitors by granting some importance to research and development. Its head created a committee in charge of accounting and auditing research. Auditors' training was undertaken internally by Arthur Andersen himself and by other senior partners. A school was created in Chicago in the 1940s to train new entrants with standard methods developed within the firm. When Arthur Andersen died in 1947, Leonard Spacek, who joined the firm in 1928 and was responsible of the Chicago office from 1945, was elected managing partner among the twenty-five individuals who formed the partnership. He was viewed as the conscience of the profession, insisting on the need to remain independent of clients and to use high-quality accounting methods. He was the one who pressed the industry to adopt national standards.

All these specific features characterised the firm and its founder from its inception. Andersen was opposed from the beginning to the more tradi-tional British-style companies that had established branches in the USA since the end of the nineteenth century. Andersen was the only one of the Big Five indigenous to the USA. The late creation of Arthur Andersen & Co. as well as its Middle West culture meant that the firm did not embrace the old-fashioned clubby world and elitist culture of the East Coast represented by Price Waterhouse, the American market leader at that time. The social ori-gins of Arthur Andersen, as well as his status as a new migrant also explain the use of more aggressive methods (price war, advertising) used by the firm, and criticised at the time by its main competitors as being unethical. This explains why the firm chose earlier than did others to consolidate and strengthen its consulting practice as a new specialised area. Andersen started working with computers much earlier than other firms,[5] so that by the 1970s, Andersen's Management Advisory Services (MAS) department clearly emerged as the largest (Allen and McDermott, 1993). In 1971, a training cen-tre called 'St Charles', located in the suburbs of Chicago, was bought by Andersen to operate as an *intra muros* academic campus, a sort of profes-sional university. New employees were sent for some weeks to be trained in the company's methodologies and to receive the same specific knowledge. It represented a kind of initiatory way to enter the firm, so that everywhere in the world, independent professionals in different locations would operate in the same way under the Andersen brand and the 'one-firm concept'. The firm also set up a large internal database aimed at resolving any question or problem encountered by a local office. This made Andersen the most centralised and integrated international network among the Big Five accounting firms.

The organisational structure and the firm's own control procedures

Like other major accounting firms, Andersen was set up as a limited liability partnership (LLP). The firm had an original structure. It was run by 3,700 independent professionals, who ran more than 300 country offices. They were not all peers. Some had *de facto* higher status because of their capacity to generate a higher amount of income. They were paid better and held more power than the others. The worldwide network employed 85,000 people and its offices were located all over the world. At the head of Andersen partnership network was a co-operative created by Andersen's partners and owned collectively by senior partners who had to contribute to a pool of capital equivalent to an entry right. 'Andersen Worldwide' was located in Geneva and every four years the entity nominated Andersen's CEO and its Board on the basis of one partner, one vote.[6] Andersen Worldwide used to centralise and divide up country office incomes and surplus (number of partner units awarded) as well as a fraction of partners' earnings as an investment required for the firm. Some resources were pooled, such as support systems, audit procedures, training and knowledge database, and quality control structures. Each office operated under the same brand name and used the same methods. They shared many more resources than did other major accounting firms.

Andersen was organised as a matrix structure based on specific business areas and regional divisions. Each country was part of one of the five large regional areas at the world level and had a country-managing partner who headed four different business units: audit; tax and legal; corporate finance; and business consulting. Each of these units was run by a partner. The USA belonged to the region of the Americas and was divided into five sub-areas. The Houston office was part of the south-east sub-area. This office was one of the most prestigious in the USA, with more than 1,400 employees. David Duncan was the lead auditor for Enron. The firm was his only client, different from other lead partners, who generally had a multi-client portfolio.

Andersen possessed its own control procedures. A sort of committee aimed at supervising professional practices called the Professional Standards Group (PSG) was responsible for audit rules and their application. To supplement this body, a practice director was in charge of audit quality, and a practice review took place every three years inside the firm, operated by another country (or area in the case of the USA). In addition, SEC required US audit firms to be subject to peer reviews, since the accounting industry was self-regulated. The form of control could only be operated by members of the oligopoly – namely, one of the Big Five. Deloitte & Touche conducted the last, and probably one of the most intensive, peer reviews at Andersen LLP in 2001,[7] the year the Enron scandal exploded. Its report concluded that Andersen's system of accounting and audit process provided reasonable assurance of compliance with professional standards, even if Deloitte faulted Andersen for not having complete documentation on some audits. Despite some earlier but not very old attempts at reform, the system of peer reviews proved its ineffectiveness once again.[8]

The wrongdoing at Andersen: not just a Houston bias

Enron was Andersen's second-largest client worldwide, employing 100 full-time employees. From 1985, the firm retained Andersen to be its auditor, providing both internal and external auditing work.[9] The Enron audit was one of its most lucrative worldwide. The Houston, Texas, office was the main provider of audit work for Enron. Arthur Andersen LLP also performed work for the firm in Chicago and in Portland, Oregon. When Enron announced in October 2001 that it was subject to a SEC investigation for accounting errors, its auditor Arthur Andersen LLP was rapidly implicated in the emerging scandal regarding possible accounting improprieties at Enron.[10] But the worst damage for Andersen arose from the news that it had started destroying thousands of documents, a day before the auditors learnt that the SEC was about to open a preliminary inquiry. This destruction started on 23 October and continued until 9 November.

It soon became clear that the Houston team had directly contravened the accounting methodology approved by the Andersen PSG. Duncan had voluntary ignored the PSG recommendations. As the lead partner, he was personally responsible for Enron audit, even if Andersen internal rules required the signature of a second partner. It remains unclear whether the decision to destroy documents and electronic files related to Enron audit was taken by the Houston office or by the Andersen in-house lawyer, Nancy Temple, in accordance with 'firm policy' although the twelve jurors at the trial had agreed that she was the one who broke the law.[11] It was reported that Enron's accounting had become highly controversial within Andersen, being the object of internal struggles. Enron had been rated in the category for 'maximum risk' by Andersen's in-house client risk analysis in 1999 and 2000. An e-mail message obtained by Congressional investigators showed that some senior Andersen executives had discussed the possibility of dropping Enron as a client in 2000 because of worries about Enron's accounting. Furthermore, in mid-August 2001, a senior Enron employee, Sherron S. Watkins, who had previously been an auditor with Andersen, raised the alarm of improprieties in Enron accounting practices in a letter to her chairman.

These facts show that there was a serious problem within Andersen's chain of command, which let local partners considerable leeway without any serious control, despite the fact that the firm possessed one of the most centralised and co-ordinated structure within the Big Five, as already described. P. A. Volcker, the Federal Reserve chairman from 1979 to 1987, who was appointed by the firm to head a special oversight Board, declared that 'it is not clear, for instance, whether the accounting for Enron's deals was approved by senior partners outside of Andersen's Houston office'.[12] This failure has certainly to be connected to the partnership structure of the firm, based on the great autonomy of partners leading regional offices that were legally and financially independent. The size of the partnership made effective control by the partners increasingly difficult and eroded the sense of collegiality. This very flexible structure appeared no longer to be efficient when reputation and revenues of local partners outside the USA were at stake because of irregularities committed by a US member of the worldwide network. The cohesion of the partnership of local partnerships was broken as soon as global interest in co-operation diminished at the expense of prevailing local interests. This has probably to do with the way partners were compensated and profit was shared among them. Andersen audit partners were rewarded according to the amount of revenue they produced from their audit clients (including the sales of non-audit services). Piaget and Baumann (2003) considered that this compensation model contributed towards maintaining a very individualistic culture that appeared to be the company's Achilles' heel during the Enron crisis. However, the emergence and accentuation of the numerous problems at Andersen must be set in the context of major changes in the auditing industry as a whole.

Concentration, diversification and loss of independence

The formation of the oligopoly

The enactment of federal securities laws in the 1930s transformed the accounting profession.[13] They gave it a critical role in ensuring the efficient functioning of US financial markets. In reducing the asymmetric information between a company's management and investors, auditors fulfilled a public duty, although they were subjected to very limited public scrutiny. Independent public accountants or external auditors had to certify the quality of large public firms' financial results in accordance with generally accepted auditing standards, to enhance public confidence in the stock market and, more broadly, to protect the integrity of the free-market system. This social responsibility linked to the defence of public interest placed auditors and the accounting profession at the core of American business life. At the same time, these laws contributed to the formation of an oligopoly in the auditing market. By redefining the auditor's role, by guaranteeing them clients and a sustainable market through mandatory annual audits, and by enhancing audit's status, these laws favoured an increasing concentration in the industry. By the early 1970s, this concentration had already led to the formation of the Big Eight audit network. A further process of mega-mergers took place as a response to growing globalisation and the complexity of multinational client operations. Mergers enabled firms to achieve greater economies of scale and were seen as the quickest way of filling gaps, not only in geographic but also in industry-specific expertise coverage (GAO, 2003a). A first wave of mergers in the 1980s reduced the number of large firms to six. The most recent mega-merger took place in 1997, between Coopers & Lybrand and Price Waterhouse, bringing the number to five. As a result, these Big Five dominated the audit market, leaving large publicly traded companies with no alternative but to deal with this tight oligopoly. Andersen, the smallest member, was the only firm not to have merged with another of the Big Eight, preferring organic growth to preserve its strong firm's culture. In 2000, it had worldwide revenue five and half times the global revenue of the biggest of the second-tier firms, Grand Thornton, and almost four times the number of the latter's staff.[14] If one takes key industry sectors for the auditing market (energy, telecom and so on), the concentration of business was even higher. With the abrupt demise of Andersen in 2002, the Big Five are now down to four, undertaking the audit of almost all US public companies. This has led to yet another increase in the degree of concentration, with ever higher barriers to entry for smaller firms: at the time of writing, the Big Four audit over 78 per cent of all US public companies. For US public companies with sales of over US$250 million as a whole, the Big Fours' combined market share is 97 per cent (GAO, 2003a). A similar trend has occurred in most other industrialised countries.

Diversification as a means of making money and enhancing professional prestige

Following the building of strong ties with the CEOs and CFOs of large US corporations, audit firms started in the postwar period to develop new practice areas and to sell new products such as tax and consulting services. Specialised departments (tax and systems departments, later renamed management advisory services) were set up. During the 1970s, management consulting services became the main source of growth, and began to create public concern about auditor independence.[15] The Big Eight controlled as much as 20 per cent of the management consulting market at that time, although, on average, such services accounted only for 11 per cent of their total income (GAO, 2003a). Simultaneously, there was a fall in the value of external audit activity. It became a rather common labour-intensive service,[16] a sort of undifferentiated and mere commodity subject to price rebates. Staffing young and inexperienced auditors supervised by a senior manager was the way to lower the cost of this routine activity in order to gain clients for non-audit services.[17] By contrast, unregulated management consulting services were much more lucrative, attractive and prestigious. This process had strong negative impacts. The scope of work performed was seriously reduced, with a consequent decline in the quality of audits. Diversifying their services and their business area, and becoming privileged dialogue partners of top managers, appeared to be a way of restoring the reputation and image of auditors. But this could only take place at the expense of existing genuine audit relationships. It was also crucial to increase income by delivering high-margin non-audit services. In this way, traditional accountants were able to convert themselves into flashy and high-profit business consultants. During the 1990s, this business area exploded at the expense of audit fees, which represented no more than 31 per cent of their revenues in 1998 (as against 70 per cent in 1976). This became the basis for strong controversies between the incumbent SEC chairman, Arthur Levitt and the profession. In 2000, Levitt proposed a new rule that would limit auditors from doing some consulting work (notably computer-system consulting) that could have impaired their independence. The Big Five campaigned aggressively against Levitt, lobbying Congressional members. Andersen and his CEO, Joseph Berardino, led this campaign (Levitt and Dwyer, 2002). They eventually succeeded in keeping the right to go on delivering these services and performing a company's internal audit up to 40 per cent for those with more than US$200 million in assets. In return, companies would in future have to disclose in their annual proxy statement the amount of non-audit services undertaken. A very similar disclosure requirement was adopted by the SEC in 1978 but was repealed in 1982 as a consequence of strong pressure from the accounting profession (Allen and McDermott, 1993).

Andersen as an example of the conflict of interests

The clash of cultures and interests between auditors and consultants is well illustrated by the Andersen inside story. Andersen Consulting (AC), the consulting arm of Andersen, was set up in 1989 as a separate division of its parent firm because of growing tensions between consultants and auditors because of asymmetric growth and revenues. This internal agreement was known as the Florida Accord. However, the growth of AC in terms of fee income continued to be so strong during the 1990s that AC partners expressed increasing dissatisfaction with the 1989 agreement and their 'second-class' status within the firm.[18] They had to continue to share revenues with auditors. But in the meantime the latter had built an entirely new consulting unit called Business Consulting, orientated towards financial information systems design and implementation. Since it rapidly became profitable, it was perceived more and more by AC as a competitor, thus feeding the resentment of consultants against auditors. Internal conflict between Arthur Andersen and AC ended in 2000, when the latter was finally spun off and later renamed Accenture. This, however, did not resolve the fact that business consulting fees were growing at the expense of audit fees within Andersen. This was particularly true in the case of Enron.

At the Houston firm, Andersen fees in 2000 soared to US$52 million: more than half (US$27 million) represented consulting fees, of which a large part concerned tax consulting. Andersen helped Enron to design a web of complicated and opaque financial arrangements, the purpose of which was to get around accounting rules and hide large debts and losses. The Special Investigative Committee of the Board of Directors of Enron came to the conclusion in what is known as the Powers Report that 'Enron accounting treatment was determined with extensive participation and structuring advice from Andersen ...'. The report also mentioned that from 1997 to 2001, Andersen received US$5,7 million in specific fees for advising Enron on the LMJ and Chewco financial transactions, in addition to its regular audit fees.[19] Between 1993 and 1998, Andersen used to perform the roles of both internal and external auditor at Enron.[20] This was a perfect example of the concern expressed by SEC about the potential conflicts of interest between these responsibilities. When Paul Volcker was appointed by Andersen to propose changes in order to save the firm in February 2002, Andersen partners showed themselves to be very reluctant to adopt one of his proposals, made a month later, namely to refocus Andersen's business on to audit (Piaget and Baumann, 2003, pp. 165–6). This reaction was largely a consequence of the prevailing tarnished image of audit among expert professionals as well as its being an insufficient source of income, both features being linked.

In their reaction to the Volcker recommendations, Andersen partners were voicing the whole industry's opinion. Providing consulting services can create synergies that improve auditors' in-depth knowledge of a client and audit effectiveness. But also, and above all, it enhances the prestige of the profession as well as its revenues. This is why large firms are so prompt to defend the need to deliver such services, external audit just being considered as an appeal product, since it has lost status for a long time. Yet when auditors become economically dependent on their clients, it is likely that this will impair their independence and objectivity in the area of audit and create serious conflict-of-interest issues.

Auditing as the 'poor relation' of professional services: the problem and its effects at Andersen

Difficulties in recruiting

In the world of US professional services, accountants and auditors remain those with the lowest profile. To become a CPA usually requires a bachelor's degree in accounting as well as passing the CPA exam. Hence their academic training is dedicated entirely to accounting. By contrast, the best and the brightest students graduating from the Ivy League universities generally join the law firms. And in the 1990s, these students were increasingly attracted by investment banking and strategic consulting, the two most preferred job opportunities of MBA graduates. Some evidence reveals the relatively poor interest of young graduates to become auditors in the USA. The number of CPA candidates decreased dramatically during the 1990s: between 1993 and 1999, numbers fell from 53,763 to 38,573 (Levitt and Dwyer, 2002, p. 130). Furthermore, the percentage of college students majoring in accounting fell from 4 per cent in 1990 to 2 per cent in 2000. The same was true for high school students who intend to major in accounting: this number decreased from 2 per cent to 1 per cent during the same period.[21] Although consulting services were developed by audit firms since the mid-1990s they were not able to stop the ongoing professional decline because of the strong attractiveness of start-ups from the Internet industry and the promise of rapid and important gains. The rather slow and hierarchical career of an auditor (the status of partners is based mainly on seniority) could not compete with the adventurous, lightning, non-hierarchical careers promised when recruited by an Internet start-up. Levitt considers that the accounting profession was responsible, because of its inability to be attractive to potential new entrants (Levitt and Dwyer, 2002). By proposing to well-qualified audit recruits lower wages than to consultant recruits, the audit firms contributed strongly to the downgrading of the profession.

At the end of the 1990s, Andersen was only ranked in the second half of the *Fortune* top 100 best employers in the USA. In attracting and retaining key professionals, firms such as Andersen had to compete with investment banks, and consulting and law firms as well as large corporations. Andersen was now considered to be as a second-best choice of place to start a career. MBAs out of the best business schools demanded high levels of compensation, notably during the 1990s. To meet this demand, accounting firms had not only to find more business; they also had to find more lucrative business than the traditional low-margin services they had previously delivered (corporate audits). The threat of litigation was also deterring new recruits to the profession.[22] Hence, consulting could be seen as a new career opportunity after working two or three years in auditing. Another major issue illustrated by the Enron–Andersen case is the status of auditors *vis-à-vis* the very large corporate clients.

The dominated position of auditors *vis-à-vis* their corporate clients

For a long time, the professional body AICPA (American Institute of Certified Public Accountants) supported the legitimacy of major audit firms to deliver consulting services under the same roof, and encouraged this trend. Even the last letter of the body's name referring to Accountants appeared to become something shameful. Some AICPA leaders would like to replace the word 'accountants' with the fancier expression 'Strategic business professionals'. AICPA argues that consulting business leads audit firms to a better understanding of the corporate client, and therefore to improving their audit work. In fact, consulting services allow auditors to get access to CEOs more frequently, whereas external auditors have traditional had long-term relationships with CFOs or chief accountants. However, to press strongly for access to CEOs as a condition of improving the quality of external audit can be costly for investors. While auditors are usually required to be appointed and paid by the shareholders they are supposed to protect, in practice they are paid by the corporation and are beholden to the managers of the companies they audit. Furthermore, the kind of close relationships they generate with top corporate managers, as a result of their common background and cosy business relationships, intensifies auditors' vulnerability and their position of being at the mercy of the client and of accepting questionable accounting practices. This risk is all the greater when the fees from a single company they audit account for a significant portion of an accounting firm's revenues, when the type of services they deliver have a direct effect on senior executives' income (tax planning services, for example), or when auditors have been serving the same company for a long period of time.

Richard and Reix (2002) stress that the audit work relationship, far from being a simple technique of doing sample check, is also a social construction. This is necessary to build the trust underlying the development of professional service markets. It is based on common social trajectories and cultural backgrounds between the outside auditor and the corporate manager involved. It is a condition of the quality of transactions in professional services while inducing the risk of harming this quality by blunting the watchfulness and the acuteness of the way auditors look at their clients. Given the characteristics of this relationship, auditors' independence – that is, professionals fulfilling a public duty required by law – is likely to appear to be a real gamble. If the auditor challenges a company's account or delivers unfavourable audits, the risk of being fired by corporate executives is real, and can be costly for both the auditor and his/her firm. By doing so, s/he puts lucrative consulting services at risk and therefore the firms revenue as well as his/her own revenue as a partner. Furthermore, individual auditors' jobs and career paths may depend on success with specific clients. Audit firms as partnerships have a very narrow internal labour market with limited career opportunities. The prevailing 'up or out' implicit rule organises staff turnover, allowing only some of the auditors to become eligible for partner status. By contrast, corporate clients offer most of the job options available to young professionals. At the time of writing, barely 40 per cent of AICPA members work in audit firms, while the majority of them (47 per cent) hold jobs in the corporate private sector.[23] Therefore, auditors have strong incentives to remain popular with clients (Bazerman *et al.*, 2002).

The Andersen's turnover rate was a good proxy of this 'up or out' rule, varying from about 17 per cent to 23 per cent in 2001 (Piaget and Baumann, 2003, p. 21). The common practice of Arthur Andersen employees taking up positions with Enron came to light with the Enron scandal. In Houston, more than 100 Andersen employees had made the move to Enron over the previous ten years, so it was difficult to find a CFO in the area who was not an Andersen alumni.[24] Among them, Richard Causey, Enron's chief accounting officer, and Jeffrey McMahon, chief financial officer, both held positions in the Houston office of the Big Five professional services firm. Mr Causey had been a senior manager at Andersen, involved more particularly in the natural gas business area. Mr McMahon began his career at Andersen in Houston; he was audit manager in the company's energy division.

As far as the Enron audit team was concerned, David Duncan, the lead partner, had a long-term cosy relationships with Enron executives. Born in Texas, he joined the Andersen local office in 1981; soon afterwards he graduated as a CPA at Texas A&M University, where he met future Enron executives. In 1995, he became one of the youngest Arthur Andersen LLP partners. Two years later, he was given responsibility for the Enron audit, one of the audit firm's biggest corporate clients. Duncan moved his office directly into Enron's building. He had close relationships with some Enron executives, notably Richard Causey, its chief accounting officer, with whom he played golf regularly and shared meals in local restaurants. The ambivalent wish to please both his firm and his client often led him to defend Enron executive choices against the opinions of his Andersen colleagues, notably those of the PSG, and to hide insider information.[25] When an Andersen member of this monitoring body, Carl Bass, reviewed some of Enron's accounting practices (notably SPE, known as the 'Raptors') in December 1999, he was the target of sharp criticism from Enron officials and the Enron engagement team, which amended its memos to correct the record of its review in an opposite way.[26] Andersen removed him from overseeing Enron as well as from the PSG at the request of Enron executives according to congressional investigators.

This evidence suggests that the Houston profit centre was stronger than in-house standards and ethic rules, aimed at enforcing Andersen's reputation and credibility. Within Andersen, the internal monitoring procedures failed to constrain local partners to act properly.

Conclusion

The independent audit function held by the accounting profession is supposed to play a key role in financial reporting and disclosure, and thus in the effective functioning of US capital markets and the optimisation of resource allocation. The profession is entrusted with a public responsibility. However, during the 1990s, the auditor's primary duty to look out for the interest of investors and further the public interest was clearly supplanted by the profession's propensity to serve primarily the interests of its clients.

Ethical guidelines and general norms of professional behaviour set up by the profession proved to be totally incapable of addressing seriously the pressures put on auditors by executives in corporations. Executives were, of course, themselves committed to shorter deadlines in terms of financial performances and intensified pressure to produce ever increasing returns.

The implication of Andersen in the Enron scandal occurred after a succession of audit failures involving its responsibility. Given its size and numerous implications, the Enron collapse and bankruptcy was akin to an earthquake. The admission of document shredding related to Enron audit by the Houston office was the beginning of the end for the firm. It caused a real shock among the public as evidence of a failure of due professional care. It also gave the US Justice Department a solid argument for the prosecution process, although the conviction of Arthur Andersen by the Texas jury in Houston in June 2002 was reversed by the Supreme Court at the end of May 2005. The latter considered that evidence that Andersen officials willfully destroyed documents was insufficient. It should be noted that this is the only point the Supreme Court ruled on.

Whatever the outcome, Andersen's indictment was undoubtedly at the time a political response to the urgent need to produce an example for the Bush administration (Piaget and Baumann, 2003). The legislative response came soon afterwards, with the Sarbanes-Oxley Act, which introduced major reforms concerning accounting and auditing issues. The most stringent measure was the creation of the PCAOB (Public Company Accounting Oversight Board), a new regulatory body under SEC supervision. For the first time in the profession's history, the power to regulate accountants and to monitor audit firms was withdrawn from the industry and placed in the hands of an independent panel under tightened federal oversight. Of course, the effectiveness of the PCAOB will depend on the will of its president and members to enforce the regulation. This will also depend on its resources, which are voted by Congress and subject to political priorities. But the Sarbanes-Oxley Act is far from resolving issues such as conflicts of interest and the level of concentration of the audit market further aggravated by the demise of Andersen. The new SEC law that came to effect in January 2004 aims to tackle the question of auditors' lack of independence. It bars auditors from providing certain consulting services, notably the design and use of financial information systems. But it does not prohibit this entirely and gives the new oversight Board a strong leeway to deal with it. It establishes mandatory rotation every five years for the lead partner in the audit of a given corporation, but not for the audit firm itself.

However, the issue can be taken a step further. As long as auditors are paid by the companies they audit and thus depend on executives for their employment, their compensation and their career opportunities, conflicts of interest are likely to continue. A more radical way of preventing this subordinate relationship than the one chosen by the US Administration and Congress would have been to create a public agency that would be responsible for the selection of auditors and to which audit clients would be required to contribute to pay the audit. The other major problem that is unresolved by the Sarbanes-Oxley Act is that of fees. Accounting firms' resources are tighter than ever given the growing complexity and cost of handling audits for multinational corporations. Audit fees should at least be increased to improve the quality of the audit process and to avoid the development of non-audit services on the back of existing audit relationships. This would also allow an increase in salaries and thus would enhance the status of audit among professional service firms. A final measure should be to renew and broaden the academic preparation of accountants in order to make the profession more attractive to the best students.

All this, of course, does not really address the main underlying issue of a once-honoured profession with strong ethical standards that has turned almost exclusively to behaving as a business driven by the bottom line and client satisfaction to the detriment of public interest. This is the gist of the Andersen story.

Notes

1   The Enron debacle has resulted in many victims, primarily the 4,500 ex-employees who saw their careers ended abruptly as well as losing their pension savings. Fastow, the former Vice-President and CFO was the first Enron top executive to be indicted and sentenced in 2003. Since then, Lay, the former President, Skilling, a former President and CEO, and Causey, the former CAO have been indicted on fraud charges by a federal jury. But the sentencing of the former Arthur Andersen partner, David Duncan, who pleaded guilty to obstruction of justice in April 2002, has been postponed several times.

2   US Senate, *Financial Oversight of Enron – The SEC and Private Sectors Watchdogs*, Special Report of the Committee on Governmental Affairs, US Government Printing Office, Washington DC, 8 October 2002.

3   Andersen was involved into several items of shareholder litigation in which it neither admitted nor denied allegations of fraud. The firm made a US$7 million settlement with the SEC for a false audit of Houston-based Waste Management, after the company announced that four years of its pre-tax profit reports had been inflated – between 1992 and 1996. Andersen also agreed to pay US$110 million to settle class-action litigation with Sunbeam shareholders in 1997. In March 2002, a few months after the Enron scandal broke, it agreed to pay US$217 million to settle claims by the Baptist Foundation of Arizona trustee, investors and state agencies after this non-profit organisation declared itself bankrupt in 1999. Andersen was accused of ignoring warning signs during annual audits and lending credibility to false financial statements.

4   The accounting industry lobbied successfully for legislation in the 1990s limiting the liability of external auditors in class action lawsuits brought by shareholders, notably the Private Securities Litigation Reform Act in 1995 and the Securities Litigation Uniform Standards Act of 1998 (GAO, 2003a).

5 In 1952, Andersen introduced the first computer capable of managing General Electric's accounting.

6 Berardino was the last CEO to be elected, in 2001.

7 The peer review covered 240 audit engagements in more than thirty Andersen offices. The Enron audit was not included in the peer review, nor were other audits that have been subjected to litigation.

8 In 1977, the trade association AICPA (American Institute of Chartered Public Accountants) had to create the POB (Public Oversight Board) in order to carry out some self-regulatory functions that were ineffective after a wave of audit failures in the 1970s. This body was expected to review the quality of audits and to oversee the peer review processes.

9 The sixteen years of Andersen tenure in the Enron case was not exceptional, since the average length for Andersen tenure at *Fortune* 1000 public companies was twenty-six years, while auditor tenures average twenty-two years (GAO, 2003b, pp. 14, 17).

10 Later, a Senate committee reached the conclusion that its professionalism was not at fault. The report recognised that the audit firm had briefed the Enron audit committee regularly about Enron's accounting practices and their high degree of risk of non-compliance with Generally Accepted Accounting Principles (GAAP) from 1999 to 2001. At the same time, the report pointed out that Andersen had never recommended Enron to change its questionable accounting practices. See US Senate, *The Role of the Board of Directors in Enron's Collapse*, Report prepared by the permanent subcommittee on investigations of the committee of governmental affairs, US Government Printing Office, Washington DC, 8 July 2002.

11 As evidence, the jurors cited an e-mail that Temple sent to Duncan, asking him to alter a memo he had written for his files about Enron public statements.

12 J. D. Glater, 'Andersen Revamp Seen Under Volcker', *Chicago Tribune*, 26 February 2002.

13 In their seminal book published in 1932, *The Modern Corporation and Private Property* (New York: Harcourt), A. A. Berle and G. C. Means recommended that more objective financial information be obtained by requiring large public companies to file audited financial statements and by mandating some accounting principles to prevent the abuses that already plagued reporting at the time. They identified public accountants as key agents in ensuring the functioning of financial markets. Many of their proposals became public policy under the Securities Act of 1933 (Allen and McDermott, 1993).

14 Andersen had a global revenue of US$9.3 billion and employed a staff of 85,000, whereas Grand Thornton had only US$1.7 billion of worldwide revenue for 22,000 employees.

15 The Metcalf Report had already stressed the problem at that time.

16 Staff time on a typical audit constitutes the bulk of the total hours worked.

17 GAO (2003a) stresses that audit firms during the 1980s and 1990s bid unrealistically low fees to obtain new clients.

18 The consulting partners were under-represented among Andersen's top managers. They were also disadvantaged by the way pay and profits were distributed among Andersen partners, based mainly on seniority.

19 See W. C. Powers, Jr. (chair), R. S. Troubh and H. S. Winokur, Jr., *Report of Investigation by the Special Investigative Committee of the Board of Directors of Enron Corp*, 1 February 2002 (http://news. findlaw.com/wp/docs/enron/specinv0201022pt1.pdf).

20 The internal audit function was outsourced to Andersen during this period, with more than forty Enron employees becoming Andersen employees in the process of outsourcing. Once the latter reintegrated Enron, Andersen auditors had then to control their 'ex-colleagues' work (Piaget and Baumann, 2003, p. 87).
21 See A. L., Gabbin, 'The Crisis in Accounting Education', *Journal of Accountancy*, September 2002, pp. 81–6.
22 A further handicap rests on the private partnership structure. It does not give partners much leeway in terms of their ability to deal with the size of potential legal claims. This entails high insurance costs.
23 See http://www.aicpa.org/.
24 'Enron Fallout Hits Workers at Andersen', *Houston Chronicle*, 21 February 2002.
25 See A., Raghavan, 'For Most of His Life, David Duncan Played the Rules', *Wall Street Journal*, 15 May 2002.
26 See 'Lessons Learned from Enron's Collapse: Auditing the Accounting Industry', Hearing before the Committee on Energy and Commerce, House of Representatives, US Government Printing Office, Washington DC, 6 February 2002.

References

Allen, D. G. and K. McDermott (1993), *Accounting for Success: A History of Price Waterhouse in America 1890–1990* (Boston, Mass.: Harvard Business School Press).
Arthur Andersen and Company. (1984), *The First Fifty Years 1913–1963* (New York/London: Garland Publishing).
Bazerman, M. H., G. Loewenstein and D. A. Moore (2002), 'Why Good Accountants Do Bad Audits', *Harvard Business Review* (November), pp. 97–102.
GAO (General Accounting Office) (2003a), *Public Accounting Firms – Mandated Study on Consolidation and Competition*, Report to the Senate Committee on Banking, Housing and Urban Affairs and the House Committee on Financial Services, GAO, Washington (July).
GAO (General Accounting Office) (2003b), *Public Accounting Firms – Required Study on the Potential Effects of Mandatory Audit Firm Rotation*, Report to the Senate Committee on Banking, Housing and Urban Affairs and the House Committee on Financial Services, GAO, Washington (November).
Levitt, A. and P. Dwyer (2002), *Take on the Street: What Wall Street and Corporate America Don't Want You to Know* (New York: Pantheon Books).
Piaget, M. and C. Baumann (2003), *La chute de l'empire Andersen. Crise, responsabilité et gouvernement d'entreprise* (Paris: Dunod).
Richard, C. and R. Reix (2002), 'Contribution à l'analyse de la qualité du processus d'audit: le rôle de la relation entre le directeur financier et le commissaire aux comptes', *Comptabilité, Contrôle, Audit*, tome. 8, vol. 1 (May), pp. 151–74.
Sauviat, C. (2003) 'Deux professions dans la tourmente. L'audit et l'analyse financière', *Actes de la recherche en sciences sociales*, no. 146–7 (March), pp. 21–41.

9
Enron *et al.* and Implications for the Auditing Profession

Anthony Travis

There are many unanswered questions arising from recent changes in legislation for the regulatory supervision of external audits of public companies. Questions concerning conflicting national privacy and commercial secrecy laws; the authorities and competencies for setting international standards for accounting, and reporting the financial statements of public companies, and for their audit across borders; the extent of access to information about subsidiaries and affiliates of public companies by government agencies of foreign states; and the extent to which auditors should be empowered to investigate, prove and publicly report the occurrence of corporate fraud without submitting the evidence to the due process of law.

Introduction

The Enron affair has been the first of a number of recent cases in both the USA and Europe where serious and in some cases terminal failures in corporate governance have given rise to public concern about the quality and reliability of the independent auditing profession.

Andrew Cornford, in Chapter 2 of this volume, refers to the legislative measures introduced in the USA in response to the Enron case (the Sarbanes-Oxley Act) and it is not intended to rehearse that subject in this chapter. It is worth noting, however, that the European Union (EU) and other legislative bodies have taken steps to respond to potentially far-reaching transnational effects of the US legislation, and that similar legislative processes are taking place in other countries, and having significant effects on the auditing profession.

The main purpose of this chapter is to raise certain issues in respect to the historic role of auditors, and to discuss the extent to which the assumptions underlying that role remain valid and necessary for the fulfilment of the audit function. This chapter assumes that until very recently the fundamental purpose of the audit was unchanged, being the expression of an objective and independent opinion on the accounts of the entity subject to audit.

A substantial number of commentators have suggested that the role and responsibilities of auditors should be much more far-reaching, but have not proposed the manner in which and on what basis such responsibilities might be fulfilled. Also discussed in this chapter are the actions being undertaken to restore public trust in auditing.

Historical role of the auditing profession

In the context of an industrial economy, the auditing profession has its origins in the nineteenth century and evolved from the role of independent accountants acting as administrators of bankrupt businesses. The role was essentially the same as it remains to this day, being the undertaking of a private-sector function to fulfil a public duty to assist in maintaining and restoring order in private-sector financial and commercial affairs. The creation, in the first half of the nineteenth century, of the joint-stock company, using limited liability structures to raise economic capital, gave rise to legislation to protect the interests of shareholders and creditors from abuse by managers and majority shareholders of the privileges conferred upon them as founders and managers of limited liability companies. Legal remedies available to minority shareholders and creditors of companies to protect their interests have evolved through an accumulation of case and company law on the basis of national legislative and judicial processes. This remains the case to this day and, as can be seen from the recent failures in corporate governance, the legislative process is far from complete and is only beginning to take place at the international level. Under most legislation, the rights of minority shareholders to challenge the decisions of boards of directors remain minimal and rudimentary. In the case of bankruptcy, the rights of creditors take precedence over those of shareholders and holders of subordinated debt, and the role and responsibilities of administrators to protect the interests of creditors is absolutely contrary to those of auditors in the case of a going concern, where the auditors' primary duty is to the shareholders.[1]

In the case of Enron, there are a number of corporate, accounting, auditing and other issues that are pertinent to reaching an understanding as to why the recent failures may be considered different from those arising in the past. These include the use of complex but apparently compliant accounting rules to mask or defer recognition of liabilities and losses; the development and sale by investment banks of complex accounting-driven structures and products to assist corporations to hide losses and liabilities, and thereby to improve their published financial condition and credit ratings; the introduction of highly leveraged employee stock option plans and other executive remuneration systems conferring on corporate management opportunities and rights to benefit in the short term from economic rewards sufficient for them to achieve genuine personal economic independence for life;[2] the deregulation of certain markets;[3] and the rapid increase in the internationalisation of corporations and their structures.[4] For the auditing profession, several trends are evident. The increasing complexity of international and transnational corporate structures and business transactions has called for a substantial extension in the scale and depth of resources necessary within auditing firms to handle multi-location audit engagements on a global scale. Because of their origins and the nature of their statutory and other responsibilities, audit firms are necessarily subject to different and conflicting national laws and regulations, which require that audit firms are organised at a national level in accordance with a variety of legal structures that preclude fully transparent communication of commercial and other private information about their audit clients across borders. In fact, in most jurisdictions, auditors are forbidden from communicating publicly information about any matters concerning their clients other than their formal audit opinion on the published accounts. In certain jurisdictions, for an audit firm to communicate information spontaneously about its audit clients outside the context of the audit mandate *per se* may be a criminal offence.

During the latter half of the twentieth century, as more professional accountants were recruited into the commercial sector from the professional auditing and accounting firms that had trained them, auditing firms came under dramatically increasing competitive pressure to reduce or discount their audit fees, or lose the work to other competing audit firms. As the published product of the audit (the audit opinion) was limited by statute to the issuance of a standard text, the audit came to be seen as an undifferentiated product where the only concrete means for the audit firm to distinguish its service offering was either to reduce its fee below that of its competitors or to offer services additional to the audit. The audit firms' rational economic reaction to dealing with increasing price competition was to develop, offer and deliver higher-margin non-audit services on the back of existing audit relationships. In this regard, Andersen was most successful at Enron. When Enron's difficulties became well known, Andersen's success in cross-selling its services to Enron caused its independence as auditor to be called into question. It may be that Andersen would not have considered the risks it apparently perceived it was running in its auditing relationship with Enron to have been worthwhile without the incentives of the rewards generated by the other, more profitable, service offerings it was providing. It may be the case that, if Andersen had been precluded from providing non-audit services to Enron, the only remedy would have been either to increase substantially the audit fee, or to resign the audit mandate.[5]

It is perhaps still too early to quantify the extent of any longer-term increases in audit fees. Two points, though, are emerging. First, it is evident that a substantial effort and cost is being incurred by corporations to meet the immediate requirements of certain sections of the US Sarbanes-Oxley Act, and that the auditing profession is carrying out extensive work in checking US-listed corporations' systems of internal controls. Second, the restrictions on providing non-audit services to audit clients has reduced the amount of such services provided by audit firms to their audit clients. What is also clear to anyone operating in the audit market, is that it is fiercely price-competitive. In general, the negotiation of fees for audit services remains the responsibility of corporate chief financial officers or their delegates, and has rarely been addressed in any detail by audit committees or boards of directors. This is now changing, but there is a strong case for suggesting that the present fee-negotiating process is inappropriate in today's corporate governance environment.[6]

The expanding role of external auditors to identify fraud

Based on reports emerging from investigations into cases of corporate failure, it is becoming clear that there are grounds for suspecting collusion between members of failed corporations' top management and their outside suppliers of services, including lawyers, tax advisers, banks and others whereby a tissue of arrangements were put in place over time to camouflage losses and liabilities that would have otherwise been disclosed earlier. It is also possible to consider that such arrangements would not have been possible without collusion between at least some of those parties. Historically, it is axiomatic to the external audit function that auditors cannot be expected to find and prove fraud where it arises from collusion, particularly where it involves members of top management. It is expected that external auditors are professionally sceptical of a client's behaviour and suspicious of its motives. In the face of collusion between members of management, it is quite another matter for an auditor to prove whether his/her suspicions of any fraudulent behaviour are justified. It is indeed hard to imagine that an auditor would publish an opinion referring to any suspicions s/he might have of the existence of fraud without clear proof that they are justified.

As is demonstrated by the already prolonged time between the time that the Enron affair first surfaced and the commencement of the trial of some of the alleged culprits (other than Andersen), even the courts, for all their wide-ranging powers, require a great deal of time, resources and access to information, far exceeding those available to any auditor, to begin the formal process of proving fraud or analogous offences. Proving such allegations is indeed a difficult and far from certain task. It can be asked, therefore, whether it is in any way reasonable to expect an auditor going about his day to day business to be more successful in far less time than the courts? It can also be asked whether governments are prepared to grant external auditors such explicit powers as would be necessary to permit them to execute adequately, and on a day-to-day basis, such an all-encompassing investigative role at all audited entities. A debate about what powers may be necessary for the successful execution of such a role will be necessary if it is to be imposed on auditors. There is no doubt that they would be substantially greater than those that exist today, and would involve issues of unfettered access to information and people in a manner that is at present not possible in the context of an audit.

Unanswered questions

With respect to Andersen, there remains at least one question. The prosecution of Andersen for obstruction of justice took place within an astonishingly short period of time, and from the moment the prosecution began it was evident that Andersen could no longer remain in business as an auditor. It is also clear that the people who decided at their discretion to prosecute Andersen were fully aware of the immediate, grave and in fact terminal consequences that their action would have on that firm.[7] It turned out that by the time Andersen was found guilty, the firm was already substantially out of business and was in terminal collapse. How interesting it would have been if the jury had found Andersen innocent of the charges. An innocent defendant would have been terminated before judgement had been passed.

Based on the speed with which Andersen's was prosecuted and terminated, compared with the long-winded pre-trial processes being undertaken in the Enron and other cases, it seems clear that audit firms are being held to a vastly higher legal standard than their audit clients. Is such asymmetry sustainable, even in the short term? Can the present state of professional liability of auditors be maintained without some form of capping? If not, what are the alternatives to the present, private-sector-based external audit role operating on a cross-border basis? Should public companies' group accounts be audited? If so, in the absence of private-sector-based audit firms, would public-sector-based audit agencies co-operate adequately and timely enough to permit the same degree of integration of auditing across borders as is undertaken by the present private-sector providers? Would any national government audit agency be willing to take on such a role? If it were to do so, would its opinions on private-sector financial statements be seen as a form of government guarantee? Would that introduce moral hazard to the private sector, thereby increasing risk? Is it reasonable to expect private-sector businesses to co-operate willingly and to provide unfettered access to state auditors who could not provide reasonable assurance of privacy of the information provided to permit the audit to be undertaken?

Today, a regulated profession

Today, public-company external auditing is a regulated profession. It is subject to wide-ranging and in-depth supervision and inspection by governmental and quasi-governmental bodies, and can no longer provide guarantees of confidentiality over the commercial and private affairs of its clients. The accounting and auditing standards to which it is held are promulgated by agencies outside its control. Looked at from the private-sector perspective, these are profoundly disturbing developments almost certainly involving conflicts with laws designed to protect privacy and human rights.

The policy response to the Enron case includes a wide array of initiatives including the US Sarbanes-Oxley Act, the draft EU 8th Company Law Directive and similar initiatives in many countries. Up to the time of writing, the auditing profession has participated and co-operated actively in providing comments to legislators on the practical aspects of implementing these initiatives. These comments have included recommendations regarding proposals for the compulsory rotation of auditors; definitions of appropriate auditing standards; auditors' qualifications and training; the provision of non-auditing services; professional liability issues; regulatory supervision; and inspections; cross-border impediments to supervision; and access to information on multinational audit clients and corporate governance issues, to name a few. Extensive internal administrative efforts have been undertaken by the audit firms to drive through programmes to ensure compliance with the independence rules, and the audit firms have undergone preliminary and follow-up inspections of their internal systems of governance and of their compliance with auditing standards. The senior partners of the audit firms have publicly recognized the need to address the issue of public trust in their profession, and have repeatedly expressed their views that this is a matter of the utmost importance to the auditing profession and the capital markets.

Seen in the light of all that has happened, it is interesting to consider whether the original model of private-sector auditors fulfilling their role on the basis of the assumption of good faith serving the longer-term interests of their clients, with limited powers of communication beyond their statutory role and guaranteeing the confidentiality of their clients' commercial affairs, is an attractive proposition when compared to the scenarios described. It is not realistic to believe that the clock can be turned back to reinstate such a situation: the corporate world has become too complex and important for this to happen. However, it is also worth reflecting on the point that this is mainly because the short-term personal economic interests of corporate management are no longer aligned with the longer-term interests of their employers.

Extra powers and vigilance are needed to control and reconcile the risks resulting from these conflicting goals, and neither the auditing profession nor investors have been granted such powers. The root cause of the Enron failure and the issue underlying so much of the corporate governance debate and legislative effort has not been resolved. It is not impossible to consider whether this may be a conscious failure of legislators to face up to the real challenges, and that they are already aware that the policy responses undertaken thus far have missed the point.

In the meantime, the auditing profession in the USA in particular has developed a number of points for consideration. These include the following suggestions:[8]

(i) recognition that the concept of exactitude and precision in an audit of financial statements is an illusion. Financial statements are not and cannot be as precise as investors have believed and expected them to be;

(ii) auditors need to address issues ranging from the potential problems or conflicts created by the consolidation of their industry to the need to restore their credibility to attract the best and brightest people;

(iii) the debate over rules-based and principles-based accounting is based on the false premise that the two systems are mutually exclusive. In fact they are tied together inextricably;

(iv) the balance sheet of the future will be a more flexible instrument, able to adapt to a wide variety of non-financial information, and should encompass a wider array of numbers so that users recognise when management and auditors are making judgements on transactions and asset valuations that are not, and cannot be, 'hard and fast';

(v) new audit attestation standards are needed. The current standard is appropriate for some, but not all, transactions. Going forward, auditors should be prepared to offer, and investors to accept, more limited attestations when the facts require them;

(vi) the consolidation of the accounting industry has come at a cost for the auditing profession. With fewer alternatives, companies may have few options to their current auditors. This may be a situation that is difficult to correct, but it is one that demands that regulators seek to maintain public confidence in the surviving Big Four accounting firms, and where auditing firms themselves strive to overcome the limitations created by their market dominance;

(vii) regulators and others must address the issue of auditor liability to enable the profession to forge ahead using more judgement and fever rule-based accounting approaches;

(viii) auditing firms must place appropriate value on the partners who conduct top-quality audits, not solely on the 'rainmakers' who bring in the most new business;

(ix) audit committees must be upgraded continually, so that their members are both qualified and able to challenge management and auditors alike on the reasons behind particular judgements and auditing decisions. Audit committees must reassert their pre-eminence in the audit process, and ensure that they provide full backing and support to independent external auditors as well as to internal auditors in the event of clashes with management;

(x)   accounting firms must seek out job candidates with a strong knowledge of business and finance, and provide them with top-quality continuing education and training; and

(xi)   company directors need to both financially literate and knowledgeable enough about the business itself to be able to challenge management when needed.

And, of the greatest importance, the accounting profession must recognise and expand its role, its responsibility and its dedication to fulfil its mission to provide accurate and complete information to the investing public. It is perhaps worth emphasising that these goals are applicable to accountants who are responsible for preparing corporate accounts, and to the accountants who audit those accounts. Under the professional rules applicable to auditors, they are precluded from acting as preparers of the accounts they audit.

Notes

1   The powers of administrators over the disposal and distribution of the proceeds of bankruptcy are generally much more far-reaching than the powers of an auditor of a going concern. In the latter case, the auditor has no powers of disposal over client assets: s/he may have a power of veto over the distribution of a dividend in certain circumstances prescribed by company law, and may be required to assist in putting a company into liquidation in the event that it is no longer able to pay its creditors.

2   The phenomenon of the existence of stock options and remuneration packages on such a scale as to provide the beneficiaries with short-term opportunities of life-time scale rewards has raised the rather obvious point that the risks and rewards for such beneficiaries are unlikely to be aligned to the longer-term interests or sustainability of their employer (it should be noted that the employer is the company and not the shareholders). Given that the financial and other criteria for measuring the extent of such employee rewards lies generally in the hands of those same persons who are also responsible for the establishment, maintenance, preparation and presentation of the company's accounts, it is self-evident that they will be motivated to ensure that short-term results are measured in as positive a manner as possible. The abundance of accounting-driven financial products offered by investment banks to assist employees of companies to achieve such goals, and the willingness of employees to buy them for their companies, is evidence that the financial market has responded very effectively to a clear demand. Auditors are not generally consulted on matters of remuneration levels and are not empowered to influence, intervene or prevent such practices. Nor should they, as to do so would affect their independent status. Their role in such cases is to examine whether the financial statements published by the company comply with the generally accepted accounting principles applicable to such transactions. As a result of major lobbying efforts undertaken in the early 1990s by the high technology industry sector, proposals by the accounting profession to expense such options in the accounts of public companies were abandoned as a result of overwhelming pressure from the United States Congress. It is interesting and disappointing to note that governmental pressures on accounting standard-setting bodies in the USA and the EU continue seriously to dilute the effectiveness of proposed accounting standards,

and therefore open the door to the occurrence of further accounting anomalies and failures in corporate governance.

3   It is difficult to imagine that the decision to deregulate Enron was the result of some action or initiative on the part of Enron's external auditor, Andersen. The deregulation was, however, a key point in the ensuing developments.

4   The scale and complexity of Enron's group structure as described in Andrew Cornford's chapter (Chapter 2 in this volume) is not uncommon in large-sized multinational corporations operating on a global scale. It is reasonable to ask whether it is possible, or even likely, that non-executive directors of such groups can be expected to understand and follow the business practices, financial and other reporting standards required and expected of large economic groups without becoming involved fully in the affairs of the business on a day-to-day basis.

5   It is reasonable to assume that an initiative by Andersen to increase its audit fee would have led Enron to change its auditor.

6   In an initial response to this concern, the draft 8th European Directive issued in March 2004 referred to the need for EU states to legislate on the issue of audit fees, to ensure that they are adequate for the purpose. This element was deleted from subsequent drafts of the Directive.

7   The consequences of a criminal indictment or conviction on a Certified Public Accountant (CPA) or licensed accounting firm practising before the Securities and Exchange Commission (SEC) are that, in the case of an indictment, the SEC would be free to initiate proceedings relating to the conduct alleged in the indictment and, after a full hearing, suspend SEC practice rights based on findings that the underlying conduct was 'improper professional conduct'. Under SEC rules, an individual accountant or an accounting firm convicted of a crime of 'moral turpitude', or whose license to practice accounting has been suspended or revoked in any US state, will be suspended automatically from practising before the SEC (which includes giving opinions on financial statements filed by SEC registrants). Clearly, obstruction of justice would constitute a crime of 'moral turpitude' and would subject the convicted party to suspension. In the case of Andersen, it would appear that an important number of its clients became fearful that if they did not make the change to another auditor they could be caught without an audit firm for the year that had already started, or at least that their choice would be very limited.

8   For a more detailed description of these suggestions, see the American Assembly Report, *The Future of the Accounting Profession*, 103rd American Assembly, Columbia University, 11 November 2003.

10

Enron Revisited: What Is a Board Member to Do?

Beth Krasna

Given the evolution of the role of the Director of the Board and the increased liability attached to the position, in particular since Sarbanes-Oxley became law, it is important to know what degree of freedom a Board member could have in a situation such as Enron. The Permanent Subcommittee on Investigations of the Committee on Governmental Affairs of the United States Senate published their report, entitled *The Role of the Board of Directors in Enron's Collapse*, on 8 July 2002. The Subcommittee examined in detail the role of the Enron Board in the company's bankruptcy, and held the Board accountable for the company's downfall. The Subcommittee believes that the Enron Board not only failed their shareholders and employees, but also did not acknowledge their own responsibility in the collapse. The main findings with respect to the role of the Enron Board of Directors are regrouped in the report under the following six headings: high risk accounting; inappropriate conflicts of interest; extensive undisclosed off-the-books activity; excessive compensation; lack of independence; and fiduciary failure.

A closer look at the six findings from a Board member's perspective, to see what possibilities of action are available, taking into account the general responsibilities and activities of Board members, their best practices and freedom of movement, is discussed below under the short summary of the findings, extracted from the report.

High risk accounting

The Enron Board knowingly allowed Enron to engage in high risk accounting practices.

In order to better control the operations and financial results of a company, Boards today need to be organised in order to be more efficient. The first aspect is Board composition, as a variety of competencies are needed to understand and develop the company's business. No large company today can afford to elect Board members who do not have extensive business experience, knowledge of Board regulations and best practices, and with considerable expertise in finance and accounting. It is also necessary to have a good understanding of, if not experience in, the company's market, to be able to challenge management and the strategy of the company constructively. Planning for replacement of members retiring or stepping down has become a more serious and important activity than previously, where Board members often co-opted their business acquaintances, and this exercise is usually undertaken with a view to the evolution of the company's business. Yearly evaluation of a Board's efficiency and the individual members is now becoming a mainstream practice. This exercise does allow individual directors to express concerns or doubts in certain areas, ask for information sessions on certain aspects of the company's business, and propose the inclusion of needed expertise to balance the portfolio of available competencies on the Board. Many Boards develop a matrix table showing the available competencies on one axis, and their distribution among the directors on the other. This allows for a good overview of the strengths and weaknesses of the Board, and makes it easier to see what expertise might need to be strengthened or added to the group. Many companies have started to use headhunters to generate and access the best possible people for the defined profile.

Once these competencies are available, most Boards create committees which meet at more frequent intervals than the full Board, and discuss items at greater depth. They also have access to the executives responsible for preparing the reports. This does allow for some interaction between the directors and management, and gives the directors a chance to get to know and evaluate the people some levels down from the CEO. Regular interaction and open discussions during these committee meetings allow for doubts and concerns to be expressed on both sides. On the one hand, management can provide additional information to assuage the directors' concerns, and on the other, the directors can listen for dissenting views and unease among management. This also provides an additional check on the information that the CEO brings to the Board.

Commonly, companies will have a permanent Finance Committee, an Audit Committee, a Compensation Committee, a Nominating Committee and sometimes an Executive Committee, a Strategy Committee and a Risk Committee (the latter is sometimes included in the Finance Committee). *Ad hoc* committees are usually created as needed (a committee to choose a replacement of the CEO, for example). These committees are usually chaired by the independent directors who have the most experience in the specific area under discussion. The Finance and Audit Committees should be composed of directors with good training and expertise in financial management and accounting, and structured finance. The Finance Committee usually oversees and approves large transactions and investment opportunities. The Audit Committee reviews the accounting and compliance programmes, approves the financial statements and reports, and is the main contact with the internal audit group and the outside audit company. The Board is ultimately responsible to the shareholders, and must then decide carefully as a group what decisional authority it delegates to the committees, and what will only be prepared and reviewed in the committees, then brought to the full Board for decision.

If the Finance and Audit Committees are composed correctly of experienced directors, they should not accept transactions that they do not fully understand. Each director can request more information, coaching sessions or an independent opinion of the external auditors regarding the proposed transaction. If the company is moving towards using instruments that the directors inexperienced in – hedging or derivatives, for example – they can ask to be briefed by a qualified member of the external auditors, who will not only explain the transaction, but also give an opinion on the appropriateness and risk level of the transaction. If the company is moving towards using these instruments on a regular basis, the Board might want to include a director who is familiar with and experienced in the subject.

The Audit Committee is the main contact point for the external auditors to reach the Board. The Audit Committee should review all large consulting contracts for conflict of interest, but in particular those mandates related to the external auditor and which might influence its degree of independence. In a perfect world, it would be optimal to use one firm as external auditors and another accounting company for consulting services. Management might be tempted to ask the external auditors for an opinion on a proposed transaction or on change in accounting policy, but this can create a problem – for example, if the auditors participate in the design of the transaction. It will then be difficult for them to indicate that this might be risky if they were involved in designing the deal. The committee needs to look out for this conflict of interest and keep management informed about this concern. If management tries to hide behind the auditors' opinion, then the committee can always ask for a second opinion from another firm before approving the transaction. This said, the committee should always listen to the external auditors, and should challenge them to make their position clear. They are not only paid to review the financial statements for the shareholders, or a change in accounting policy for the Board, but their comments on detected weak points described in their management report can be of great help for the company to improve, and raise the necessary red flags for the Board of Directors.

Boards today must try to define a company's risk profile and match it to its strategy and mission. There is most often a risk/reward ratio, and with little risk there might be no reward. But there are acceptable levels of risk a business can support that do not jeopardize the going concern. The level of acceptable risk in the various businesses should be discussed, quantified and decided upon. Worst-case scenario planning should be carried out to determine maximum risk. The Board must require the tracking and monitoring of all of the risks of the company, and the establishment of regular risk reports, which will be reviewed by the appropriate committee, if not by the whole Board. If the transactions a company is carrying out are so complex that management is not able to provide an adequate risk report, then the company should probably not be involved in these transactions. It is the Board's responsibility to ensure that the company is able to manage its risks, and to stand up to management when it believes managers are not taking the interests of the company into account. When positions between management and Board differ greatly, or when positions between the directors differ, it is not uncommon to bring the issue to the shareholders' meeting for a decision; this happens quite often in the case of company takeovers. If their views are not being followed or their concerns addressed, directors can always resign. The outside stakeholders should view a director's resignation as a sign of dissent, and demand that the reasons for the resignation are explained.

In large companies it is now also common to have an internal audit group, which reports directly to the Board and not to the CEO. Again, it is usually the Audit Committee that has the most interaction with this group, approves the annual internal audit plan, and reviews the reports and follow-up. It is the Board or the Audit Committee that fixes the compensation of the internal audit group, which is thus independent of management interference and pressure. Internal audit groups are very useful to review departments and processes, and suggest areas of improvement or deviation from internal rules and regulations. They can raise the red flag on dubious practices, perceived risks, and even misdemeanors and fraud. If a Board member has requested information that management has failed to supply, then the director should insist on the delivery of this information. If, after repeated requests, the information is still not forthcoming, the question should be raised as to 'cannot or will not?'. If management is not able to furnish the information because the internal system cannot provide it, the director can review the request in the light of the necessity versus the effort needed to provide it and, if it is a priority, request management to implement this part of the system. If the director suspects that management does not want to deliver the information because it does not care to disclose it, then the director can request an internal audit to find out why the information is being withheld. As with the external auditors' reports, the findings of the internal auditors should be reviewed with the greatest of care, and all high-risk areas given full Board attention and addressed with an action plan to lower the risk, if not eradicate the issue totally.

Inappropriate conflicts of interest

Despite clear conflicts of interest, the Enron Board of Directors approved an unprecedented arrangement allowing Enron's Chief Financial Officer to establish and operate the LJM private equity funds which transacted business with Enron and profited at Enron's expense. The Board exercised inadequate oversight of LJM transaction and compensation controls and failed to protect Enron shareholders from unfair dealing.

It is generally accepted that, when an executive accepts a full-time position with a company, then s/he will devote all his/her efforts to this activity. Most companies have rules and regulations that determine what a company executive might accept as a 'side activity', or this is defined in the code of conduct of the company. Senior executives who sit on the Boards of affiliated companies are generally not compensated, as looking after the interests of their employer is part of their main job.

Some companies require their senior executives to declare all other remunerated activities, and to request authorisation to accept, say, a Board position in another, unrelated company. Some companies in Europe even require executives to give up any remuneration they might receive from authorised, but unrelated, activities performed during company hours. This is to ensure that executives will not have any conflict of interest between the different activities, or favour one activity over another for personal gain. Most regulations or codes of conduct determine that the acceptance by senior executives of activities in other companies is usually subject to the authorisation of the Board of Directors. Internal controls that could be part of the internal audit activities, or part of the compliance group, can be used to detect irregularities in the application of the rules and regulations, or code of conduct. Care should be taken to protect the reporting of misconduct, as well as to give it adequate attention. It takes courage to stand up and denounce a practice, and if corrective measures are not taken after the reporting, whistle-blowers will not expose themselves to potential retaliation by their superiors and/or peers.

There can be cases where the Board authorises, and even encourages, a senior executive to accept an outside position, such as a directorship of another company; this could be at a point when the position would reflect positively on the executive, and thus also on the company; or when the executive could learn a lot in this position, which would benefit the company indirectly. These cases can usually be authorised by the Board without necessitating a waiver of the codes of conduct. Board directors and management must set an example and 'walk the talk'. Waivers of the codes of conduct should never be granted, because the message this gives to the rest of the company is that the Board and the management are above the law and do not believe in the code of conduct. And if management does not respect it – why, then, should the rank and file? So the Board's and management's credibility disappear, and the company culture accepts disrespect of the rules. The Board must ensure that the senior executives are aligned with the goals of the company, and act in its best interests. If the case is very complex, an outside opinion can be sought, but all decisions should be postponed until this opinion is received. Conflict of interest situations can arise, and must be fully disclosed and managed. Even though pressure from management might be high, and an urgency situation initiated, the Board should never accept a situation where a conflict of interest has been created deliberately, and where the other entity will benefit to the detriment of the company. Standing up to management on this type of issue can be both unpopular and unpleasant, but must be done by the independent directors as part of the trust conferred on them by their election by shareholders. If a sole director or a minority of the directors object to the authorisation, but the majority vote to let the senior executive go ahead, these individuals should insist that their objection be noted in the minutes of the meeting, and that some form of monitoring of the case be implemented.

Extensive undisclosed off-the-books activity

The Enron Board of Directors knowingly allowed Enron to conduct billions of dollars in off-the-books activity to make its financial condition appear better than it was and failed to ensure adequate public disclosure of material off-the-books liabilities that contributed to Enron's collapse.

Off-the-books liabilities can arise through several types of operation, such as non-consolidation of subsidiaries with intercompany loans; guarantees given to other subsidiaries, other companies or banks; and the use of structured financial instruments such as complex derivatives transactions. Off-the-book financing is anything that is not equity or debt financed; it can be legitimate and acceptable, and represent a rather low risk to the company. However, when used to finance operations or expansion, and when there is an incomplete transfer of risk to the other entity, then the company will eventually be liable, so it will be necessary to track contingent liabilities at regular intervals and to disclose all material off-the-books liabilities in the footnotes of the financial statements. Obligations that are not on the books to guarantee bank loans to unconsolidated entities such as subsidiaries, joint ventures, partnerships or unrelated companies such as institutional investors, can totally destroy shareholder wealth if things go wrong. Lease contracts also belong to this category, as the value of the assets might not cover adequately the debt financing that has been removed from the books (the leasing of aircraft in the Swissair bankruptcy is a case in point).

The Board of Directors must thus review all equity and debt of an investment nature, or ensure that all these investments are followed by management, and that the appropriate controls for all these transactions sit in the correct divisions. The consolidation perimeter should be reviewed at least once a year, and all unconsolidated entities categorised. The auditors should be asked to give an opinion as to the adequacy of the perimeter. The Board of

Directors is responsible to the shareholders, who will take the financial statements at face value; so disclosure of all material liabilities and obligations in the footnotes must be reviewed, discussed and approved by the Board.

If the transactions are so numerous and so complex that a review by the Board is not possible, the Board must ensure that the company has a structure in place to monitor and manage these risks, and that this structure is capable of providing a picture to the Board of the global risk to the company. If the risks cannot be quantified, they can't be managed, and the Directors should be wary of conducting business in this way, and insist on the company acquiring the necessary expertise to manage their risks. Risk assessment is not a precise science, so there is some leeway for interpretation, depending on the ongoing situation and expected evolution. It is customary for the Risk Committee to review the scenario planning prepared by the company's risk group, and the worst-case alternative will usually give the maximum risk that might arise. The work of the risk group should be reviewed by the external auditors, who should express an opinion for the Board, not only from a compliance to regulatory directives point of view, but also from an adequacy and benchmarking position. The Board must question the external auditors as to the current practices in the company's industry, and to their assessment of the company's risk profile. Pressure from management to improve the balance sheet for short-term reasons should be scrutinised carefully, and the possible impact evaluated. The Board of Directors should keep in mind a clear view of their mandate, and their fiduciary responsibility to the shareholders and employees in the long term.

Excessive compensation

The Enron Board of Directors approved excessive compensation for company executives, failed to monitor the cumulative cash drain caused by Enron's 2000 annual bonus and performance unit plans, and failed to monitor or halt abuse by Board Chairman and Chief Executive Officer Kenneth Lay of a company-financed multi-million dollar, personal credit line.

Executive compensation appears on the Board agenda at least once a year, and the desire to retain and provide the proper incentives for good management is strong and justified. The problem is that the CEO proposes the salary increases and bonuses of senior management, following which, the CEO's compensation will naturally be higher. The CEO thus does have a conflict of interest: on the one hand s/he wants to promote the expectations of his/her team, as well as his/her own progression, but on the other hand must balance this with the need to improve the operating profit of the company. This conflict of interest can be intense if several members of the Board hold executive positions, which is one of the reasons why shareholder groups are pushing for independent directors on the Boards of large companies.

There are several ways for the Board to judge the level of incentives: first they can request the human resource department to provide a benchmark of compensations from the previous year in a corresponding industry and in the geographical area. This data is available because the compensation of top management is disclosed in most annual reports of publicly-traded companies. For companies that are not publicly-traded, the human resource director can attempt to benchmark by asking his/her peers to share this type of information. If not obtainable otherwise, a small study can be requested from a headhunter company, as these organisations usually track salaries and compensations; however, they usually quote on the high side. The Board can then align compensation with the company's culture and values – and how they want to position their employment practices in the industry. When reviewing the CEO's and management's compensation packages, the Board should request the previous year's package – that is, all forms of remuneration broken down, including fees, such as Board fees, from related and unrelated companies; the benchmark figures; the company's results; the individual results of the area for which the executive is responsible; and the CEO's evaluation of the executive, based objectively on the attainment of his/her yearly objectives.

The granting of credit facilities to management is not part of the compensation package, and does not usually depend on individual performance or company results. Most companies have rules and regulations in place that cover this type of benefit to employees. Employee credit lines create huge problems for the company when the employee resigns or is fired, and with the exception of the financial industry, most companies are not in the business of lending money to their employees, and actively discourage, if not forbid, it. There are exceptions in European countries where there is a mandatory pension scheme, and transferring from one country to another can have a negative impact on future benefits; this type of loan is usually negotiated upon hiring. All credit lines to employees should be mentioned on the balance sheet (or in the footnotes if guarantees are given to banks for the employees), and disclosed in the notes as part of the executive compensation description.

Furthermore, the Board must take into account the interests of the shareholders. The total variable compensation package of the CEO and management should be compared to the amount of dividends the company intends to distribute to the shareholders. There must be some fairness in this ratio, and it would be unseemly to favour the executives over the shareholders, as management is compensated for their work by the fixed portion of their salary. Originally, the variable part of the remuneration of the executives was to let them share in the business cycles of the company, and to profit along with the shareholders in the exceptionally good years, or else to recompense true value creation. However, variable compensation that exceeds value creation in fact destroys shareholder wealth. Shareholder activists are becoming more vocal about this subject, and many countries already have regulatory guidelines that require individual disclosure of the compensation of the top executives (fixed, variable and in the form of shares, share options and credit). Now that disclosure is mandatory, shareholders have sufficient information to question the level of executive compensation. In some cases, institutonal investors have spoken out at shareholders' annual general meetings against the high amounts of compensation (the Disney company being a good example of this); and some people think that it will only be a matter of time before a shareholder meeting will vote to require that Board and executive compensation be submitted to shareholders for approval. It would be difficult not to see this trend as a compensation for the failure of some Boards in their fiduciary duties to shareholders, and the outrage of the public at large at the levels of salary paid to certain executives.

Lack of independence

The independence of the Enron Board of Directors was compromised by financial ties between the company and certain Board members. The Board also failed to ensure the independence of the company's auditor, allowing Andersen to provide internal audit and consulting services while serving as Enron's outside auditor.

Independence of Board members means that there should be no financial connection whatever between the members and the company other than their Board compensation. Types of relationships that would compromise independence would be directors receiving consultancies or fees from the company; directors being employed by or sitting on the Board of charities and foundations that receive donations from the company; or directors being employed by a third party that derives financial benefit from doing business with the company. If directors were engaged in these types of practices, they might not wish to challenge management in order not to lose the side benefits. They would thus effectively become part of the management team, and will have problems in exercising independent judgement. Boards should be strong, well-functioning work groups whose members trust and challenge one another and engage directly with senior management on issues facing the company. This will be difficult to do if the truly independent members suppose that some of the other directors have conflicts of interest, and suspect their position on certain issues.

Basically, the higher the position in a company, the more transparency is required. Some Boards ask their members to fill out a form every year, where they disclose the Boards they are on (profit and non-profit, charities and foundations); their consultancy contracts (with all parties); the associations and interest groups to which they belong; their official or political functions; the environment of their current employer, and his/her eventual relations with the company; and family connections who might have a particular relationship with the company. These completed forms are then distributed to all the Board members, so that in case of conflict of interest, a process can be put in place ensuring that the decision-making is not affected (for example, the Board member concerned could leave the room while this point is being debated, so that s/he does not influence the discussions). Once the standards of behavior have been set, it is easier to measure compliance with them.

In most cases, it is the Audit Committee that is responsible for tracking these conflicts of interest, and monitoring compliance with the guidelines. It is also the Audit Committee that can obtain information regarding conflicts of interest that would lead to loss of objectivity and independence of the external auditors. The Audit Committee should review annually the list of the main consulting mandates (the top ten or twenty), with particular attention being paid to the mandates of the external auditors. It is becoming increasingly common to split auditing and consulting work between different firms to avoid any loss of objectivity, as it would be difficult for auditors to audit their own work – for example, to design a complex financial transaction – and then to claim that it is risky accounting. The Audit Committee must insist on obtaining a list of the main consulting mandates company-wide, as often these are given by individual divisions in large companies and no one is responsible for tracking the global picture. The Audit Committee should also question in detail the changes in senior personnel that the external auditors have working on their account, to ensure that they are not being removed at management's request because of the auditors disapproval of company practices. The Audit Committee must also question the auditors about their level of confidence in management's practices and procedures. The Board cannot claim ignorance of these issues; it is their job to obtain the necessary information for the oversight of the company, and this role is often delegated to the Audit Committee, who works more closely with the external auditors, the internal audit group, and the compliance group.

Fiduciary failure – a Board is not a team

The Enron Board of Directors failed to safeguard Enron shareholders and contributed to the collapse of the seventh largest public company in the United States, by allowing Enron to engage in high risk accounting, inappropriate conflict of interest transaction, extensive undisclosed off-the-books activities, and excessive executive compensation. The Board witnessed numerous indications of questionable practices by Enron management over several years, but chose to ignore them to the detriment of Enron shareholders, employees and business associates.

When a company such as Enron (or Swissair, WorldCom or Tyco) fails in such a fashion and in such a short period of time, a lot of effort is spent on trying to understand how this could have happened, and what type of oversight could ensure that it will not happen again. The directors of these companies are often highly regarded professional individuals with appropriate skills, expertise and experience, but for some reason, things did not work when they were united as a group. A Board is not a team. There should be respect and a common goal between the members, but they need to keep their independence and individual competencies focused on exercising their oversight role. There must be a certain chemistry between the members that allows for respect and trust to flourish, for the sharing of difficult information and the working out of a common solution, but that also allows for the need and right to challenge and question other members' positions or the information provided by management. There is a fine line between dissent and disloyalty, and this must be managed. Achieving this climate of trust, yet maintaining critical objectivity is probably the most difficult and important role that the Chairperson of the Board plays, and goes beyond the careful selection of the individual Board members.

The distribution of roles is neither rigid nor fixed, so the Board and the individual members must play a variety of roles as the company evolves and progresses. Depending on various internal and external conditions (for example, effectiveness of management, short- or long-term perspectives, insignificant to significant changes in externalities), the role of the Board will be shifting between coaching, steering, auditing and supervising. The Board as a whole will have to balance the need to focus on external demands while continuously improving internal Board processes. Yearly evaluations by the individual members of the efficiency of the Board and of their own performance, as well as that of their colleagues and chairperson, allows for the correction of attitudes and behaviour and the refocusing of their roles and objectives. Enforcing accountability of the individual members can be done by their peers. This is important, and the board should not be above yearly evaluations, as it is difficult for individuals to learn and improve without feedback. Recognising and attempting to anticipate changes in externalities that affect the company and the Board's governance focus should now be the concern of all members.

The sense of responsibility of Board members is inversely proportional to the size of the Board, and many companies are reducing the number of directors. Regular attendance is no longer a problem, but rather a condition of acceptance of the position. It is now a commonly held view that strong corporate governance is best exercised by a highly experience, diverse and wise group of independent directors governing the company on behalf of its long-term shareholders. As the requirements rise for this type of position, as well as the responsibility and level of accountability, there is a trend towards 'professionalizing' the job of director. This is being done not only on a more careful selection basis, but can also be seen through the development of director education that is now being offered by selected professional bodies as well as some business schools.

Given the increasing liability exposure of Directors and media coverage of the bad cases, the passive role of Boards faced with a strong CEO is becoming a thing of the past. Individual Board members have a duty to speak up and insist that best practices be implemented and followed, and need to make their views heard during meetings. If they hold a dissenting position they can always insist that it be stated explicitly in the minutes. Ultimately, if they are not capable of convincing the rest of the Board and believe that the company is engaging in risky or doubtful practices, they have the option to resign. Resignations of board members are often signs of dissent and are being scrutinised more closely by large shareholder groups, who should not only be concerned about appointing their representatives, but also about their views of the level of governance being exercised.

11
How to Restore Trust in Financial Markets?

Hans J. Blommestein[1]

Introduction

Without trust, financial markets cannot function efficiently. Trust and integrity depend to an important degree on the reputation of financial markets to generate reliable valuations of companies and business ventures. This perspective makes clear why the integrity of the gatekeepers of the public trust to vouch for accurate and reliable information about public companies is at the heart of the proper functioning of financial markets. And since the 'garbage in, garbage out' principle also prevails in financial markets, public trust in the functioning of financial markets has declined as a result of major financial reporting scandals involving Enron, Tyco, WorldCom, Parmalat and others. Also, massive overvaluations of equity that occurred in the second half of the 1990s and in the early 2000s have been singled out as being caused by misinformation and manipulation of financial results (Jensen, 2002). More generally, when information about the operation of public companies is false, misleading or opaque, trust in financial markets is likely to be affected adversely. This gives financial market participants a stake in the disclosure of timely and meaningful information, including by assuring that the quality of financial reporting by public companies is as high as possible. And this in turn puts the spotlight on the role of the gatekeepers of the public trust, in particular accounting firms, banks, rating agencies, supervisors and regulators.

This contribution addresses the key questions of why public trust is in decline, why agency relations have broken down within companies and within gatekeepers, and how trust in financial markets can best be restored. It will be argued that, in answering these questions, it will be necessary to go beyond recent corporate scandals. Gatekeepers of the public trust play a central role in modern, complex markets. However, we shall show that they are facing extraordinary new challenges that have not only reduced their effectiveness in safeguarding public trust but also in a number of cases have resulted in spectacular governance failures. Against this backdrop, we shall also argue that, for financial markets to continue to function effectively and efficiently, gatekeepers of the public trust will need to tackle a number of key structural obstacles associated with the new business landscape, and in particular the (consequences of the) downward shift in ethical standards.

Public information, valuations and financial market efficiency

A key function of financial markets is the valuation of public companies and the debt instruments issued by these companies. A related function is the pricing of financial instruments used in connection with the risk profile of public enterprises such as derivatives. These functions require that financial markets collect and process a great multitude of information. An important part of this public information flow is produced by the public companies themselves in the form of audited and non-audited financial statements, quarterly projections of profits and cash flow, and so on. No one expects that financial markets are perfect processors and evaluators of information, but investors and other market participants may expect that, more often than not, financial market valuations are reliable. We also expect that financial markets are (weakly) efficient.

The concept of market efficiency is useful to clarify the link between public information and market valuations. Market efficiency – made precise in the efficient market hypothesis (EMH), formulated by Eugene Fama in 1970 – suggests that, at any given time, prices fully reflect all publicly available information on a particular stock and/or market. The nature of information does not have to be limited to financial news and research alone; indeed, information about political, economic and social events, combined with how investors perceive such information, whether true or rumoured, will be reflected in financial market prices. Thus prices only respond to information that is publicly available, while stock prices incorporate in an unbiased way all publicly available information regarding a company's value. However, market efficiency does not say that all financial instruments are valued precisely – 'only that at any point in time we cannot tell from publicly available information whether a particular firm is over- or under-valued' (Jensen, 2004, p. 2). But market efficiency can be used as a bench-mark for assessing mistaken valuations in the sense that insiders (managers and others) can determine in an efficient market (using superior information that is not publicly available) whether their company is over- or undervalued.

When public information is reliable and accurate, it can be trusted. In efficient markets with reliable information, systemic under- or overvalua-tions are less likely to occur. Systemic under- or overvaluations are more likely to occur in inefficient markets, especially when the available (public) information is not reliable. Unreliable public information is information that is distorted, manipulated, misleading or plain wrong. Information can be wrong as a result of a (honest) mistaken belief shared by most market participants. For example, societies more often than not overvalue important innovations – the dot.com bubble being a recent historical example.[2] We shall not study this source of overvaluation here, but focus on the causes and consequences of misleading, distorted or manipulated information.

The central role of the gatekeepers of public trust in the new financial landscape

Trust in financial markets is dependent on a complex web of laws, regulations, supervisory procedures, institutions and market practices. In this web, the primary role of the gatekeepers of public trust is to make sure that public information is as reliable as possible. This role is crucial for the efficient functioning of modern, complex financial markets, as reliable public information constitutes the basis of savings and investment decisions. To that end, gatekeepers of the public trust act as reputational intermediaries (Gilson and Kraakman, 1984). Among the important institutions are accounting firms, securities firms, commercial and investment banks, law firms, rating agencies and exchanges. The key financial market function of these intermediary institutions is to vouch for the integrity and quality of information, transactions, procedures and financial instruments on the basis of their reputation.[3] By acting as the gatekeepers of public trust, they form the core of a strong market framework for protecting investors. For example, many investors rely on financial statements audited by a reputable accountant, shares underwritten by reliable investment bankers, prospectuses drafted by honest securities counsels, and new issues listed on a reputable exchange.

Why have the gatekeepers of public trust failed?

Against the backdrop of the many corporate scandals worldwide, there are prima facie indications that some of these gatekeepers have failed in a fundamental way in safeguarding public trust. At first, it was the accounting profession that came under heavy fire, even resulting in the demise of one the major global accounting firms, and leaving just four major players. But then attention shifted to the financial sector. Banks soon became a target of investigations concerning their role in the financing[4] and advising of companies that were accused of manipulating their books. The role of bankers in initial public offering (IPO) allocations also came under scrutiny, leading to criminal investigations. This was followed by accusations of conflicts of interest and lapses in the regulatory duties of stock exchanges. Then it was the turn of the mutual fund industry. At the time of writing, the insurance industry is the latest part of the financial sector to have come under the intense scrutiny of regulators and prosecutors. As a result, the reputation of auditors, accountants, bankers, regulators, mutual funds, exchanges, insurance companies and other gatekeepers of the interests of the investing public have been (seriously) damaged. This raises the follow-up question: why have they failed?

Leaving aside highly personalised situations or very special individual cases of fraud or greed, the focus in this section is on the identification of structural reasons why gatekeepers have failed. Although we shall use the Enron case to illustrate several points, our analysis goes far beyond the Enron saga. An important conclusion is that overvaluations were not under all circumstances the result of ill intent or neglect of fiduciary duty by managers, boards of companies or the gatekeepers of public trust. More particularly, it will be shown that a number of structural changes in the new financial and business landscape have made the work of the various gatekeepers much more challenging than in an earlier era. Four (in part interconnected) structural developments stand out.

A downward shift in ethical standards

The ongoing scandals in the insurance industry have much in common with the breakdown in corporate governance systems in corporations, banks, exchanges and mutual funds, amplified by (or reflected in) accounting irregularities and excessive pay of top management since the start of the 2000s. Control by investors (shareholders) of the directors of companies was clearly ineffective, while many of the gatekeepers of trust failed in their core duties. As a result, at the time of writing, financial market integrity is under great stress.

The threat to the integrity of markets causes uncertainty, increases risk and raises the cost of capital. Urgent action is therefore needed to restore confidence in financial markets. What to do? The widespread failure of corporate governance systems seems to argue in favour of a redesign of corporate governance rules[5] and/or a stricter compliance with existing ones. Michael Jensen has identified breakdowns in agency relationships within companies and within gatekeepers as the leading causes of excessively high stock valuations that in turn have led to 'massive destruction of corporate and social value' (Jensen, 2004). He argues that agency relations are flawed because of counter-productive, target-based corporate budget and compensation systems. These systems provide adverse incentives to manipulate both the setting of targets and how to meet them, and encourage an 'earnings management game' with the capital markets (Jensen, 2001). Jensen's studies provide important insights into the mechanics of recent corporate governance failures. The main objective of this contribution is to take one step back by answering the following fundamental questions. Why did agency systems break down in the first place? Why were rules, regulations and codes of conduct changed, broken or discarded? The breaking of corporate governance rules and financial market rules and conventions stem in large part from a fundamental shift in ethical standards in business and society at large. It is true that recent 'excesses' are related in part to 'normal' business behaviour during boom times such as the 'roaring 1990s'. Excess, greed and the hunt for fast money always end with a crisis or a major 'bust', followed by (political pressures for) regulatory interventions and a number of high-profile criminal court cases. They are circular phenomena – returning repeatedly.

But evidence is starting to accumulate that on top of this 'history repeating itself', a deeper transformation of business attitudes has also occurred. Companies are changing the way in which they operate in increasingly fluid marketplaces, with new opportunities but also with new moral temptations. In this emerging, fast-moving business environment with its growing trend of individualism, whereby traditional (moral) restraining influences on the behaviour of people have become largely obsolete, unethical behaviour is likely to flourish. Many new rules have yet to be written for doing business in the new techno-market order, while enforcement of existing rules has become more problematic because of the lack of moral guidance. The spread of secular ideas is weakening the traditional influence of religion. Codes of conduct promulgated by associations for doing business in specific, local areas have become less effective or even irrelevant in a global market place.

The information and communication revolution has created new opportunities for honest individuals but, unfortunately, also for those with looser morals and, of course, for outright criminals. There is an emerging new business climate in which increasingly moral standards and associated procedures that were considered previously to be ethically dubious, are now considered 'normal' and acceptable. This shift in ethical standards inspired even business-friendly magazines (well before the crash of tech stocks in 2000) to focus on 'doing business the dot.com way' by questioning the ethical standards of the standard operating procedures in the brave new world of the Internet. Other business insiders have pointed out that the desire to become instantaneously rich in this brave new world has also affected the behaviour of consulting firms, law firms, and even executive search firms. These service providers have been accused of (potential) conflicts of interest because they are getting involved directly in the 'new economy' companies by accepting equity instead of cash for their services. This behaviour is the result of a paradigm shift in the brave new business landscape in the form of a lowering of ethical standards. This paradigm shift has a negative influence on breakdowns in agency relations within both companies and gatekeepers.

Creative and aggressive accounting[6]

The use of creative but questionable accounting practices inflated revenues of Enron and many other companies. Leaving aside the cases of pure fraud, why did many companies engage in new, sometimes highly questionable, accounting practices? To an important degree it reflected probably the greater complexity of many of today's business concepts, operations and management tools. The new business landscape is characterised by the extensive use of new technologies, including the use of innovative financing techniques. Complexity creates opacity, while the management of risk becomes more challenging. Meaningful disclosure of corporations' risk-management tools and positions, and performance indicators of new types of business operations (for example, Internet-based companies) has therefore become a great challenge. Traditional accounting standards have not kept pace with these developments. Financial analysts have pointed out that Enron's accounting structures were opaque to the market (Ross, 2002). 'Aggressive accounting' was used to keep losses and risk off Enron's balance sheet by the extensive use of offshore special purpose vehicles (SPVs – see further discussion below).

In this increasingly complex and opaque business landscape, accountants are facing extraordinary challenges in fulfilling their essential gatekeeper's role of public trust. Audit quality and audit oversight have emerged as key policy issues, and auditor firms will have to respond in an effective and credible way to show that they are capable of dealing with a more complex task. Accounting standards need to be updated so as to capture the sometimes very complex risk profiles of companies. Audit procedures need to become more effective by incorporating these updated accounting concepts (including appropriate risk accounting rules). Audits of companies with complex organisation and financial structures need to result in reliable and transparent insights of corporate activities and risks. To provide additional confidence in companies and markets, regular audits may have to be supplemented by ethical audits that capture the integrity of business operations, especially those with highly complex organisational structures.[7] Companies subject to those more rigorous or extensive audits and disclosure standards may be rewarded by attracting extra customers, and face lower spreads when issuing financial instruments.

Banking in the new business landscape

Banks soon became a target of investigations concerning their role in the financing and advising of companies that were accused of manipulating their books. The role of bankers in IPO allocations also came under scrutiny, including criminal investigations. The scrutiny of banks by supervisors and others is justified because of their central gatekeeper's role. They are like spiders in the web of listed companies, brokers, exchanges, institutional investors and other financial market players. Accordingly, they are expected to play a central and active gatekeeper's role to monitor the behaviour of their clients and other counter-parties. In fact, there are indications that society expects them to take on increased gatekeeper responsibilities in the new business landscape. This means that banks have to bear greater monitoring responsibilities as part of their (expanded) gatekeeper role in the brave new business landscape. This view is a sea-change compared to the way that banks used to operate in the past. In the words of the Vice-Chairman of J. P. Morgan, 'Our view historically was that our clients and their accountants were responsible for the clients' proper accounting and disclosure of transactions.'[8] However, the greater complexities of markets and clients have made this (expanded) gatekeeper role more demanding. Moreover, many banks have failed in their (expanded) gatekeeper role (Blommestein, 2003–4).

More complex organisational structures and risk profiles

Over the past few decades, corporations (including financial companies) have acquired spectacular new tools to manage all sorts of risks. Securitisation helps a company to manage the risk of concentrated exposure by transferring some of it outside the firm. Companies can obtain liquidity and reduce funding costs by pooling assets and issuing marketable financial instruments. But moving assets off the balance sheet and into SPVs also have potential drawbacks in the form of greater complexity, more opaqueness, higher agency costs, and significant risk residual interests retained by the company.[9] In short, although securitisation is an important risk management tool, it generates its own risks and potentially reduces transparency. Additional steps are needed to overcome these adverse side-effects.

Derivatives are another class of new financial instruments that is employed by an increasing number of companies. These tools are used to manage more effectively and efficiently the risk exposures of companies, including derivative contracts to deal with market risk (exposure to price fluctuations in currency, interest rates, commodity, energy and so on) and credit risk. For the latter risk, a new market (the market for credit derivatives) has developed at an astounding pace. Credit derivatives allow financial and non-financial firms to reduce their exposures to particular borrowers or counter-parties more efficiently.

But derivatives also make companies and markets more complex and potentially more opaque. For example, credit derivatives allow financial companies to achieve a more diversified credit portfolio by acquiring exposure to borrowers with which they do not have a lending relationship. Another source of complexity and opaqueness is where new financial instruments have been used extensively in tandem with highly complex organisational structures. For example, Enron's basic business strategy was to modernise markets (first energy, and later steel, telecommunications, the Internet and so on) by the introduction of financial instruments and derivatives for trading and hedging (Ross, 2002). The strategy was implemented by using offshore SPVs. There was a great deal of leverage inherent in the resulting highly complex organisational structure. Complex derivatives have also been used to paint a better picture of the financial health of companies. Reportedly, self-referenced credit-linked notes (CLNs) have been used to this effect.[10]

Further improvements in information and communications technology, the fast pace of financial innovations and the evolving science of risks management, will allow companies 'to use almost limitless configurations of products and services and sophisticated financial structures'.[11] In this new, more complex business landscape, outsiders (including some of the gate-keepers)[12] will have ever more difficulty understanding the operations and risk profile of the larger and more complex organisations. Clearly, gatekeepers of the public trust (in particular auditors, banks, banking supervisors and rating agencies) have a special monitoring role to play here. At the same time, greater complexities and opaqueness have made gatekeepers' activities more challenging.[13]

A fundamental response is needed to restore public trust

Enron and other corporate scandals have acted as wake-up calls that trust in gatekeepers and financial markets cannot be taken for granted. Analysts have highlighted various conflicts-of-interest situations for accountants, security analysts, company lawyers, mutual funds, exchanges and banks. The loss of confidence in the integrity of the gatekeepers of the public trust has affected market trust. Indeed, repeated assaults on the integrity of markets have damaged trust in financial markets, causing great uncertainty, increased risk and rises in the cost of capital.

The downward shift in ethical standards (in business and society at large) means that we cannot simply rely on more aggressive enforcement by regulators and prosecutors. A more fundamental response to the paradigm shift in ethical standards is needed as well. In addressing the loss of trust in financial markets it is necessary to go beyond the recent spectacular fraud cases and other irregularities.[14] To regain public trust it is essential that corporations, financial markets, regulators and supervisors address in an effective fashion the new, fundamental problems associated with the new business landscape. Indeed, our analysis indicates that structural changes in the new business landscape have created extraordinary challenges for the gatekeepers of public trust. At the same time, their monitoring role has become more important. But for the various gatekeepers to function properly, a great many obstacles related to the structural changes in the business landscape need to be addressed. For example, traditional accounting standards need to be adjusted to overcome the difficulties in incorporating in a reliable fashion the risk-management tools employed by sophisticated corporations.[15] New conflict-of-interest situations have been identified and, in response, new laws and regulations have been adopted. Unfortunately, there is considerable controversy as to how best to address conflicts of interest, including those related to the difference in incentives between the management and the board on the one hand, and the shareholders on the other. Some legal reformers advocate expanding liability to gatekeepers to induce gatekeepers to monitor clients and prevent them from committing misconduct (Coffee, 2003).[16] Others have argued that rules prohibiting gatekeepers from providing certain services may be a less costly method than making gatekeepers liable for client fraud (Hamdani, 2003). In response, financial analysts have pointed out that some of the new laws and regulations that prohibit certain activities in fact create further barriers to entry to the capital markets, reduce competition within and between the various categories of gatekeepers, and raise the overall costs of doing business (Ross, 2002).[17] Other studies have focused on the implication that some regulatory responses to corporate scandals 'interfere with freedom of contract ... are likely to increase legal costs, waste board time and deter future companies to go public'.[18] More generally, some analysts and policy-makers are warning against taking too-hasty regulatory steps by arguing that market forces will cleanse the system more effectively than will regulatory interventions. They point to the capability of markets to exact a terrible price for unacceptable conduct by companies in the form of a drop in their stock price, raising their cost of capital and punishing their competitive positions. There is also a loss of reputation by CEOs, auditors, accountants, bankers, regulators and other gatekeepers of the interests of the investing public, while many of them are also likely to suffer financial loss.

Whatever one's position is in this debate on regulation versus gatekeeper liability versus the market, greater attention by policy-makers, gatekeepers and investors for higher ethical standards is required. The need to deal with the deep transformation of business attitudes in the form of a lowering of ethical standards has important consequences for policy-makers. A key policy implication is that we cannot rely only on more aggressive enforcement by regulators and prosecutors to restore market integrity. A more fundamental response to this paradigm shift in ethical standards is needed as well. It is therefore encouraging that politicians, regulators, prosecutors, investors and the general public do not any longer accept a morally neutral approach to business, in particular in the financial sector.[19] Adherence to higher moral standards would have prevented many of the recent corporate scandals. The monitoring role of gatekeepers has become more important because markets are becoming more complex and therefore opaque. Clearly, higher and more meaningful disclosure standards will be helpful in operating more efficiently in complex markets. But the adoption of higher ethical standards is also a much needed and fundamental response to the new challenges and temptations of doing business in the 'new global techno-market order'. High ethical standards provide the glue between rules, regulations and business behaviour. Only in this way can we be assured that high corporate governance standards and other regulations are adhered to, and that sound agency relations prevail. An important practical step would be to supplement regular audits with ethical audits. This move would enhance the efficient performance of complex businesses guided by honest managers, and make a contribution to restoring trust in financial markets.

Notes

1 The views expressed in this chapter are strictly personal and do not represent those of the OECD or its member countries.
2 Michael Jensen refers to railroads, canals and telephone companies as earlier historical examples (Jensen, 2004).
3 This reputation is based on acquired licence, expertise and track-record.
4 This included questioning the responsibility of banks in the allocation of bonds of a major company under criminal investigation.
5 Thomas Landon, Jr., 'N.Y.S.E. Chief is Planning to Split Board', *The New York Times*, 29 October 2003.
6 It has to be acknowledged that sometimes there is a thin line between creative or aggressive accounting on the one hand, and fraudulent accounting on the other. For example, derivatives that are not marked-to-market can be either an example of aggressive or creative accounting, or of fraudulent accounting. However, as noted, we do not focus here on outright fraudulent motives and activities such as the recording of credits with customers that do not exist.
7 See, for a concrete proposal, Blommestein, 2003.
8 *International Herald Tribune*, 'Warning to Banks that Aided Corporate Fraud', 30 July 2003.
9 Enron's use of SPVs is a case in point.
10 CLNs have been used to paint a flattering picture of Parmalat's financial health (*The Economist*, 'Skimming off the Cream', 24 January 2004).
11 Susan Schmidt Bies, Member of the Board of Governors of the US Federal Reserve System, Financial Markets and Corporate Governance, 'Remarks at the Economic Club of Memphis Dinner', Memphis, Tenn., 9 February 2004.
12 Gatekeepers are to different degrees outsiders, including the external auditor of the company. But even among insiders (including those with a public trust role such as internal auditors, lawyers and so on), knowledge and understanding of the company may be quite uneven.
13 For example, organisations with offshore affiliates and SPVs complicate not only audits but also effective consolidated supervision.
14 This conclusion also gets indirect support from Robert Shiller's assessment that the number of recent corporate scandals such as Enron and other fraud cases is relatively small, and that their adverse impact on the integrity of US financial markets should not be exaggerated (Robert J., Shiller, 'How Corrupt Are US Capital Markets?', *Project Syndicate*, December 2003). However, as noted above, this paper goes beyond fraud as the leading cause of having had a major impact on the integrity of markets. Instead, the spotlight is on the lowering of ethical standards.
15 Susan Schmidt Bies, as note 11.
16 Coffee notes that the Sarbanes-Oxley Act did *not* adopt the strategy of enhancing gatekeeper liability.
17 Ross points out that 'not permitting auditing firms to offer this expertise as consultants is certainly not efficient' (p. 24).

18   Oliver Hart, 'The Wrong Way to Avoid a Corporate Scandal', *Financial Times*, FT.com, 9 January 2004.
19   This is especially the case for banks. See Blommestein, 2003–4.

References

Blommestein, H. J. (2001) 'Etica nel nuovo mondo mirabile' ('Ethics in the Brave New World'), *Il Regno Documenti. Quindicinale di Documenti e Attualità*, vol. 884, no. 13 (1 July), pp. 457–64.

Blommestein, H. J. (2003) 'Business Morality Audits are Needed', *Finance & the Common Good / Bien Commun*, no. 15 (Summer) pp. 51–7.

Blommestein, H. J. (2003–4) 'Unethical Markets Distort the Remuneration of Capital', *Finance & the Common Good/Bien Commun*, no. 17 (Winter), pp. 66–71.

Coffee, J. C., Jr. (2003) 'Gatekeeper Failure and Reform: The Challenge of Fashioning Relevant Reforms', Columbia Law and Economics Working Paper, No. 237 (September).

Gilson, R. J. and R. Kraakman (1984) 'The Mechanics of Market Efficiency', *Virginia Law Review*, no. 70.

Hamdani, A. (2003) 'Gatekeeper Liability', *South California Law Review*, no. 77 (November), pp. 53–122.

Jensen, M. C. (2001) 'Corporate Budgeting Is Broken: Let's Fix It', *Harvard Business Review* (November), pp. 94–101.

Jensen, M. C. (2002) 'The Agency Cost of Overvalued Equity and the Current State of Corporate Finance', Keynote Lecture, European Financial Management Association, London (June).

Jensen, M. C. (2004) 'Agency Cost of Overvalued Equity', Harvard NOM Working Paper, No. 04–26 (April).

Ross, S. A. (2002) 'Forensic Finance: Enron and Others', Fourth Angelo Costa Lecture, pp. 9–27.

Part 4

Corporate Culture and Ethics

12
Enron: The Collapse of Corporate Culture

John Dobson

Introduction

One of the fascinating aspects of the Enron Corporation's collapse is the speed with which the company went from being one of corporate America's paragons to become its chief pariah. Up to the time that Enron's stock price peaked in August of 2000, the company's name had appeared many times in leading business publications such as *Fortune*, *Forbes* and *Business Week*. The articles generally marvelled at some aspect of the 'Enron Miracle', such as its establishment of an energy derivatives trading platform, or its pioneering use of the Internet to market energy through Enron Online. For example, Enron won *Fortune* magazine's 'America's most innovative company' award for an unprecedented six years between 1996 and as recently as 2001; the prestigious *Financial Times* awarded Enron the 'energy company of the year' award in 2000.

Senior Enron executives, such as Kenneth Lay, Jeffrey Skilling and Andrew Fastow, frequently appeared in these business publications, sometimes even as the cover story. These men were invariably held up as paragons of everything good and right about corporate America. They were idolised for their drive, ambition, innovativeness, deal-making skills, and in general for their entrepreneurial spirit. The two men generally recognised as masterminding the Enron miracle, Skilling and Fastow, both had MBAs from top American business schools: Harvard, and Northwestern, respectively. Lay, Enron's avuncular CEO, possessed a PhD in Economics from Rice University. Indeed, Enron's managerial ranks were replete with top MBA graduates; Enron had a reputation among recruiters for hiring the best, and rewarding them commensurately. In short, up to August 2000, the Enron Corporation was viewed almost unanimously as being a corporate culture *par excellence*.

Within eighteen months, however, Enron was bankrupt. Nowhere is its rapid demise reflected more dramatically than in its share price decline, from a high of US$90 per share in August 2000, to a low of 20 cents per share on 30 November 2001, three days before the official bankruptcy filing. This share price decline represented a loss of about US$50 billion in equity market value; it also represented the largest corporate bankruptcy in history.

Hardly surprisingly, by the time of Enron's bankruptcy filing, the pendulum of public opinion had swung dramatically against Enron, and particularly against its senior executives. These individuals were once again making headlines in the major business publications, but this time they were of a very different tenor. Lay, Skilling, Fastow and their cohorts were being vilified as personifications of everything that is wrong with American corporate culture. Corporate character traits such as drive and ambition, which just eighteen months before were being hailed as virtues, were now damned as vices. From representing everything that was right about corporate America throughout the 1990s, Enron was, almost overnight, seen as representing everything that was wrong. How could Enron's corporate culture have encompassed both of these extremes in such a short period of time? Was Enron's internal culture always rotten, or did something change subtly in the latter half of the 1990s to corrupt an otherwise sound organisation? In terms of the broader implications of the Enron collapse for American corporate culture, was Enron an aberration – a 'freak event' – in an otherwise sound corporate milieu, or does the Enron story signal something rotten at the heart of American business?

The remainder of this chapter addresses these questions. First, I define the concept of corporate culture, and outline the basic organisational problem that any corporate culture must address. Second, I show how Enron's corporate culture not only failed to address this basic problem, but in fact exacerbated it. Third, I broaden the discussion to include American corporate culture in general, and argue that Enron's problems were by no means unique; they should be viewed rather as a dramatic manifestation of a problem that exists throughout contemporary American corporations. Finally, I look to the future by suggesting several ways in which, in shaping corporate cultures, we can learn from Enron's collapse. Specifically, I outline a morally broadened foundation for corporate culture that builds on the virtues of Enron, while avoiding its economically and ethically lethal vices. I hope that this chapter, and indeed this book, will be one step towards ensuring that those who suffered by Enron – whether employees, stockholders, or whomever – did not suffer in vain.

Enron's corporate culture

Visitors entering Enron's head offices on Smith Street in downtown Houston were often struck by the large banners hanging in the foyer. The banners were emblazoned with Enron's 'R.I.C.E.' principles: respect, integrity, communication and excellence. A naïve visitor may thus have been fooled into thinking that this RICE acronym in fact had some bearing on Enron's corporate culture. Indeed, such a deception might have been the motivation behind hanging the banners, because history has proved that such moral sentiments as respect, integrity, communication and excellence in reality had no bearing on Enron's corporate culture.

Given what we now know about Enron, RICE should more appropriately have stood for risk-taking, individualism, contempt and exploitation. In a recent article in the *Journal of Accountancy*, for example, William Thomas describes Enron as characterised by 'individual and collective greed born in an atmosphere of market euphoria and arrogance' (2002, p. 41). This statement describes pretty succinctly the essence of Enron's corporate culture. But from where did this culture spring? In the previous section I observed that corporate cultures are built from the top down. It is the ethical principles guiding the actions of top management that filter down and shape the corporate culture. What were the ethical principles guiding the senior executives at Enron?

Enron Corporation was created in 1985, shortly after the federal deregulation of natural gas in North America. Enron was formed by the merger of two natural-gas pipeline companies, one based in Houston, and the other in Nebraska. This merger was primarily debt-financed, which meant that Enron started life with a large level of debt on its books that required interest and principal repayments. So from its inception, Enron was a company characterised by risk: high business risk resulting from the highly competitive, recently deregulated, natural gas market; and high financial risk resulting from the merger-induced heavy debt load.

Kenneth Lay, Enron's first CEO, knew that his firm would have to be innovative to survive. He hired consultants McKinsey & Co. to assist in developing Enron's business strategy. Not only did McKinsey give Enron a business strategy, they also gave it the seed from which Enron's corporate culture would rapidly grow. That seed was a McKinsey consultant named Jeffrey Skilling.

Skilling joined Enron officially in 1990 to head the newly created Enron Finance Corp. Shortly afterwards, Skilling hired Andrew Fastow, a specialist in financial derivatives. Skilling and Fastow had much in common. They had both obtained MBAs from leading US business schools, as noted above – Harvard and Northwestern respectively; they both had expertise in sophisticated financial instruments; but above all they both had an overwhelming drive for short-term wealth creation. Their 'ethic' appears to have been simple and unambiguous: maximise Enron's short-term stock price appreciation at any cost, and in any way possible.

Enron, guided by Skilling, aggressively hired top MBA graduates from leading US business schools, promising them rapid advancement and rapid wealth. The notion of stock price maximisation as the ultimate goal of the corporation would have been something with which these individuals were very familiar from their classes – particularly their finance classes – in their recently completed MBA programmes. The 'short term stock price appreciation' ethic was disseminated rapidly through these ranks of new managers in a startlingly sophisticated yet simple manner. It was disseminated by something called the Performance Review Committee (PRC).

Superficially, the PRC might sound harmless enough; after all, every business has some form of peer performance review. Enron's PRC, however, under the guidance of Skilling and Fastow, rapidly became notorious as the harshest employee-ranking system in corporate America.

The PRC created and sustained Enron's corporate culture. It promulgated, ruthlessly, the ethic of short-term stock price appreciation at any cost, and in any way possible. Those who contributed to this goal were rewarded handsomely, mostly in stock options, which of course further motivated the manager to focus on short-term stock price appreciation. Whether managers were identifying and undertaking projects that were really profitable, or just superficially profitable, mattered not one jot to the PRC. Managers who were either unable or unwilling to create or fabricate profitable 'deals' did not last long. Skilling's division alone replaced about 15 per cent of its workforce every year. As Skilling himself put it, 'you eat [only] what *you* kill'! As one Enron manager put it: 'Good deal versus bad deal? Didn't matter. If you could give it a positive Net Present Value it got done.'

Certainly, there were positive aspects to Enron's corporate culture. Many managers found Enron to be a very dramatic and stimulating place to work. In focusing on stock-price performance, net present nalue (NPV) and financial innovation, these recent MBAs were able immediately to apply the skills they had honed in graduate school. Enron encouraged and rewarded innovation. Enron provided employees with excellent leisure and exercise facilities. Lay was an acknowledged philanthropist and supporter of the arts in the Houston area.

As regards Enron's corporate culture, all these were on the plus side of the ledger. The ethic that drove the minus side, however, far outweighed them. This negative ethic was the overwhelming drive for short-term personal wealth accumulation. Managers were encouraged to pursue this goal with, if necessary, guile and deceit. In forming this corporate culture Enron's senior executives ignored the fundamental problem that a corporate culture, guided by a corporate ethic, must overcome.

Enron's corporate culture failed to sustain the organisation because it lacked any method of contractual enforcement. Enron's ethic gave managers no rational justification for choosing 'honour trust' over 'abuse trust'.

Explicit enforcement

Explicit enforcement mechanisms, such as disclosure rules and the auditing of accounts, were treated with contempt. Enron's generous reward structure and unwillingness to tolerate dissent essentially bullied auditors and directors into being accomplices in Enron's acquisitive excess. Lured by promises of undreamt-of-wealth, many Andersen (Enron's auditor) employees aspired to work for Enron and were therefore very reluctant to 'rock the boat' with the company.

Enron's board of directors simply did not understand what was going on; they trusted that Jeffrey Skilling's and Andrew Fastow's labyrinthine special purpose entities (SPEs) made sound financial sense; after all, both Skilling and Fastow had graduated from top MBA programmes. Thus neither the auditors nor the Board of Directors performed effectively their function of monitoring the activities of insiders for the benefit of outsiders. Rather than performing their proper role as controllers of it, both these supposed monitoring groups became witting or unwitting accomplices in Enron's excesses of guile, deceit and personal greed. In short, Enron's executives effectively short-circuited any explicit enforcement mechanism that might have induced them to 'honour trust'.

Implicit enforcement (the reputation effect)

What about the implicit enforcement mechanism of reputation? Why did Skilling's, Fastow's, and other managers' concern for their personal reputations – not to mention the reputation of Enron itself – not induce them to 'honour trust'? The answer to this question takes us to the heart of Enron's cultural failing: its obsessive focus on the short term.

Enron's executives seem to have acted as though the future did not exist. Whether this was because they believed they could continue their deceptions for ever, with the aid of a never-ending bull market in stocks, is not clear. Certainly, many of Enron's managers were young (with the obvious exception of Lay), and had never experienced anything but a booming stock market. Or perhaps these executive knew that the bubble would burst, but planned to be long gone when it did. Whatever the reason, Enron's financial myopia effectively made the 'reputation effect' discussed above entirely impotent. Enron executives appear to have cared little for their long-term reputations, and in the short term the veil of secrecy surrounding Enron's activities – not to mention outright fraud and deception – rendered the activities of Enron's managers opaque, to say the least. Through its labyrinthine array of offshore partnerships, and mark-to-market accounting, Enron took the concept of 'informational asymmetry', defined above, to new heights. Like many of their supposed profitable deals, the activities of Enron's managers were clouded in obfuscation and secrecy. No hope for the implicit-contractual-enforcement mechanism of reputation here!

Enforcement through corporate culture

If Enron's senior executives had in fact taken its RICE principles to heart, then no doubt Enron would still be around today. As it is, these principles of respect, integrity, communication and excellence stand as a mockery of what did transpire inside Enron. Enron's ethic of an obsessive focus on 'short term stock price appreciation at any cost' ensured that its culture would be one incapable of contractual enforcement. Enron's individual executives, concealed under a shell of impenetrable creative accounting, effectively milked the corporation for all it was worth. Premised on an ethic of pure individualistic greed, Enron's was a culture hell-bent on self-destruction.

America's corrupt corporate culture: an educational failure

Was Enron's morally bankrupt corporate culture of greed unique, or is it symptomatic of a trend in US corporate culture in general? The first casualty of war may be the truth, but if revelations since the end of the 1990s stock-market boom are any guide, the first casualty of a bear market is unethical behaviour. Specifically, the stock-market downturn brings to the surface ethical transgressions committed during the euphoria of the preceding boom. Some of these transgressions are being brought to light through litigation: individual investors who fell victim to recent market volatility have sought restitution through the law. A typical example of this is the suit brought by Debasis Kanjilal, an individual investor with a brokerage account at Merrill Lynch. During the year 2000, Kanjilal's account dropped from a market value of US$1.2 million to about US$95,000. Mr Kanjilal's complaint centres on his assertion that Merrill Lynch's brokerage arm was urging him to buy stocks – namely InfoSpace and JDS Uniphase, which Merril Lynch's consulting arm had a vested interest in supporting. To back up his assertion of a conflict of interest, Mr Kanjilal notes that during the time he was being urged to buy by Merrill Lynch's broker, the CEOs of both InfoSpace and JDS were heavy sellers. A spokesman for Merrill Lynch counters that 'Mr Kanjilal was an experienced investor who made his own investment decisions'... the case continues.

Ongoing litigation is highlighting similar conflicts of interest in the underwriting of initial public offerings. Several class action suits have recently been brought by individual investors against major investment banks. Underwriters at Morgan Stanley, for example, are accused of soliciting and receiving commissions from certain investors in return for a larger portion of the offering than is legally allowed. They are also accused of reaching pre-offer agreements with some wealthy customers to allocate preferentially to these customers a portion of the initial public offering (IPO) shares. As a sweetener, the suit alleges, these customers were guaranteed the opportunity to buy additional shares in the after-market at predetermined and preferential prices.

Scrutiny of these and similar conflicts of interest is not limited to private litigation. In the public sphere, various government and judicial authorities are currently investigating the behaviour of investment bankers, securities analysts and other individuals engaged in the finance industry. The Securities and Exchange Commission (SEC), US Justice Department, and a Congressional subcommittee on capital markets, have each initiated investigations that focus primarily on the existence and extent of conflicts of interest faced by finance professionals such as analysts, brokers and underwriters. Although many specific issues are being addressed in these investigations, two broad questions are attracting the most attention: How do underwriters of initial public offerings make share allocation decisions? And why do financial analysts and brokers so rarely give 'sell' recommendations, even in an established bear market?

The implication of all this attention being lavished on the financial services profession, and indeed on corporate America in general since Enron, is clearly not very flattering. Although some of the allegations being levelled may prove to be unfounded, the evidence already brought to light provides sufficient cause for concern. For example, in the case of the ongoing SEC investigation, Laura Unger, acting chairman of the SEC, has already made public findings that the agency has uncovered numerous conflicts of interest in its review of full-service brokerage firms. In testimony before a congressional subcommittee, Ms Unger said that 28 per cent of a small sample of fifty-seven analysts reviewed had made their own investments prior to an initial public offering of a company the analyst later followed. The analysts initiated research coverage with a 'buy' recommendation.

This and similar evidence calls into question the very notion of securities underwriting or financial analysis as a 'profession', in the sense of being an activity in which the practitioner places the interests of the client before his/her own interests. The evidence points to many individual finance professionals acting, at best, in the interests purely of their company's shareholders; or, at worst, purely in their own narrow material self-interest. The behaviour of these individuals, whether acting on there own or under the auspices of some organisation, appears in many cases to have fallen well short of what would generally be regarded as professional conduct. More alarmingly, this behaviour is being undertaken at a time when ethical rules and guidelines have never been more omnipresent in the securities industry: all professional bodies in finance now educate and examine candidates on an array of such rules and guidelines designed to define the parameters of professional conduct.

Why are these omnipresent codes of conduct failing to influence sufficiently the behaviour of finance professionals? In essence, they are not working because they represent just a superficial gloss on the very different and far more pervasive education in ethics that individuals entering the management suites of corporate America receive. This different and more pervasive ethics education is supplied through the behavioural notion of rationality contained in theoretical finance, which in turn is derived from economic game theory.

This economic, game-theoretic rationality construct focuses on the persistent, atomistic, exclusive and endless pursuit of personal material wealth as the only conceivable justification for individual on group behaviour. In short, in finance theory, 'rational' agents are always assumed to be material opportunists who will readily jettison honesty and integrity in favour of guile and deceit whenever the latter is more likely to maximise some payoff function; indeed, to act other than opportunistically in this manner is immediately labelled as 'irrational'! Used out of context in an educational setting, this rationality construct, which forms the foundation of all finance theory, inculcates business students and professional trainees with an implicit moral agenda – an agenda very different from that espoused by professional codes of conduct. This is the real ethics education that those entering the finance professions receive. What passes officially for ethics education is too little, and too late. MBA graduates such as Fastow and Skilling already know – or think they know – what the behavioural ideal is, since it has been drummed into them, subtly yet conclusively, throughout several years of education. It is material opportunism.

Individuals, whether finance professionals or others, cannot be expected to respect or adhere to behavioural concepts that appear to be irrational and inconsistent with their pursuit of self-interest. Sadly, in the harsh light of material opportunism, this is just how ethical guidelines appear. Ethical guidelines are viewed in the same way as legal or accounting rules: they are constraints to be (whenever possible) circumvented or just plain ignored in the pursuit of self-interest, or in pursuit of the interests of the organisation.

For ethical concepts such as honesty, fairness and integrity to have any impact on the behaviour of finance professionals, this state of affairs must be altered radically. Those engaged in business-school education – either directly as teachers and trainers, or indirectly as mentors and peers – must recognise and disseminate a broader notion of rational behaviour, and hence, by implication, reasonable and acceptable behaviour in financial markets.

Rising from the ashes of Enron: building a sound foundation for corporate culture

Economic rationality undoubtedly has its uses, but it also has its limitations. As a game-theoretic construct developed originally by von Neumann and Morgenstern in the 1940s, it is a simple behavioral rubric that facilitates mathematical analysis. It was never intended as a guide, and indeed is not a guide, to professional life. As J. von Neumann and O. Morgenstern themselves put it in their original paper published in 1947: 'We wish to find the mathematically complete principles which define "rational behavior" for the participants in a social economy, and derive from them the general characteristics of that behavior' (p. 31). These 'complete principles which define "rational behavior" in fact involve the logical and consistent ordering of preferences – all preferences. In short, they concern themselves purely with instrumental rationality; and they say nothing about the substantive issue of which goal or goals this rational preference ordering will serve. Unfortunately, because finance professionals and students are not generally exposed to broader discussions of rationality, narrow economic rationality is stretched beyond its appropriate role as a descriptive tool into the prescriptive arena of a moral prerogative. This prerogative is increasingly forming the foundation of corporate cultures in America, as Enron's collapse amply illustrated.

To take a specific example, finance theory generally prescribes that decisions within the organisation be made on the basis of stock-price maximisation. Thus stock-price maximisation is proffered as an ethic – *the* ethic: it is the correct justification for decisions made by individuals within the organisation. Finance theory justifies this ethic by observing that stockholders are the residual claimants; they supply the risk capital and so should be compensated accordingly.

This argument is fine as far as it goes. Certainly individuals within an organisation should pursue the interests of stockholders in preference to their own material interests when the two conflict. But what is generally not made clear is that, in many decision situations, it is very difficult to determine what the affect of an action will be on stockholders. A broad spectrum of factors affect a firm's stock price: as a decision criterion, stock price maximisation is the ultimate 'blunt instrument'. Individuals within organisations are often faced with an array of decisions, the economic impacts of which are uncertain. Finance theory would address this uncertainty quantitatively. Probabilities of stock-price impacts would be assigned to each outcome, and sensitivity and scenario analysis would be employed. There is nothing wrong with that; but, given this uncertainty, might not other decision criteria also be usefully applied? Criteria that are not so dependent on quantitative estimates, and that are sensitive to other considerations?

Professional codes of conduct should provide just such criteria. They provide sound guidelines for behaviour that, far from conflicting with the organisation's financial goals, should guide individuals operating in complex and uncertain environments towards achieving these goals. As noted earlier, if Enron's executives had in fact taken to heart and abided by the firm's RICE principles, Enron would still be around today.

As any cursory scan of the financial press reveals, the economic cost of ethical transgressions can be substantial. John Swanda, for example, notes that '[t]he value of the firm's moral character ... can result in a market value of the firm that is greater than the firm's net assets'. He conjectures that '[e]ven in the short run one can argue that the firm with an excellent ethical reputation can have a special economic advantage' (1990, pp. 752–3). Swanda characterises this ethical reputation as both an asset and a source of income – as both a stock and a flow:

> While morality as a resource cannot be considered in the same context as
> tangible assets or goods, it can be considered, however, as a highly

valuable but volatile asset, one which reflects the perception of the community . . . In this sense, it will use outflows of resources to establish stocks of morality in order to encourage various publics to hold the firm in trust. (p. 757)

Finance professionals and initiates need to be made aware of this financial value attached to 'stocks of morality'. It is not a case that ethics versus profits, but rather a case that ethics leads to profits. For example, in his recent book, *Competing with Integrity in International Business* (1993) Richard DeGeorge notes:

Competing with integrity does not imply either a reluctance to compete or an inability to compete aggressively . . . In fact, it demands precisely the institutional discipline that often gives a competitive edge. Competing successfully with integrity is in fact the aim and the norm of individuals who compete with integrity. (p. 7)

Thus, attributes such as integrity or honesty need not conflict with the individual's or the organisation's pursuit of material self-interest; in fact quite the reverse. In *The New World of Business: Ethics and Free Enterprise in the Global 1990's*, Robert Solomon states that 'ethics is not a burden or a business disadvantage but the very ground rules of business as such and the key to business success' (1994, p. xv).

But the most fundamental and crucial educational lesson is that ethics must come first. For honesty and integrity to become truly instilled in an organisation and to become the foundation of the organisation's corporate culture, such values must be recognised as possessing intrinsic worth. As Robert Frank points out in his influential book, *Passions Within Reason*: 'Satisfaction from doing the right thing must not be premised on the fact that material gains may follow; rather it must be intrinsic to the act itself' (1988, p. 254). This is important because, if honesty or integrity are seen merely as efficacious means to an economic end, then they will be jettisoned as soon as the economic calculus dictates; they will be merely pseudo-honesty and pseudo-integrity. This is where education into a broader notion of rationality comes in. Business professionals need to be made aware that, to be honest simply because being honest is generally the best foundation for behaviour, is eminently rational. Honest people will tend to be happier, more successful, and will tend to engender successful organisations and societies. Honesty, fair-dealing, integrity; it is upon these premises that successful careers in business are built.

The solution therefore lies in reconciling this logical and pedagogical inconsistency between the implicit behavioural prerogatives of economic rationality on the one hand, and the explicit behavioural guidelines of professional codes of ethics on the other. The crucial lesson here is that the type of behaviour espoused by professional codes of ethics is rational: self-interest, when correctly defined, is best achieved by adherence to these professional guidelines. Furthermore, organisations populated by individuals who respect and adhere to ethically sound guidelines will develop sound cultures, and will excel in long-term financial performance. In short, the best way to maximise personal wealth and corporate stock price is to act ethically. This is an observation made repeatedly in the strategic management and business ethics literature, and it is one that needs to be made more often in business schools and business organisations. Perhaps then professional guidelines will prove to be an effective antidote to the false prophet of economic theory, preaching its material opportunism.

Furthermore, to return substance to the notion of 'professionalism' in business requires, first and foremost, a commitment to those ethical principles already laid down in corporate credos and codes of ethics. These promote a primary responsibility to the integrity of the profession, whether it be business management, securities analysis, investment banking or financial planning. Just as in the medical or legal professions, this integrity is nurtured and sustained by a concern not primarily for the self or the shareholder, but for the patient/client/investor who has placed his/her trust in the professional's expertise, integrity and honesty; in short, trust in the individual's 'professionalism'. As Aristotle observed in *The Nicomachean Ethics*: 'The life of money-making is one undertaken under compulsion, and wealth is evidently not the good we are seeking: for it is merely useful and for the sake of something else.' That something else is the intrinsic reward to be obtained from a life of professional service. This is the notion of rationality that requires dissemination and discussion within business schools and business organisations. It is a notion of rationality entirely consistent with a sound corporate culture, as well as being entirely consistent with long-term financial success.

Some concluding thoughts

In concluding their seminal work on the theory of the firm, Jensen and Meckling (1976) note that 'whatever its shortcomings, the corporation has thus far survived the market test against potential alternatives' (p. 357). But what the Enron collapse illustrates clearly is that the success of the public corporation 'against potential alternatives' cannot – indeed, must not – be taken for granted. In this chapter I argue that a crucial foundation for the ongoing success of the public corporation is a healthy corporate culture.

This healthy corporate culture is created and nurtured, not merely by economic theory, but by a sound managerial ethic – an ethic built from our inheritance of some 2,000 years of moral philosophy. Future business leaders must be made to realise that simple material opportunism, of the type often espoused in business schools, is an insufficient ethic for the sustenance of a healthy corporate culture.

No one has made this point more clearly than moral philosopher Alasdair MacIntyre. MacIntyre illustrates the shortcomings of the economic ethic by considering two fishing communities, which differ in terms of context. MacIntyre precedes his description of the crews by admitting '[m]y descriptions of these will be of ideal types, defining the extremes of a spectrum on which there are many points' (1994, p. 284). He describes two types of fishing business as follows (p. 285):

> A fishing crew may be organized as a purely technical and economic means to a productive end, whose aim is only or overridingly to satisfy as profitably as possible some market's demand for fish. Just as those managing its organization aim at a high level of profits, so also the individual crew members aim at a high level of reward . . . When however the level of reward is insufficiently high, then the individual whose motivations and values are of this kind will have from her or his own point of view the best of reasons for leaving this particular crew or even taking to another trade . . . management will from its point of view have no good reason not to fire crew members, and owners will have no good reason not to invest their money elsewhere.

MacIntyre then describes another fishing community:

> Consider by contrast a crew whose members may well have initially joined for the sake of their wage or other share of the catch, but who have acquired from the rest of the crew an understanding of and devotion to excellence in fishing and to excellence in playing one's part as a member of such a crew . . . So the interdependence of the members of a fishing crew in respect of skills, the achievement of goods and the acquisition of virtues will extend to an interdependence of the families of crew members and perhaps beyond them to the whole society of a fishing village.

MacIntyre's second fishing community encapsulates beautifully the essential characteristics of a healthy corporate culture – one built on more than simplistic economic logic, yet more capable of sustaining long-term economic success. In the first community, individuals pursue personal material wealth with no explicitly recognised further objective, and in an environment designed to facilitate this pursuit. In the second community, individuals also pursue personal material wealth, but this pursuit is recognised as just one facet of a morally inclusive nurturing corporate culture, based on a sound corporate ethic. In his invocation of a 'craftsmanship ethic', Sherwin Klein recently enumerated a managerial ethic along these very lines (1998, p. 55):

> The ideal of craftsmanship is to create that which has quality or excellence; personal satisfaction, pride in accomplishment, and a sense of

dignity derived from the consequent self-development are the motivations. In an 'excellent' company it is this ideal that permeates the firm, and management should provide the moral example of such an ideal; a business management craftsman attempts to create a quality organization, and quality products and services are the result of such an organization.

Scholars, educators and practitioners in business face a fundamental challenge. How to enlighten business executives as to the inherent superiority of a corporate culture based on the values espoused in MacIntyre's second fishing community, based on Klein's craftsmanship ethic? How to imbue current and future managers with those traits of character necessary to sustain such a culture? The key is education. But it must be education beyond the confines of a morally impoverished contemporary business school. The actions of the highly educated individuals at the head of the Enron Corporation should help teach us the true meaning of 'highly educated'.

References

Aristotle (1991 edn) *The Nicomachean Ethics* (Oxford: Oxford University Press).

Bowie, N. E. (1991) 'Challenging the Egoistic Paradigm', *Business Ethics Quarterly*, vol. 1, no. 1, pp. 1–21.

DeGeorge, R. T. (1993) *Competing with Integrity in International Business* (New York: Oxford University Press).

Frank, R. (1988) *Passions Within Reason* (New York: W. W. Norton).

Jensen, M. C. and W. H. Meckling (1976) 'Theory of the Firm: Managerial Behavior, Agency Costs and Ownership Structure', *Journal of Financial Economics*, vol. 3, no. 4 (October), pp. 305–60.

Klein, S. (1998) 'Don Quixote and the Problem of Idealism and Realism in Business Ethics', *Business Ethics Quarterly*, vol. 8, no. 1 (January), pp. 43–64.

MacIntyre, A. (1994) 'A Partial Response to My Critics', in: C. Taylor (ed.), *After MacIntyre* (Oxford: Oxford University Press).

Raghubir P. and S. Das (1999) 'A Case for Theory-Driven Experimental Enquiry', *Financial Analysts Journal*, vol. 55, no. 6 (November), pp. 56–80.

Solomon, R. C. (1994) *The New World of Business: Ethics and Free Enterprise in the Global 1990's* (Lanham, Md.: Rowman & Littlefield).

Swanda, J. R., Jr. (1990) 'Goodwill, Going Concern, Stocks and Flows: A Prescription for Moral Analysis', *Journal of Business Ethics*, vol. 9, no. 9, pp. 751–60.

Thaler, R. H. (1988) 'Anomalies: The Ultimatum Game', *Journal of Economic Perspectives*, vol. 2, no. 4 (Fall), pp. 195–206.

Thaler, R. H. (1992) *The Winner's Curse: Paradoxes and Anomalies of Economic Life* (New York: The Free Press).

Thomas, W. C. (2002) 'The Rise and Fall of Enron', *Journal of Accountancy* (April), pp. 41–8.

Von Neumann, J. and O. Morgenstern (1947) *Theory of Games and Economic Behavior*, 2nd edn (Princeton, NJ: Princeton University Press).

13
Ethics, Courage and Discipline: The Lessons of Enron

Robert G. Kennedy

The ethical challenge facing us in the wake of the Enron scandal is not one of analysis. The problem at Enron, as with the problems that emerged at Tyco, Parmalat, Adelphia, Worldcom and other prominent corporations, was not one of isolated bad judgement. At Enron, as at the other companies, there were patterns of behaviour that were widespread, persistent and systemic. While perhaps they did not always disobey the *letter* of the law, Enron's executives quite deliberately and cleverly violated the *spirit* of the law, to say nothing of their fiduciary duties as professionals. They engaged in many acts of deception and manipulation, enriched themselves at the expense of their shareholders and employees, and corrupted or intimidated the people who might have prevented these abuses.

No profound analysis is needed to reveal such behaviour as unethical. Despite some claims to the contrary, the ethical challenge that business faces does not derive from the inherent difficulty of distinguishing between ethical and unethical behaviour. In a great many cases, this is easy enough to do, at least if one is not personally involved in the situation and its implications. The real challenge is related to the difficulty of recognising consistently morally sound courses of action despite the organisational pressures and temptations that can so easily obscure a person's moral vision. It is also connected to the way in which personal character is shaped and sustained (or eroded), first by education and later by organisational culture.

Modern business organisations have the potential to do both great good and great harm. Since these organisations have, in the last century or so, taken on an unprecedented importance for social life, the breadth and depth of this potential is something relatively new and demands of us new thinking about management. The recent corporate scandals are a reminder that society has too much at stake not to take an active interest in the conduct of managers.

This active interest generally manifests itself in two kinds of social responses, one external to business and the other internal. The external response normally takes the form of laws and regulations that reshape the environment in which business operates. These rules are designed to define bad business behaviour and to discourage it, both by requiring transparency and by punishing violations. The internal response, by contrast, seeks to use education to shape the thinking and character of managers. Each response has its limitations, and even taken together they cannot prevent all management misbehaviour without smothering the potential that business has for improving the human condition. Nevertheless, both are necessary and both must be understood.

The external response: law and regulation

The natural inclination of a community following major business scandals is to pursue a regulatory response. This is encouraged by public opinion and political expediency. What results is the enactment of new statutes (such as the so-called Sarbanes-Oxley Act) or the imposition of new rules (by such bodies as the American Financial Accounting Standards Board). Passing laws and promulgating regulations can be done swiftly; such actions satisfy the need to do something. However, while these may offer concrete correctives to certain bad behaviour, they may also create additional problems of their own.

The law itself is never enough to ensure sound behaviour; laws and rules are constraints on bad choices, not formulas for good choices. At best, in a law-abiding community, laws and rules function as practical guidelines about what to avoid. Citizens and professionals who are committed to the common good respect laws and rules, adjusting their choices and behaviour to conform to them. Additional problems are created when conforming to the law (or providing evidence that one is conforming to the law) directs resources away from productive activities. Worse yet, ill-conceived laws can make managers risk-averse and stifle creativity and innovation throughout a company. Moreover, laws and regulations by their very nature can rarely prescribe the management behaviour that is necessary to make a company successful. Laws and regulations tend to be reactive; they cannot anticipate new circumstances and unexpected challenges. To use a loose analogy, they are like the rules governing highway traffic. Speed limits, lane markings and barriers all serve to establish constraints on driving that are important for the sake of safety. Nevertheless, safety provisions cannot help drivers who do not know how to get to their destinations, or who lack the necessary driving skills. Constraints and skills are both necessary if highways are to serve their purpose and contribute materially to the common good.

Similarly, laws and regulations must achieve a difficult balance which sharply constrains a set of bad behaviour while not impeding sound management judgement. This is rarely accomplished, in part because legislators and regulators are under considerable pressure to find means of preventing managers from making bad choices, and little corresponding pressure to ensure that they are free to make good choices. Responsible legislators and regulatory officials will recognise that their duty is not only to prevent harm but also to set free as far as possible the potential of business organisations to provide benefits. This is a delicate balance and its achievement is made more difficult where business leaders cannot demonstrate the integrity that is a necessary condition of freedom. Attending to this integrity is an essential complement to the external, legal response of society to business.

The internal response: professionalism

Discussions about business ethics from ancient times to the twentieth century have almost always focused tightly on questions concerning commerce: sales, money lending and so on. The normal assumption was that merchants acted as individuals and that the issues to be considered concerned transactions between individuals. The organisational dimension was rarely, if ever, explored. Today this has changed dramatically and the relevant ethical questions are both individual and organisational – that is, we have moved beyond questions of fairness in transactions to include questions relating broadly to the leadership and management of organisations of all kinds. The concept of professionalism is the key to understanding this change.

As we move into the twenty-first century, responsible management has become critical to modern life. As Peter Drucker has pointed out, in *Post-Capitalist Society* (1993), we have become a society of institutions, organisations and corporations. In the developed world, it is nearly impossible for an individual to accomplish anything without collaborating with or depending upon an organisation of some kind. Few doctors, for example, remain in private practice; they are absorbed into managed care organisations. Writers depend on publishers; farmers work with co-operatives and depend on seed companies and pesticide and implement producers (to say nothing of government organisations). No one is truly independent today.

The sheer size of organisations, and the benefits to be derived from incorporation, have ensured that organisations, even non-profit and privately-held companies, are rarely managed by their owners or founders. Instead, organisations depend on legions of hired managers, and in many ways it is the skills of these managerial employees that have made possible the revolution in modern life, and the benefits (and burdens) that flow from it.

These skills, however, are morally neutral, which is to say that they can be used for various purposes, some good and some bad, and they do not in themselves determine for what purposes they will be used. The skills of the physician can heal or they can kill. It is the moral vision and the character of the physician that determines how they will be used. Similarly, because the skills of management are so powerful when applied to the resources of organisations, the moral vision and the character of managers must be properly shaped. As in other professions, we aim to achieve this through a social response that focuses on what is internal to sound business practice.

The internal social response is more subtle, less immediate, but potentially more effective than the external response. Because ethical behaviour in practice depends not only on knowing what choices are morally sound but also on being able to make those sound choices in the face of conflict and other pressures, this response aims at internalising standards of behaviour in professional managers and developing the sort of character that disposes them to make sound decisions, even in difficult circumstances. It depends on formal education to introduce it, and community expectations to reinforce it.

As stunning as the misbehaviour of the executives of these corporations has been, it is not really new to the human experience. This is all a modern retelling of the perennial story of greed: for money, for power, for celebrity and for honour. It is a story of the abuse of knowledge and trust. Fortunately, we do know something about how to deal with this sort of challenge. In the past, a number of occupations have become sufficiently important to society, both in terms of the value they could contribute and the harm they could cause, that amateurs were prohibited from engaging in them. In one way or another, the occupations became *professional*.

Professionals, in a sense, live on the 'cutting edge' between the tried and true, and the new and uncertain. Society depends on professionals to provide reliable fixed standards (of health, of justice, of truth ...) in situations where the facts are murky or temptations too strong. Their principal contribution is an ability to bring sound judgement to bear on these situations. They represent the best a particular community is able to muster in response to new challenges. By employing a knowledge of causes and principles, they are able to draw an increasing number of problems within the category of what is predictable and manageable. Modern society, in many important ways, is the product of professional activity.

Professionals do not so much occupy a special place in a society as play a special role in it, a role they may play well or poorly. The indispensable function of a professional is to exercise sound and reasonable judgement about important matters in conditions of uncertainty. The ability to do this, in turn, depends on three other factors that must be present for someone to exercise this sort of judgement. The professional must possess specialised knowledge, must make critical commitments and must be permitted (and deserve) autonomy in decision-making. When these three foundational elements are present, and a person has developed the necessary judgement, we are justified in speaking of this person as a professional, regardless of whether s/he has joined with his/her colleagues to form a profession. Consider what these elements involve.

Specialised knowledge

The *sine qua non* of professionalism is specialised knowledge, and not just any sort of specialised knowledge. It is an accumulated and ordered knowledge, built up over time by the experience, analysis and insight of predecessors in the field. It is knowledge that penetrates to the root of the matter and gives its possessor an understanding not only of *how* things are, but *why* they are. It is also hard-won knowledge that requires time and effort to possess, knowledge that many people cannot achieve. Finally, it is powerful knowledge, and historically those in a position to pass it on have ordinarily demanded some evidence from students that they are worthy of receiving it.

The professional, as a result, is the opposite of the 'self-made person'. The professional is a man or woman who is deeply indebted to others from the start. Principal among these others are predecessors in the field who have discovered and systematised the knowledge and who have passed it on. Furthermore, the professional is indebted to the community. Virtually all professional education these days takes place in the context of a university, and universities are heavily supported in many ways by the community (tax exemptions, land grants, donations and tax deductions for donations and so on). The community offers this support because it values the contributions of the professional so highly, and because it expects a reciprocal dedication.

The professional is therefore obligated to use his/her knowledge well. In addition, s/he must add to the accumulated knowledge where possible, correcting it, refining it, and generally had to increasing its depth and breadth. Because this knowledge is so powerful, professionals have generally had to be careful throughout history to share their knowledge only with those personally committed to using it well. This remains true to some degree in professional areas such as medicine, the ministry and the law, where technically competent candidates may be dismissed from schools if it is seen that they lack the necessary moral integrity. As an important element of the internal response, business schools need to consider more seriously that the techniques they teach and the skills they develop also require a demonstration of moral integrity.

Commitment to service

To be a professional, to 'profess', is to stand for something in a public context, to make a public promise to the community. The first thing a professional professes is commitment to address problems according to the principles and accepted practices of the discipline. The priest or minister accepts the doctrines and liturgical practices of a particular church community, just as the physician (at least in the Western tradition) adopts an approach to medicine that depends on the physical sciences and the scientific method. As a result, someone relying on a professional knows in advance something about how that person will deal with matters related to that professional area.

Second, and more important, the true professional also professes service to others. Professionals commit themselves publicly to using their special knowledge principally to serve others and not primarily to serve themselves. They are public persons and so have an obligation to consider the public implications of their private professional acts. The competent architect designs buildings that are structurally sound and aesthetically pleasing even if this might create tension at times with a client. No ethical architect or engineer, for example, could produce a structure that would endanger the public in order to indulge a client's desire for cheapness.

This does not mean that professionals must be selfless in their practices. Quite the reverse, in fact: they may be well compensated in a variety of ways for what they do. However, their first concern in making decisions will always be the benefit to the person served, and only secondarily the consequences for themselves. Furthermore, it would be a mistake to see professional practice primarily in economic terms. As some writers have observed, the relationship between professionals and those they serve is not a transaction (which would imply an exchange of equal values), but rather a transformative encounter. While the professional is rewarded, the client, patient or student is benefited in more than material terms. Professionals of all kinds must keep in mind that, however much they may be paid for what they do, the real objective and the real value of their work is non-material and thoroughly human.

Calling attention to the genuine human goods that are served by management is another duty of business schools. Professionals are in constant danger of becoming mere technicians, highly skilled but insensitive to the goods their skills ought to serve. At worst, they become 'hired guns', employed for their ability to achieve certain kinds of goals or produce certain kinds of results with no regard for the human values involved. It would not be too much to say that a number of top business schools bear some remote responsibility for Enron and other scandals, on the grounds that they focused too sharply on developing skills and paid too little attention to developing character.

Moreover, it is probably not to much to say that business worldwide suffers from a lack of confidence in the real value of what it does. Physicians aspire to save lives, lawyers to see justice done, architects to build cities, but what do business people aspire to do? If not to make money (and we know that in the end money is not enough), what gives value to a business career? Business schools must be able to answer this question in a variety of contexts if they are to elicit a truly professional commitment from their students.

Autonomy in decision-making

Autonomy, or self-rule, is the liberty to choose concrete goals and specific courses of action without interference, or at least to make such choices within fairly expansive boundaries. The assumption that underlies the autonomy permitted to professionals is the belief that the real circumstances in which professionals are called on to make decisions are potentially so varied that they cannot be described adequately in advance. In other words, the conditions in which problems present themselves in real life are inherently unpredictable, and so it is not possible to develop routines and detailed plans for coping with every contingency. Instead, we rely on people who understand thoroughly the principles that are the foundation of successful solutions to crafting a workable plan in the context in which the problem occurs. The value of professionals to a community lies precisely in their ability to devise successful plans for new situations, and in order to do this they must have the freedom to break out of existing patterns when necessary.

Fundamentally, this freedom also depends on trust, and trust depends on the sincerity of professional commitments. As a practical matter, we are willing to permit professionals a great deal of liberty as long as we believe we can trust them to place the welfare of those they serve (clients, patients, students and so on) ahead of their own interests, and to practice competently. This often comes down to being a matter of personal contact, and faith in a particular person. This is very obvious in medicine, where establishing a rapport with a patient can be critical. Less obvious, perhaps, but often equally important, is the trust we personally place in individual architects, engineers, teachers, lawyers, and even managers. This trust is sometimes betrayed by professionals, and the community is rightly sceptical of the power of those with special knowledge. The external response to incidents of betrayal is litigation, and if it seems common enough (or too serious to tolerate, even if rare), the more public response is regulation (which has the effect of further restricting the professional's liberty). Business professionals, and those who train them, have a particular interest in reducing as far as possible the incidents that provoke these responses. This means that business schools must go beyond pointing out the difficulties with external responses. They must communicate to students the importance of being trustworthy, and take any steps necessary to develop the character necessary to sustain autonomy.

Sound judgement

The distinguishing mark of a true professional is the ability to make sound judgements in conditions of uncertainty. Anyone trained in first aid will know how to deal with a minor cut or sprain. When faced with a more serious or less common injury, we turn to someone who has much more extensive knowledge and experience, and eventually that means turning to a doctor. We have good reason to believe that the combination of knowledge and experience allows the professional to make good decisions even when presented with something new and different, perhaps even unprecedented. And what is true in medicine is also true in the law, in science and scholarship, engineering, architecture, war, and other professional areas (needless to say, while a particular professional might be a person of sound judgement generally, this does not mean that his/her judgement is *professional* judgment outside that person's area of expertise.)

In moral philosophy, the general ability to make sound judgements is called *prudence*, or *practical wisdom*, and involves knowing both what goals are worth pursuing and what means will be most likely to achieve those goals. Furthermore, each professional area has its own specific prudence (medical prudence, military prudence). The architect, for example, should have a good idea of what makes a building both functional and beautiful, and a clear conception of what materials and techniques will be required to construct the building both efficiently and effectively. Or the general directing a battle should have a clear sense of what can be accomplished and of how best to use his resources of personnel and material to produce the most favourable result. If his judgement is really sound, he must also be able to adapt his plan during the battle in response to unexpected developments.

Ultimately, the continuing (and even expanding) need that society has for genuine professionals is a function of the sound judgement they contribute in unpredictable and chaotic circumstances. If everything about life were controlled and predictable, or if professionals were unable to deal effectively with the new and the different, we would have no need of them. As it is, modern society is more dependent on professionals than ever before, and has an unprecedented capacity to support the development of professionals in new areas.

The character of business professionals

Many business people evidence the four marks of a professional. Since around the 1950s, our understanding of business has become fairly sophisticated and the prevalence of organisations has effectively required that companies, non-profit organisations and government agencies be managed by people possessing specialised knowledge and firm commitments – that is, that they are managed professionally. As signs of this, note that it is practically impossible for someone to move into a management position without a college education, and that organisations of all kinds spend enormous sums of money on the continuing education of managers.

As society has come to depend more heavily on organisations, so organisations have come to depend more heavily on professional management (in accounting, marketing, finance, operations and many other areas). For various reasons, it may be some time before management is organised into a profession in the way that, say, medicine, the law and the ministry are now. These are characterised not only by the professional behaviour of their members, but also by the organisation of these members into bodies responsible for such things as certification, discipline, research, continuing education and so on. Still, society has a great need of professionals in this area, and there are many signs that the foundations are being laid for the future development of management as a genuine profession. Among these developments must be a stronger appreciation for the sort of character professionals in business must have.

Once again, the Enron episode demonstrates the need for character. In this case, the Board members, the auditors and the analysts had clear duties. Each had a responsibility to determine the truth about the company's financial condition and to report that truth to an appropriate constituency. The Board had a further duty to examine proposed business activities, to deny permission for activities that would mislead or harm investors (to say nothing of employees and customers), and to curtail suspicious practices when discovered. In fact, the Board did none of these things; nor did the auditors complain too loudly, or soon enough, about irregularities; and neither did the analysts demand explanations or issue warnings.

The Enron debacle is an example of a cascade of failures. Unscrupulous executives probably engaged in improper and perhaps even illegal acts. Those who were charged with preventing the harm caused by these acts failed to do so, because in each instance incentives existed that discouraged them from fulfilling their responsibilities, incentives that proved to be irresistible. They each faced a test of character and, one by one, failed that test.

This does not mean that they were wicked people. While there may have been a few real scoundrels at Enron and the other notorious companies, most of the people who effectively facilitated the unethical projects were probably people of goodwill who were either confused about what was morally sound or were unable to manage conflicts of interest very well. These are issues that external regulatory responses are not well-equipped to handle.

Internal responses, located in business schools and corporate and professional cultures, are, on the other hand, appropriate means of addressing issues of character. In the first place, practical wisdom, as mentioned earlier, is a necessary component of professionalism. It is, or should be, the general purpose of business education to develop authentic practical wisdom in students. As I have suggested, however, business schools do quite well in training students in technical skills but are, as a group, seriously deficient in focusing the attention of their students on the goals that professional management ought to serve. As a consequence, students are loosed upon the organisational world with a set of powerful skills they are eager to exercise but without the moral vision that is indispensable to a fully developed practical wisdom.

While society should demand urgently that business schools repair their defective curricula in this regard, other factors come into play as well. Clarity of moral vision is a rather fragile possession, subject to corrosion by a variety of pressures and temptations. To resist these very real pressures, a person of moral integrity needs also to develop two other character traits: courage and discipline.

In talking about moral problems in business, we are often inclined to emphasise dramatic situations – where, for example, a person's job or career is at risk. We rightly honour those people who do the right thing even in the face of significant hardship. We applaud their courage and perhaps hope secretly that we might be able to summon up the same kind of strength in a similar situation. While such actions are genuinely courageous (and there were certainly courageous people, in the end, at Enron and the other companies), courage does not emerge only in dramatic situations.

Courage is a moral virtue, a human perfection. It can be defined in a number of different ways, but at its root is part of a person's character that makes it possible for that person to endure discomfort or pain for the sake of a good goal. Like all moral virtues, it is acquired, built up over time and experience. It exists in a sort of symbiotic relationship with practical wisdom, for courage requires a clear vision of the human goods at stake in any situation. A person who lacks this vision, who is not practically wise, can perhaps be tough and endure hardships, but s/he cannot be truly courageous. It is this focus on what is really good and worth achieving that leads some people to call courage 'right tenacity'.

The courageous person becomes so by small increments, choosing well even when some discomfort, however small, is the price. Confronting an employee with a performance problem rather than hoping the problem will go away, or telling a superior what s/he needs to hear rather than what s/he wants to hear can be courageous acts. Such acts reinforce one another and build character in the individual. Those who resisted the unethical practices at Enron were genuinely courageous individuals, but their courage was not created by the situation, it was merely demonstrated there.

Courage is complemented by discipline. Where courage resists external pressures (fears and risks, for example) that incline a person to make bad choices, discipline deals with internal factors (desires and temptations). In other words, where courage helps a person to deal with pain (even small pains), discipline helps a person to deal with the pleasant things that can distract him or her into making bad choices.

Discipline is 'right passion'. Business needs passionate people, but their passion must be directed towards the accomplishment of worthwhile goals, not towards self-indulgence. People who cannot moderate their personal desires are unlikely to be able to bring the right passion to their management responsibilities (the recent scandals have certainly given us a number of examples of both self-indulgence and incompetent management).

Courage and discipline are essential to sound management but they are also fragile traits of character. In healthy companies, such virtues are nurtured and in turn strengthen the organisation. Some companies, however, create an environment toxic to virtue, and the slow corruption of the managers undermines the effectiveness of the enterprise.

Business schools and corporate cultures

The development of moral virtues is not something that can be accomplished in a classroom. Business schools are well-suited to developing practical wisdom in their students (though this wisdom will be deepened by experience and maturity). They are not, however, as well-suited to developing courage and discipline, since these traits of character are strengthened only through real-world practice.

Nevertheless, even in the classroom, moral virtues can be celebrated and their importance explained. Students can be encouraged to embrace virtues, but in the end much will depend on the moral environment of the workplace – the corporate culture – in which young managers find themselves.

We now know that one of the characteristics of the culture at Enron was a climate of fear and destructive competition. Those whose performance was judged to be in the lowest quintile were subject to dismissal, even if looked at objectively they were otherwise competent. This focused the attention of young managers not on accomplishing worthwhile goals, but rather on satisfying their superiors and defeating their colleagues. Employees were not developed, they were culled. Survivors were also drawn on by the prospect of lavish rewards. At the same time, the entire company was subject to waves of propaganda, which had the effect of distracting employees from what was really being done and fixing their attention on phantom goals. It takes a strong person – and there were some – to place both fear and reward in context in a workplace like this.

It has often been said, especially in the context of finance, that ethics and sound management practice are inconsistent with one another. Ethics, in this view, imposes a set of constraints that retards the proper functioning of business organisations. The view has a certain superficial appeal, but only if one focuses on an artificially narrow set of goals, such as efficiency or maximisation of shareholder wealth. Organisations, however, are not closed, mechanistic systems; they are human communities of a sort and therefore depend on and affect the people who work within them. These people, the employees, are whole beings, with strengths and weaknesses, fears and desires. No organisation can function at a sustained level of excellence without being populated by a strong majority of employees who are virtuous and mature.

The failure of Enron, like the failures of several of other large companies, had a number of causes. It would be foolish to try to identify one cause as primary and the others as merely being contributory. Still, as one reviews the history of the problem, it is hard to escape the conclusion that Enron's difficulties would not have arisen if its managers had been genuinely professional and its employees virtuous.

14
Developing Leadership and Responsibility: No Alternative for Business Schools

Henri-Claude de Bettignies

Today, the demand from many corporate stakeholders for leadership and responsibility is inducing business schools to reposition these dimensions in their education process and research activities. When the voyage becomes more perilous, the crew demands more of the captain. As 'perfect storms' gather on the horizon of the world economic scene, captains of industry are coming under increasing pressure to live up to the expectations of more nervous and demanding crews. What are the visible 'clouds' of such incoming storms?

* *Uncertainty is increasing*: hundreds of millions of new workers entering the global work force threaten the jobs and livelihood of the middle classes in the developed countries, and the frequency and severity of natural and human-caused 'extreme events' – tsunamis (December 2004) to terrorist attacks (11 September 2001, Madrid and so on), market bubbles (Japan 1991, dot.com) to financial scandals (Enron, Parmalat and so on) cause worldwide shock and distress. Even positive events tend to be ambiguous; and this ambiguity feeds uncertainty, which in turn fosters a pervasive sense of insecurity. We live, as Ulrich Beck puts it, in a 'risk society' (1992).
* We also live in a *complex, interconnected world*, where many things can go wrong in many ways, and local breakdowns quickly produce global effects. Work in this world requires the integration of many interdependent parts, and the combination of diverse individuals and groups, each contributing a share of the knowledge required to achieve objectives and reconcile the often opposing interests of diverse stakeholders.
* We live in a *world of conflicting values*. Secularism and relativism spread, and notions of what is good or bad, right or wrong, fair or unfair blur and clash as European societies increasingly question the traditional core values (family, marriage, work, religion, country of origin) serving as anchors to individual behaviour. The globalisation process confronts corporate

values to the challenge of different (at times conflicting) national or corporate culture norms and values, requiring managers to make choices to cope with complex dilemmas.

- *Affluence*, beyond a certain level, *bears little relation to satisfaction with life*; the search for 'meaning' beyond material goods leads the despairing to dangerous palliatives (drug-taking, for example) or to a search for escape (into sects, extremisms, religious fanaticism, nihilism, violence and so on). Citizens, reduced to being primarily 'consumers' (if they can afford to consume!), are faced with an excess of choice among competing goods and services and increasingly come to perceive their options as constituting a handicap, inducing anxiety (so many more errors we can make with only ourselves to blame), stress and even paralysis (Schwartz, 2004).
- *Uneven access to development* – the gap between rich and poor at both international and national levels – and its impact on migration pressures, its potential for nurturing violence within and between countries, cannot but enhance concern about our capacity to manage a safe society in the future.
- *The experience of violence*: resource wars, class, ethnic and religious conflicts (clashes of civilisations?) but also violence as our daily companion, seen via television, in urban ghettos, in stadiums or schools, in the family, induce tensions – latent or explicit – that contribute towards explaining this thirst to reduce uncertainty.
- The *explosion of science and technology* is another factor. Simultaneous advances in – and the convergence of – nanotechnology (the manipulation of matter at the atomic or molecular level), information technology, biotechnology (Joy, 2000) and neurotechnology create a plethora of new possibilities for good and bad, the veritable realisation of Francis Bacon's programme 'the effecting of all things possible' (*New Atlantis*, 1627), but not all are socially desirable. The promise is of a future when humankind will be able not only to treat previously fatal illnesses, but also to change to modify its genetic heritage, to clone or 'download' humanity, and to alter fundamentally what it means to be human.
- The *rapid depletion of the planet's natural* (often non-renewable) *resources* and the endangering of nature's services (the climate, ozone layer, water and so on) will affect humanity for generations to come. Insufficient mastery of the negative externalities of 'growth' raises concern about sustainability.

The 'leadership' dimension

In such a context, indeed, the crew will demand more of the captain. Whether leadership is becoming a 'global obsession' (Coutu, 2004) or not, leadership development seems to be in short supply and has become an 'industry': books, journals, conferences, seminars, courses, institutes and centres based on leadership skills have mushroomed all over the world. They aim towards the development of leadership competence, to mastering the skills necessary to turn any organisation into a great one, to manage effective corporate transformation and to induce change – in fact, *to reduce uncertainty*.

The leaders are indeed expected to reduce ambiguity and uncertainty, to reduce the sense of insecurity, to articulate a vision, to propose *meaning*. At international, national and corporate levels, we are short of trustworthy leaders who can attract followers through their vision, the role model they provide and the confidence they inspire. Excellent captains of industry are in particularly short supply, yet we still do not know how to produce such skilled leaders, despite some corporations eternally attempting to create 'leaderful organisations'.

There is a very rich literature on leadership, yet we still do not have the answer to these organisational or societal concerns. Groping for reliable models and methods, we talk of charismatic leaders (Martin Luther King, Jr. or Richard Branson, for example); of 'primal leadership' (Goleman *et al.*, 2002); of 'situational leadership'; of 'tipping point leadership' (for example, William Bratton, the police commissioner of New York City who transformed the city) (Kim and Mauborgne, 2003); of 'breakthrough leadership' (Harvard Business School, 2002) and so on. What do all these labels have in common? Warren Bennis, author of twenty-five books on leadership, founder of the Leadership Institute at the University of South California (Los Angeles), says: 'Leaders share a number of similarities among which I, personally, single out: a *love of learning* and a *strong sense of values* as being paramount.'

Leaders share discipline, integrity, vision, imagination, self-knowledge and willingness to learn and to question; they have the capacity to raise difficult questions which people are willing to make their own. They have an agenda for the journey, and strategic courage all along the road. They know that the reward is often more in the journey than in the destination (for example, Moses proposing to cross the desert to reach the 'land of milk of honey'). Leaders are able to cope with loneliness at the top and blows to self-esteem, to distance themselves from deputies (clones, sycophants and/or jockeying for the top job), and – as Professor Kets de Vries emphasises (1984) – can sense the non-rational side of organisational life, manage their narcissistic wounds and balance the different dimensions of their life (Coutu, 2004). The effective CEO – who knows who s/he is – can manage the tension (or conflict) between idealism and pragmatism, both necessary ingredients clearly visible among effective men and women at the top.

The 'responsibility' dimension

Like leadership, 'responsibility' too is in fashion. Why is there a public debate on responsibility at the individual, organisational and societal level?

As the power to cause effects increases, society increasingly demands that individuals and organisations be held accountable for the intended and unintended consequences of their actions, for outcomes and impacts. An ethics of good intentions will not do; an ethics of results is demanded and this means taking responsibility. In today's post-industrialised, post-modern society, complexity brings vulnerability, and while actors only seek to maximise their own benefit, quite understandably, society emphasises 'responsibility'. The globalisation process raises awareness of dependence on finite resources, of interdependence among nations, both of which require 'responsibility'. Scientific knowledge (for example, in genetics) and technological evolution (for example, in robotics or nanotechnology) push further the limits of our capacity to make the impossible possible, while raising new questions of responsibility (for example, GMO, cloning). Information technology has changed our way of communicating, reshaped our perception and understanding of the world, and raised new questions of responsibility for the media, including the spectre of 'Big Brother', as in George Orwell's *1984*.

If complexity, globalisation and technological evolution have brought the responsibility issue to the forefront of the public debate, it is current corporate behaviour that has given more visibility to the responsibility issue. There is so much talk about 'responsibility' in the corporate world today because of the role of the corporation as the most important value-creation mechanism in our society. Products and services, R&D and innovation, job creation, taxes paid, contribution to the community, charitable activities, patronage and so on make the corporation the most visible and important value-creating institution in society, and its responsibility is commensurately large. Furthermore, when accidents or ecological disasters do occur (from Bhopal in India to AZF in France, from Amoco Cadiz to Erika or Prestige, from Three Mile Island in the USA to TEPCO in Japan), the issue of 'responsibility' comes to the fore: who is to blame? Responsibility has also become prominent following the recent scandals in the USA (Enron, WorldCom, Tyco, ImClone), in Europe (Vivendi Universal, Crédit Lyonnais (Executive Life), Elan, Ahold, Adecco, Lernout & Hauspie, and now Parmalat), and in Asia (SK in Korea, BNI in Indonesia, China Aviation Oil in Singapore, Bank of China, Sagawa Kyubin in Japan and so on), and the list could include many – if not all – regions of the world.

These events have had a considerable impact on public opinion – not only in rich OECD countries, but also in emerging or developing economies – and have destroyed trust in corporate leaders. As Felix Rohatyn has said: 'Enron's failure was a failure of particular people and institutions but it was above all, part of a general failure to maintain ethical standards that are, in my view, fundamental to the American economic system. Without respect for those standards, popular capitalism cannot survive' (Rohatyn, 2002).

If some business leaders behave irresponsibly, we should not be surprised to see the media and public opinion debating how responsibility is 'mismanaged' in the corporate world. Furthermore, if the corporate gospel of free trade – with the (now *late*) 'Washington Consensus' of liberalisation, deregulation and privatisation – is seen as one of the two horses driving globalisation (along with technology), it is hardly surprising to see the responsibility issue fuelling criticism from the growing anti-globalisation crowd (now repackaged altermondialists preparing an agenda of 'alternative globalisation'). They denounce the mishandling of the 'responsibility' issue, not only in reaction to recent responsibility lapses by a few top level criminals (with *cordon bleu* in the art of cooking the books). Rather, theirs is a more radical criticism of the global 'system', which they perceive as destroying the planet's natural resources, creating a global apartheid, endangering a fragile, highly sophisticated, global financial system, and nurturing a technology-driven change which refuses the 'precautionary principle'. The corporation is taken to task for not fulfilling its obligations towards society: it is seen as the villain, colluding with international institutions supposed to oversee (or regulate?) the globalisation process, and fuelling the global system – a perverse mechanism driven by profit maximisation, with the market as god, inducing the commoditisation of everything.

Corporate leaders cannot go on ignoring 'the Seattle crowd', and the mixed bag (but big and growing) of dissenters who devastated downtown business centres in Genoa or Geneva (instead of Evian ...). Responsibility requires them to make sense of the noise in the street, to decode the messages of Porto Alegre and Mumbai as effectively as those of Davos. It demands Wall Street's attention to Main Street. The absence of an alternative model to the current dominant neo-liberal paradigm, the delay in coming up with such an alternative, realist model, does not justify shutting one's ears to dissent or 'subversive' voices.

The questions business leaders need to ask are: What if they were right? At least 'partly'? What if globalisation, indeed, did not deliver its benefits to the largest number of stakeholders of our planet? What if the objectives and operational mechanisms of international institutions (for example, the World Bank, IMF, WTO and so on) had, indeed, to be redefined? What if those who think that the globalisation process is irreversible – a mega-machine without a driver on a planet-wide journey reaping benefits for only a small minority – were wrong?

Perhaps, today, we see a number of early warning signals that must be properly decoded:

- development of the small, community-based, local economy;
- pressure to decentralise in order to bring citizens closer to economic and social decisions affecting them (applying the subsidiarity principle);

- the emergence of regional economic entities that may act as filters to, or buffers in the globalisation process;
- resistance against uniformisation by claims of 'cultural exception'; and
- attempts to preserve a local or regional cultural context and heritage (Scotland, Brittany, the Basque region and so on).

Sustainable development may become progressively incompatible with globalisation, as the moving of goods around the world to implement the comparative advantage model may become too costly – financially or environmentally. This may not be for the current generation, but we are already seeing negative reactions to population migration, which is bound to increase as globalisation proceeds. Should the responsible leader continue to regard our current model of globalisation as being sustainable? (Madaule, 2004).

Leadership and responsibility: two facets of the same challenge

Developing leadership and responsibility: there is no alternative – it has to be the mission of business schools. As our world searches for leaders and demands that more of them be developed (as not enough are born!) and our society expects more accountability (particularly) from corporations, business schools have a critical role to play, a major 'responsibility' to fulfil. Observing our current globalisation process, growth-driven, market led, shareholder-centred, assessing its current consequences and anticipating its future, we may come to the same conclusion as Charles Handy, that 'the current model is no longer sustainable' (Fisher, 2003, p. 87). If continuation of the present path leads to a blind alley, our master plan must change.

But who can induce such a paradigm shift, the questioning necessary to avoid getting the blame from the grandchildren of our grandchildren for what we did to *their* planet? We can hope that governments will regulate more to correct market imperfections, business leaders' shortcomings and misbehaviour, and introduce more Sarbanes-Oxley regulations to redefine corporate governance. We can expect a further spate of criticism from public opinion – along with boycotts from consumers – while some NGOs will blow the whistle to induce a dramatic change in corporate behaviour. A 'world government' may emerge that will redefine global rules of the game and police multinational corporations. Corporate leaders may take the initiative to redefine processes and rules of corporate governance, along the lines of the Derek Higgs report in the UK (2003). We can do nothing and let the current 'winner takes all' approach, 'markets know better' principle and 'free trade has no better alternative' belief to guide the next step of our globalisation. Many see this path as leading to suicide.

There is no single solution to the predicament in which we find ourselves, but there are only a small number of paths open to us. Change has to start at the top, change must come from leaders, and change must be first in the mindset. Where are business leaders' mindsets influenced, shaped and – to some extent – 'programmed'? Business schools have a key responsibility as they prepare business leaders through their MBA education, retool managers through their executive programmes, and influence leaders (CEOs, chairpersons, managing directors) through their top executive seminars. Their capacity for influence through those functions is significant. They cannot find an 'alibi' to escape their responsibility, arguing that an individual's values are determined by the family environment at an early age, in primary education, not at the age when an MBA or an executive education is undertaken. Management education is value-loaded: there are dominant paradigms in business schools; and they tend to be shared by the instructors, implicitly (though, indeed, often not made explicit in the teaching).

If we want to change our ways of creating value for the long-term benefit of our planet, we need to start with those who have power, those who run the effective corporations today. They have a significant capacity of influence. Their decisions at the top have many externalities (not all positive): in defining and implementing a corporate strategy, in defining investment priorities, in deciding to outsource some processes, in plant closure, in accepting advertising campaigns, in engaging with lobbying and so on.

Business schools – as institutions producing and sharing knowledge for the business world – cannot escape their share of responsibility for the state of (and the dominant mindset in) today's corporate world: it is a world managed – to a very significant extent – by our alumni, by managers and leaders who have spent as students weeks or months (up to two years), during which time the business schools have tried to give them the technology and tools to manage organisations effectively. What are the values behind the models? What are the values embedded implicitly in the methods? Can business schools dodge responsibility for the state of our planet, shaped so much by corporate behaviour, itself so much the offspring corporate leaders' values and mindset? For decades, business schools have influenced managers who came to recharge and equip themselves for the tough race to the top. Have they been engaged with the 'why', beyond the 'how'? Since the 1980s, business leaders have been invited to go to business schools to refresh their knowledge, to stop and think: since when have modules been included on the responsibility inherent to power, on corporate social responsibility (CSR), on corporate citizenship, on sustainable development? Since the early 1990s, schools have designed their clones in the PhD curriculum, taking four or five years to programme them with the trainers' intellectual software, and to equip them with the schools' values. Furthermore, through the schools, very significant (if not huge) investment in research, they have produced *knowledge* in areas that they have selected as important (or, in business school jargon, 'strategic'). The research undertaken is the fuel of the teaching. It is the source of the knowledge shared with those who come to learn but the research resource allocation process is far from neutral: business schools influence knowledge creation through selective research investments and priorities. Where has there been investment?

If leadership and responsibility are strategic dimensions of tomorrow's management, this is where we need to invest. This is where business schools – as institutions – could play the responsible part that society expects of them. They can promote more CSR to rebuild trust, teach the usefulness of triple bottom line, induce a debate on sustainable development, learn from alternative corporate governance models, encourage socially responsible investment, give models of codes of conduct, and encourage whistle-blowing. All this will be relevant but, beyond, tools and gimmicks, we must *question* our own mindset, our own values, the 'robust' models we build and share, the theories we elaborate, and the paradigms we propose.

This is a challenging task, perhaps an uphill battle, but we have little choice. Lucid analysts and well-known scholars have also blown the whistle (for example, Etzioni, Pfeiffer and Fong, Mintzberg), and now the Aspen Institute illustrates the nature of the change necessary in business schools (Gentile, 2003). The road will be long.

We see a number of companies demonstrating commitment to 'responsibility': they build strength through corporate responsibility commitments in their various roles (for example, as an insurer, investor, employer, and as a corporate citizen). Leadership and responsibility are today a condition not only for building a strong and attractive corporate image, but also for ensuring the development of a 'community' sharing common values and creating value for its many stakeholders.

To move towards the development of the responsibility dimension in managing the interface between the individual, business and society is essential. Aligning the interests of the three will remain a challenge for ever. We shall have to go beyond the management of contradictions, beyond the necessary reconciliation of idealism and pragmatism. We shall need to ensure that, progressively, our research work and our teaching bring a change in our institutional culture towards a real integration of the responsibility dimension in our knowledge production and in our development of leaders. Business schools have to make this possible, welding together leadership development and responsibility enhancement, through research – not only in the insurance and financial services sectors (though issues and dilemmas in these areas are many) – and through teaching and experience-sharing.

Their excellence tomorrow, and their continuous leadership, will be based on their capacity to truly internalise the responsibility dimension throughout their research and teaching (de Bettignies, 2003). We shall have no choice: society will demand it, competition will induce it, and corporations will require it. For a business school, it could also be an opportunity to further enrich its image: developing men and women of character and producing responsible leaders. Then it will make a difference, for which future generations will be grateful.

References

Beck, U. (1992) *Risk Society, Towards a New Modernity* (London: Sage Publications).
Cornelius, P. K. and B. Kogut (2003) *Corporate Governance and Capital Flows in a Global Economy* (New York: Oxford University Press).
Coutu, D. L. (2004) 'Putting Leaders on the Couch: A Conversation with Manfred F. R. Kets de Vries', *Harvard Business Review* (January), pp. 68–75.
de Bettignies, H.-C. (2001) 'The Corporation as a Community: An Oxymoron? Can Business Schools Re-invent Themselves?', *Concept and Transformation*, vol. 5, no. 2 (January), pp. 165–211.
de Bettignies, H.-C. (2003) 'Business Schools and Society: The Limits of Responsibility', *Link*, no. 5 (Spring), pp. 33–7.
Etzioni, A. (2002) 'The Education of Business Leaders', *The Responsive Community*, vol. 12, no. 4 (Fall), pp. 59–68.
Fisher, L. M. (2003) 'The Paradox of Charles Handy', *Strategy & Business*, vol. 32 (Fall), pp. 76–87.
Gentile, M. C. and J. Samuelson (2003) 'The State of Affairs for Management Education and Social Responsibility', Keynote address to the AACSB International Deans Conference, 10 February (available from The Aspen Institute).
Goleman, D., R. Boyatzis and A. McKee (2002) *The New Leaders. Transforming the Art of Leadership into the Science of Results* (New York: Little, Brown).
Harvard Business Review in Breakthrough Leadership (2002) (Boulder: Harvard Business School Press).
Higgs, D. (2003) *Review of the Role and Effectiveness of Non-Executive Directors* (London: Department of Trade and Industry, January).
Hutton, W. and A. Giddens (eds) (2000) *On the Edge: Living with Global Capitalism* (London: Jonathan Cape), pp. 1–51.
Isaak, R. A. (2005) *The Globalization Gap: How the Rich Get Richer and the Poor Get Left Further Behind* (Upper Saddle River, NJ: Prentice Hall).
Joy, B. (2000) 'Why the Future Doesn't Need Us', *Wired*, no. 8.04 (April), pp. 238–62.
Ket de Vries, M. F. R. and D. Miller (1984) *The Neurotic Organization* (San Francisco: Jossey-Bass).
Kim, W. C. and R. A. Mauborgne (2003) 'Tipping Point Leadership', *Harvard Business Review* (April), pp. 3–11.
Madaule, S. (2004) 'La mondialisation n'a-t-elle qu'un temps?', *La Croix* (26 February).
Mintzberg, H., R. Simons and K. Basu (2002) 'Beyond Selfishness', *MIT Sloan Management Review*, vol. 44, no. 1 (Fall), pp. 67–74.
Pfeffer, J. and C. T. Fong (2002) 'The End of Business Schools? Less Success Than Meets the Eye', *Academy of Management Learning & Education*, vol. 1, no. 1 (September), pp. 78–95.
Prahalad, C. K. and K. Lieberthal (2003) 'The End of Corporate Imperialism', *Harvard Business Review* (August), pp. 1–11.
Rohatyn, F. G. (2002) 'The Betrayal of Capitalism', *The New York Review of Books*, vol. 49, no. 3 (28 February), pp. 12–15.
Schwartz, B. (2004) *The Paradox of Choice: Why More Is Less* (New York: Ecco Press).

15
Ethics for a Post-Enron America[1]

John R. Boatright

The high profile scandals at Enron, WorldCom, Global Crossing and Tyco, among others, combined with the spectacular dissolution of the accounting firm Arthur Andersen, are more than business failures. Voluminous news reports have revealed egregious failures by top executives and their advisers – including accountants, investment bankers and lawyers – to fulfil their basic fiduciary duties to serve the interests of shareholders and the public.

Executives are pledged to serve the interests of shareholders, for example. Yet some have manipulated earnings, hidden debts and falsified accounting records, all in order to exercise their lavish stock options at their shareholders' expense. Accountants who perform audits for the benefit of the investing public have permitted many instances of so-called 'aggressive accounting' and approved financial statements that subsequently proved false. Investment bankers have helped executives to develop complex financial transactions that generate phantom earnings or remove unwanted debts from the balance sheet.

All the while, the banks' analysts, who were supposed to be objective, were giving favourable evaluations of the securities of companies with which the banks were doing deals, and the banks' brokers were filling their customers' portfolios with these same securities, even as they denigrated them in internal communications. And the lawyers who blessed many of these accounting and financial shenanigans were acting as though their clients were the executives who hired them, and not the shareholders, who were ultimately paying for their services.

In each of these cases, the moral wrong is simple: a failure to fulfil a fiduciary duty, generally because of serious conflicts of interest. That this kind of behaviour is immoral, and often illegal, is clear, but what challenge does it pose beyond recognising that it is wrong and attempting to prevent it? Some argue that existing laws and the force of the marketplace are sufficient, and nothing more needs to be done. Indeed, many of the wrongs in the recent scandals are slowly being rectified. Congress has mandated new rules to ensure that directors and auditors are 'independent', which is another way of saying 'free of conflicting interests'. Among the many provisions of the Sarbanes-Oxley Act, for example, are the requirements that audit committees be composed entirely of independent directors with no ties to management, and that accounting firms doing audits refrain from performing certain non-audit services that could bias an audit. Similarly, Eliot Spitzer, the New York State attorney general, has forced some major investment banks to increase the independence of analysts in order to reduce the risk that their ratings of stocks will be influenced by the banks' deal-makers.

Although these efforts to reinforce fiduciary duties by removing conflicts of interest and restoring objectivity may produce some improvements, they do not address the most important challenge posed by the recent scandals. The effectiveness of fiduciary duties as a regulator of business conduct has been undermined seriously since the 1980s by several developments in the American business system. In particular, executive compensation tied to performance, the combining of auditing and consulting by accounting firms, and consolidation in the financial services industry have produced powerful new incentives that have been major factors in recent scandals. Restoring the traditional fiduciary duties in the face of these developments will be a difficult, if not impossible, task.

There are alternatives, however. Imposing fiduciary duties is one form of regulation that relies heavily on moral force, but market-based regulation that seeks to alter the incentives is another form. The challenge in this post-Enron era, then, is to determine which form of regulation, or what combination of these forms, can best secure the kind of ethical business environment in which future 'Enrons' will not occur.

What went wrong?

We cannot propose reforms to prevent another Enron, much less understand the post-Enron world, without a firm grasp of why the recent scandals occurred. The stories are complex, and each one is different, but they all share some common features. Each case involves a business strategy gone awry, executives determined to boost short-term stock price by any means, directors who failed to detect warning signs, accountants who acquiesced in aggressive accounting, investment bankers who structured questionable financial deals, and lawyers who showed how to achieve the desired results with a plausible legal veneer.

A major factor in the scandals of 2001 is an increased focus on share price. This began in the early 1980s, during a period of hostile takeovers when a high price was the best defence. The impetus for high executive compensation tied to performance came originally from companies taken over that needed to raise share price quickly. Institutional investors encouraged this trend because it seemed to promote good corporate governance by aligning executives' interests more closely with those of shareholders. Finance theorists, most notably Michael Jensen, further supported this idea with arguments drawn from agency theory, which studies the problems of a principal (in this case the shareholders) controlling an agent (the CEO). Reducing the loss from an inadequately controlled CEO would more than offset the high executive compensation – or so the theory goes. Executives also became enamoured with rising stock prices, not only because of their option-rich pay packages, but also because a high stock price opened up a growth strategy of making acquisitions.

A second important factor is the deregulation that has occurred since the 1980s. Market deregulation, especially in energy and telecommunications, started a scramble to develop business models for a future that no one could predict accurately. It is significant that the biggest bankruptcies occurred at Enron (an energy trading company) and at WorldCom and Global Crossing (both telecommunications). The novelty of these companies required new accounting methods that tested Generally Accepted Accounting Principles (GAAP). How should Enron price long-term contracts for delivering energy, for example? Or how should WorldCom and Global Crossing classify unused telephone lines and optic fibre cable? (WorldCom counted lease payments for idle capacity as capital investments, which is garden-variety accounting fraud.) At the same time, investment banks were developing sophisticated financial instruments that permitted, to cite just one example, loans that could be booked as trades. In this deregulated financial environment, Enron became more like a hedge fund than an energy company.

In addition to market deregulation, a reduction occurred in the 1990s in the legal liability of accounting firms and investment banks. It is difficult for a company to commit massive fraud without the complicity of its accountants, bankers and lawyers. However, a 1994 court decision held that accounting firms and investment advisers could not be held liable for 'aiding and abetting' fraud in securities transactions, and the 1995 Private Securities Litigation Reform Act protected investment banks from class action suits for alleged securities fraud. Although this liability deregulation was introduced to make business more efficient, it had the unintended consequence of reducing a powerful constraint on accounting firms and investment banks.

The third factor, and perhaps the most significant, is simultaneous changes in the compensation structures for executives, accountants and investment bankers. The rapidly escalating pay for CEOs has become heavily weighted with stock options that must be exercised within a narrow time period. This, combined with the importance of meeting analysts' expectations, produced great pressure to achieve short-term results. In order to accomplish this, earnings management, which had long been used to iron out small wrinkles in financial statements, came to be used to fashion figures out of whole cloth.

Accounting firms had discovered that it was lucrative to sell consulting services to their audit clients, thus tempting them to go easy on audits lest they lose the consulting business. And investment banks found that there was more money to be made in doing deals with large companies than in servicing individual brokerage clients. As a result, analysts touted the stock of companies with whom the deal-makers were doing business and encouraged the firm's brokerage customers to stuff their portfolios with these stocks. Individual investors were further shunted aside as investment banks made their most lucrative opportunities, such as shares in hot initial public offerings (IPOs), available to their CEO clients. These CEOs received thinly disguised kickbacks for bringing their company's business to the investment bank.

The effect of these changes was that, what had previously been a system of healthy checks and balances became a united front at the expense of investors. Instead of having opposed interests that served to protect investors, they now had an unhealthy common interest. The fiduciary duty that executives owed to shareholders took a back seat to the pursuit of a short-term increase in stock price. Accountants, who had formerly policed financial reports in order to protect the public, now had a strong incentive to help executives to do whatever it took to boost share price in order to keep them as consulting clients. And investment bankers no longer served as trusted advisers to their customers, scouting out the best securities. They found it more advantageous to work with executives and accountants to finance deals that raised stock prices, even if it meant selling out their customers.

This is a broad-brush indictment that also overlooks many factors, but it paints a picture of a systemic failure with multiple causes. It is like a major industrial accident, which usually happens when a number of small mishaps, inconsequential by themselves, occur together with catastrophic results. Although the individual failures are predictable, their occurrence together is highly improbable and hence not easily foreseen. Lacking an understanding of the convergence of factors that led to the Enron collapse and other bankruptcies, the people involved could not easily appreciate the risks they were taking. For the most part, they were playing the game with which they were familiar, but were unaware of how treacherous the playing field had become.

What is to be done?

The American business system is divided, in that it combines a market system built on the pursuit of self-interest with a system of fiduciary duties, in which one party is pledged to serve the interests of another. This system has worked because of the compartmentalised professional roles of those with fiduciary duties. Public accountants, stockbrokers and lawyers have operated as professionals who serve clients – or, in the case of public accountants, the public. Even CEOs and other top executives have generally viewed themselves as being quasi-professionals, and taken their fiduciary duties seriously.

However, the compartmentalisation of those with professional roles has been seriously eroded in recent years, by several factors. One is the enormous compensation packages that have become common. These are designed to align executives' interests with those of shareholders, to solve the agency problem of how to induce executives to serve shareholders' interests. Whatever the merits of this strategy, one effect is to replace a moral and legal mechanism with a purely market mechanism. Fiduciary duties are now less important as a means for restraining executive behaviour because the market is now being employed to achieve the same end.

Another factor is the consolidation of multiple services in accounting firms and investment banks. Accounting firms now provide many internal accounting and auditing services, set up accounting and financial information systems, advise on tax strategies, and offer appraisals and fairness opinions. In a similar manner, investment banks that mainly served large corporate clients merged with those that offered brokerage services, mostly to small, individual clients. As a result, brokers and analysts, who have always operated with both fiduciary duties and market mechanisms, now find themselves with even greater conflicts.

A third factor is the devaluation of some professional services. Auditing is a cost that must borne by companies because the service is mandated by law. The cost is passed along to the intended beneficiaries, the investing public, but investors have little control over the price or the quality of audits. Similarly, securities analysis is a cost for brokerage firms that is also passed on to investors. Thus corporations have an incentive to skimp on audit costs – and investment banks to economise on the costs of analysis. In the recent bull market, investors had less interest in both the quality of audits and the quality of research, because they found that everything they bought unfailingly increased in price. As a result, accounting firms and investment banks have tended to treat auditing and analysis, respectively, as loss leaders to attract more lucrative business. These professional services have thus become peripheral to the more basic business services of consulting and investment banking.

This erosion of professional roles and decline of fiduciary duties is the reality of the post-Enron era. Although efforts can be made to reverse this development, doing so might require changing executive compensation and breaking up accounting firms and investment banks. Congress has grappled unsuccessfully with the issue of executive compensation, and the proposal by Arthur Levitt, the former chairman of the Securities and Exchange Commission (SEC), to separate auditing and consulting services was soundly squashed. And the consolidation of the banking industry has so collapsed the distinctions between investment banks that serve large clients and those engaged in retail brokerage that any return to the past would be very difficult.

Would we really be better off if we could put on the brakes and go into reverse to the pre-Enron period? High executive compensation tied to performance may provide greater protection for shareholders than a sense of fiduciary duty. The problem in the recent scandals is not that the pay packages were too large, but rather that the right incentives were not created. Arguably, corporations and shareholders are better served by multi-purpose accounting firms that can attract the best people and provide economies of both scale and scope; and financial supermarkets that offer a multitude of services might serve everyone better. In any event, the market is telling us that these kinds of consolidation are more efficient and that they can be undone only at a price.

What is the alternative? Despite their importance, fiduciary duties are a second-best means of regulation. They are generally employed in relations in which one party agrees to serve the interests of another. If the obligations in question can be fully specified and embodied in contracts, there is no need for fiduciary duties. Fiduciary duties, which are general, open-ended obligations to act for the benefit of another, are employed, when precise rules are not possible. For example, the main reason for imposing a fiduciary duty on executives to serve the shareholders' interests is that shareholders cannot specify in detail what executives should do to serve their interests, because the situations that might arise are unpredictable. However, the use of executive compensation tied to performance gets round this problem without the use of fiduciary duties. A market mechanism that appeals to self-interest, rather than an ethical and legal duty, is used instead.

Although accounting is a highly rule-bound activity, the rules still leave considerable discretion that accountants can use to benefit one party over another. The fiduciary duty of public accountants to serve the public is one way of ensuring that the public is served. However, the new Public Company Accounting Oversight Board (PCAOB), created by the Sarbanes-Oxley Act, is charged with creating yet more rules as well as with conducting reviews of audits. The results of such efforts may further constrain the accounting profession and reduce the need for fiduciary duties. In addition, more accounting information is now available from corporations, and it may be possible in the near future for investors to have real-time access to company books. Such a development would reduce the need for audits and provide an external check on their quality.

Some people argue that there are already too many rules in accounting, and that their number merely encourages the search for creative ways of getting round them. An alternative is the European approach, of employing accounting principles instead of rules. A principle-based accounting system which prescribes general goals instead of specific means allows accountants to choose, and auditors to approve, the accounting methods that provide the truest picture of a firm's financial situation. However, the European system requires a greater reliance on the integrity of the people doing accounting and auditing. American accountants already have the authority to depart from GAAP if doing so provides a truer picture, but few take advantage of this opportunity because it imposes a burden of proof that can be avoided by merely following the rules. In addition, the pursuit of principles should lead to the best methods of accounting, which can then be codified in rules. In return, these rules prevent unnecessary disagreements over the best methods. It is probably better to have precise rules where they are possible and leave principles for difficult cases that are less amenable to rules.

The problem of biased analysis by investment banks admits of a very easy solution. Instead of guarding the independence of analysts or requiring analysts to disclose any conflicts, which are among the current proposals, encourage the development of a larger market for analysis. If analysis has value, it will be purchased by investors, and analysis from a provider with a reputation for objectivity will bring a higher price. Part of the problem with analysis at investment banks is that top-notch analysts receive more in pay than brokerage customers are willing to pay for, and so the money for their high pay can be generated only by adding value to the bank's deal makers, which creates a conflict of interest. The best solution is to invest only as much in analysis as buyers will pay for in the marketplace.

Both fiduciary duties and market-based regulation aim at a common goal – namely to reduce risk. In particular, investors run the risk that executives will enrich themselves at the shareholders' expense, that a company's financial statements will not be accurate, and that a broker's advice will not be sound. In each case, the solution has been to impose fiduciary duties that reduce the risk with a promise, in effect, not to take advantage of investors. Executives, accountants and brokers each promise to act in the investors' interests. Rules on conflict of interest further reduce the risk to investors by prohibiting situations in which the parties might be tempted to break this promise.

However, the goal of reducing risk can be achieved in a number of ways. A market-based system of regulation would shift the risk away from investors and back to the parties that now have fiduciary duties. For example, if accounting firms cannot be held liable for 'aiding and abetting' clients in fraud, then they bear little risk in facilitating 'aggressive accounting'. Removing this protection would require accounting firms to engage in more extensive risk management so that they would, in effect, be regulating themselves more closely. In short, if accounting firms and investment banks bore more of the risk of the activities for which they now have a fiduciary duty, then investors would have less need to rely on this kind of obligation to serve their interests.

There are drawbacks to such a regulatory approach. An increased risk burden would lead to less risky behaviour, which might not be in the investors' interest, given that greater risk leads to higher returns. This burden involves a cost that would most probably be passed along to investors, as accounting firms, for example, might spend more money on audits or buy more insurance. However, fiduciary duties also have a cost, and so in the end the choice of regulatory approaches may depend on a trade-off between effective protection and the cost of that protection.

However, this issue is ultimately decided, it is clear that in this post-Enron era the fiduciary duties of the various players in the American business system have become less effective protections for investors and the public. This erosion of a traditional means of regulation is a result of many changes that have taken place in recent years, some of them highly beneficial. The challenge we face, then, is whether to strengthen these fiduciary duties, in part by reducing effectively conflicts of interest, or to find other means of protection against the kinds of scandals that Enron represents.

Note

1   Reprinted with permission from *Phi Kappa Phi Forum*, vol. 83, no. 2 (Spring 2003).

Part 5

Conclusion

16
Enron: Visiting the Immersed Part of the Iceberg

Paul H. Dembinski and Jean-Michel Bonvin

According to the thousands of pages of official reports, enquiries and studies that have already been devoted to Enron, its collapse can be attributed to a coincidence of a number of dysfunctions and malfunctions within the firm, but also in its immediate environment. Each of these 'local problems' has been scrutinized, analysed and, in some most visible cases, addressed at a regulatory level. Despite all these efforts, however, a more fundamental question remains on the internal composition of the multi-causal knot that led to Enron's collapse. Was the collapse exceptional, resulting from an accidental combination of unrelated, independent and unique incidents, or was it the spillover of a chain of linked, correlated, interdependent or even mutually reinforcing routine events? In the latter case, Enron's collapse would have been much more than an accident. It would be symptomatic of deep systemic dysfunctions, the suspicion of which may, in the last analysis, put trust in the financial system in doubt, and thereby put the system's very survival at risk. This systemic concern may grow deeper once it is acknowledged on one side the cementing role trust plays in any financial relation, and on the other the everyday longer list of corporate malpractices or wrongdoings on which Enron will remain a milestone for a long time.

Enron, a multi-causal reading

Without any shadow of a doubt, the Enron affair has yet to finish leaving its mark. Even so, a number of events have already been transformed into memories: first of all, the American giant's US$50 billion market capitalisation, which has gone up in smoke; then there is the Andersen empire which, in a directly related disaster, vanished even before the wrongdoings it was accused of had been proven; and, finally, the stock market euphoria that gripped America progressively and, subsequently, the whole world, before running out of steam at the end of 2001. As well as the memories, there has been some more direct fallout: first, the increased vigilance of operators who had their fingers burnt by Enron; this has contributed to the fuelling of a series of scandals, as well as the adoption of new regulations and laws, of which the Sarbanes-Oxley Act is the best-known, but by no means the only, example.

At the heart of this legacy, hidden among all the other elements, lies buried the real crux of the affair, and the issue that is going to prey on people's minds for a long time: questions on the why and how of the Enron affair, and the direct and indirect responsibilities involved. The 'why-problem' does not disappear simply by attributing a mechanical, or technical, causality to the disaster; even if the various court actions drag on for years, the mechanical causality will eventually be established. Technical causality, which covers all the mechanisms – technical, legal, accounting and so on – that have led to the scandal, is the issue that receives the most attention not only from the media, but also from the courts and the specialists commissioned by them. Such a strictly technical interpretation tends to amalgamate and confuse elements that belong to different levels of reality. Another reading is needed in order to distinguish strata of reality and the processes that belong to each of them. For this purpose, Aristotle's 'multi-causal' methodology is more suitable, as it identifies four causes or fashions: the efficient cause, the material cause, the formal cause, and the final cause (Lear, 1998).[1] More explicitly, it aims at showing how and why (the objectives pursued or the final cause) an acting subject (the efficient cause that can be individual or collective) gives a specific shape or form (the formal cause) to an amorphous and raw material (the material cause). The classical example of the equestrian statue illustrates this 'multi-causal' approach: the sculptor acts as the efficient cause as he gives to the piece of marble (material) the shape of an equestrian statue (formal) in order to celebrate the represented person's memory (final). In doing so, he actuates a potential present in the matter.

In this drama, the efficient cause relates to the actors: Enron's management and shareholders, Andersen's partners and auditors, and the whole range of stakeholders. None of them sees the big picture, and each operates within a framework of limited and partial rationality. This is why the issue of causality attains such a high degree of complexity here, inasmuch as it is difficult to apportion blame and to untangle the web of responsibilities.

The material cause refers to the raw ingredients that were mixed together and moulded to produce the affair with which we are concerned. To put it simply, we are talking about the fabric of modern, highly 'financiarised', market economy and society. A number of commentators favour this reading of the case, which allows them to dispose of the question of specific responsibilities (the efficient cause) by underlining the role played by the prevailing culture and business climate. According to this line of argument, the Enron affair is just one of many other potential affairs that have the similar ingredients, the only distinction being that Enron has turned sour and in consequence attracted a massive media coverage. According to this view, the 'matter' or 'fabric' of contemporary society is pregnant with thousands of fundamentally similar situations. Therefore, it is incorrect – the argument goes – to consider Enron as an accident when it is only scapegoat for the whole system.

The formal cause has a more direct relationship with the situation at Enron because it seeks to emphasise the specific form adopted by the capitalist economy in the case in point. Attention is then focused on the joint-stock company as a formal organisation, on the rules of accounting, on the logic and rationality behind them, as well as on the use of financial techniques and regulations that govern them. Delving deeper into this aspect of the problem, the seeds of the collapse of Enron are clearly revealed in the way it functioned, its procedures (or lack of them), its governance structures and its relationship with the immediate economic environment. Most contributions in this book skilfully highlighted this dimension of the Enron case.

The search for the final cause poses the question of *telos*, that is to say, the ultimate aim of the principal protagonists: the directors of Enron and the auditors. So the quest will go on to analyse the underlying motives and the value systems and hierarchies of the protagonists, now for the most part appearing in court. The search will also focus on trying to establish the psychological profiles of the individuals involved, and their deep-rooted aspirations.

The methodology proposed by Aristotle is useful in grasping the complexity of a situation where differing rationalities interact and intertwine, and where the twists and turns of retroaction replace linear and mechanical causalities. A tool such as this for laying out the facts and issues is indispensable, as is abundantly illustrated by the contents of this book. The various contributions demonstrate repeatedly the extraordinarily tangled nature of the Enron affair, in which totally different strata of reality come up against each other, some wholly subject to the affair while others go far beyond it. Our main purpose in this closing chapter is to enlighten the reader as to the relationships between the four causalities in the Enron case. We shall then strive to go beyond this specific case in order to adopt a systemic view on contemporary finance. The next section will be concerned with 'financiarisation' (the multiplication of assets and of financial transactions) and its impact on the way finance and society at large are being envisaged (the material cause and its evolution). Then we shall tackle the problem of individual responsibility in such a context. The issue of 'conflicts of interest', which is at the very core of the Enron scandal, will be addressed in detail (the efficient cause in the context of 'financiarisation').

Finally, the last section will open some avenues for reflection on the finalities, values and objectives prevailing in highly competitive, individualistic and secular society. Two main issues are at stake here: first, the dominance of opportunistic values; second, and most important in our view, the dramatic change in the presently prevailing conception of the 'common good'.

Indeed, many of the dimensions of the 'Enron affair' and reactions to it indicate the growing role of the procedural dimension of the common good, namely the importance the rules and modes of operation and decision, and the symmetrically eroding bearing of more substantial considerations, such as shared values and ethical principles. In Aristotelian terms, such a shift means a deep transformation of the relationship between the formal cause and the final one. Indeed, the Enron case and other financial scandals exemplify what is more generally present in other contemporary social practices, namely a way of conceiving the final cause as being centred on procedures alone. Indeed, in shaping social and economic reality, the quest for efficient or equitable procedures hides more often than not more substantial concerns. Our concluding section will emphasise that, in such situations, the formal cause (or process) tends to overshadow the final cause (substantial values), which in turn empties the very concept of 'common good' of all its content.

'Financiarisation': trust in finance

'Financiarisation' is one of the most visible changes in contemporary societies, thus the material cause is discussed in relation to the most important aspects of 'financiarisation'. The first two aspects – the fusion of money and finance, and conditions for trust – point to the dominance of long-term trusting relationships. They are in sharp contrast with the short-term impersonal and often anonymous relationships promoted by the third aspect, namely the impoverishing 'financiarisation' of mentalities.

When money becomes finance

In the everyday world, money is a 'purchasing power' endowed with the potential to trigger exchange and transaction, whereby objects and ownership rights change hands. Perfectly fungible, transmissible and in constant motion, money is especially adapted for settling those transactions that are impersonal and instantaneous.

In contrast to money, finance implies time. Rather than transactions, finance builds links and lasting interdependencies. While monetary transactions allow for anonymity of protagonists, in contrast, in financial relations – at least to some extent – identity matters. The written commitments exchanged in a financial transaction promise or guarantee future payments and, in the meantime, become 'financial assets'. Whether it is a matter of national debt, a bank deposit, a company share or a derivative, the identity of at least one of the parties is known and permanent, although the other can change.

Finance lubricates monetary circulation because it allows operators with surplus cash to put it back into the economic circuit in a way that is both temporary and redeemable. At the same time, it enables operators with a cash flow problem to have the necessary means to realise their projects.

Because it secures long-term transactions, 'finance' is an extension and a complement to money.

Because of the growing importance of financial intermediation, the clear conceptual limit between money and finance has today become blurred. Between the perfectly liquid asset, best represented by a coin or banknote, a bond, or even a derivative contract, there is a whole range of gradations that make a clear distinction between money and finance impossible. This fusion has very important consequences since it blurs the boundaries between the responsibilities of the public sector, traditionally in charge of the monetary side, and the private sector concerned with finance. The regulatory dilemma was made clearly visible in Enron's case but also, with a totally different regulators' reaction, in the Long Term Capital Management case. The so-called 'Basel II' is symptomatic of the difficulties regulators have to deal with this fundamentally new situation, where the classical distinctions between public and private spheres are impossible and thus pragmatically irrelevant.[2]

Blind trust in the future

Trust gives potential to money and finance as it defines the limits within which money can be converted into desired goods. For finance, trust has two main dimensions. The first corresponds to collective or social trust in a future that can be anticipated, and in which it is possible to imagine oneself both individually and as part of a group. This trust opens horizons for building this common future through a fabric of financial relations that establish interdependency between today and tomorrow. Such confidence in the financial scaffolding that paves the way for the future is somewhat rare historically, even if today it can appear to be quite 'normal' in the Western part of the world.

The second dimension of trust that ties partners to a common financial transaction can be qualified as 'mutual trust'. It boils down to a feeling of mutual understanding and the ability to anticipate, with strong accuracy, the other's behaviour in unforeseen circumstances. It is based both on collective values that are either shared or at least known to each other, and on the guarantee given by mutual membership of a network, or social constellation, from which it is difficult or impossible to escape unilaterally. The membership of one partner in a social circle limits the risk taken by the other partner when entering into a financial relationship.

With the rise of the modern state, 'mutual trust' has been institutionalised, but its nature has not changed. The state is the expression of common membership and future, while the public laws produced and implemented by the state have become the guarantee of contractual respect, and therefore – to all appearances – replaced the reference to common and shared values.

Since around 1980, the Northern nations have expressed, with a force that has been without precedent, their trust in both financial institutions and in the ability of financial scaffolding to secure the future. Banks, pension funds and even financial markets have been the main beneficiaries of this feeling of total confidence and security, to the point that they have been endowed with the function of custodians of the personal and collective future.

The uninterrupted expansion of finance during the last quarter of the twentieth century is best explained by the progressive emergence of an ever-stronger feedback loop linking unprecedented and lasting economic performances to an ever deeper trust in the future, best materialised by finance. The Enron scandal clearly helped by overstretching this 'institutional trust' almost beyond its limits. Enron's collapse could potentially have back fired. The fear of such a retro action, with the possible destruction of institutional trust, explains the rapidity and rigour of the political reaction that overlooked the collateral damage it caused.

A feeling of security – the 'financiarisation' of the economy and of mentalities

Considered from a strictly economic viewpoint, finance is an economic subsystem expected to fill very specific functions: assuring that payments are made; collecting savings and making them available for investment projects; assessing risk and giving it a price; and enabling the efficient allocation of financial resources. If the handling of payments and the transformation of savings are traditional duties of finance, the large-scale management of risk is a relatively new function, the importance of which has grown as a result of an ever-higher complexity of financial assets and transactions, to the reduction of related transaction costs, and to the increased social role of finance as the custodian of the future.

Since the Second World War, conditions have been particularly favourable to economic development. Uninterrupted growth coupled with unprecedented technological advances have been accompanied by widespread changes in both individual and collective imagination and mentalities. Step by step, the economy has grown to become the dominant dimension of social life. In consequence, what until a generation ago was used to be known as a 'market economy' has been turned progressively into a 'market society'. Today economic concerns are at the centre of the social sphere, but financial concerns are at the centre of everything economic. This change is reflected in the structure of social cohesion: monetary exchange and financial links are as much operators of social inclusion as their absence contributes to exclusion. Social cohesion is less directly interpersonal as relations to things tend to replace bonding. As a result, both at individual and social levels, economic and financial activity has ceased to be a means to reach an end. Consequently, the monetary and the financial have been invested with new functions, especially those of helping to assure a minimum of social cohesion.

Three observations epitomise the recent change of finance's role in society: at the heart of market society, assets are today one of the main guarantees of personal security. Capital-based pensions and life insurance have thus become both depositors of a utopian search for security and the main actors in the world of finance. The feeling of security is based on an individualisation of assets, and therefore of destiny. Assets have been established as the most important operator of trust, often to the detriment of interpersonal ties that require obligations and can thus be seen as a burden.

In an open and mobile society, finance contributes to making social cohesion increasingly fleeting, because it gives assets a virtual content. In this sense, finance 'liberates': it dissolves traditional connections by creating alternatives. It transforms interpersonal trust into a trust in the future, of which financial institutions are supposed to be the guarantors. If security of a financial relationship used to be based on the mutual trust of operators, but today it rests on the liquidity of the markets, which has become a substitute for interpersonal trust.

The place devoted to finance in the Western vision of society has increased, together with the growing confidence in serenity of the social system based on market-cum-democracy. The feeling of having arrived at a final and stable state is best expressed by the absurd thesis of the 'End of History'. The 'financiarisation' of the economy is only the economic extension and expression of the other less visible aspect of the same process, namely the 'financiarisation' of mentalities.

A relatively recent phenomenon, large-scale 'financiarisation' started during the 1970s. From then onwards, the supply of financial assets increased considerably. It was fuelled in the first place by the unbridled capacity of the Western economies to increase the level of debt of governments, but also of companies and individuals. Petroleum products, agricultural goods and commodities were used increasingly as financial assets and, after 1971, the same thing happened to national currencies. These new assets proved to be useful in the framework of sophisticated investment strategies, relying increasingly on derivatives and other financial innovations.

On the demand side, the parallel thirst for financial assets gives an indication of the progressing 'financiarisation' of mentalities. It was fed by the channelling on to the corresponding financial markets of a growing part, not only of traditional savings, but even more so of pensions and other insurance products. Thus the 'financiarisation' of the contemporary economy is not an external or technical event, but in fact the result of economic processes driven by deep changes in mentalities.

Loss of bearings – the conflict of interest example

Such changes have a strong impact on the way that the efficient cause is conceived in contemporary society. Indeed, in a society where the feeling of security depends on the ownership of financial assets, questions of meaning, of ethical limits and of responsibility lose all points of reference. The long list of financial scandals that has rocked liberal society highlights the frailty of the anthropological presuppositions at the root of the 'financiarised' society. In the present context, the requirements of ethical and responsible behaviour become ever more blurred, as the issue of conflict of interest aptly evidences.

The notion of conflict of interest is entering the public arena, keeping pace with the lengthening list of financial and economic scandals that began with Enron. Western society is waking up progressively to the devastating potential of conflicts of interest, and of its own unpreparedness in the face of the sickness that threatens to corrupt the heart of the market economy. For is this very market economy not founded upon an act of faith, according to which the rule of the free market transforms 'private vices', notably the selfish pursuit of personal interests, into 'public virtues'? If this is taken as the truth, the efficient cause loses its role, is discarded and replaced by a *deus ex machina* known as the invisible hand, beyond the reach of ethics or responsibility. However, recent scandals show that conflicts of interest may derail the market and undermine the usual virtuous circle. Even worse, in such a case this same market amplifies a vicious circle that threatens its very foundations. Conflicts of interest are at the centre of a paradox that, while by no means new, is currently reaching alarming proportions. The damage runs deeper than we care to admit, and it is high time to start the process of offering a diagnosis.

Modern society is increasingly complex and knowledge-based, and thus offers particularly propitious framework for the spread of situations known as 'conflicts of interest'. It is very easy for a medical doctor, armoured in authority and knowledge, to prescribe medicines that are at best unnecessary, and at worst harmful. In so doing, doctors betray their patients' trust in the name of the incentives offered by pharmaceutical companies. In societies where two-thirds of the national income derives from services and is generated by manipulation, if not of knowledge or information, reliance on proxies and experts is omnipresent. The expert – lawyer, vehicle mechanic, banker, accountant, doctor and so on – often acts a the prescriber, frequently of his or her own services. The same applies to proxies, who are agents for the interests of third parties for the purpose of a service or transaction. The clashing motivations between respect for the client's mandate and concern for one's own turnover is as old as the professions themselves.

Conflict of interest is not only a matter that affects individuals, it also affects companies and enterprises: the bank that generates additional commission income by 'churning' client portfolios more than is necessary; the manufacturer of cars or other products that limits the lifespan of a product artificially in order to force clients to make a further purchase in due course; the food or cigarette manufacturer whose products, unbeknown to the customers, include a dependency-creating ingredient and so on.

The truth is that conflicts of interest comprise situations where one and the same actor (person or business) is caught between conflicting loyalties: loyalty to a function or mission, and loyalty to personal/corporate pecuniary interests. Looked at in greater detail, the issue is in fact one of a conflict of motivations – one pecuniary, the other not – rather than a strict conflict of interest in the monetary sense. Thus the notion of the conflict of interest is revealed as a euphemism used to disguise the ethical dilemma that lies at the true heart of the problem. The contemporary malaise has its origins in the fact that, by relying on ethics to suppress ever more widespread conflicts of interest, we are recognising, although not wanting to admit it, the limits of the market project. This project would have us believe that it can do without ethical and responsible behaviour, proposing that these are replaced by the arithmetic of self-interest, which alone would be sufficient to ensure the social optimum thanks to the 'invisible hand'.

The agency theory, the cornerstone of the modern economy, views remuneration of the agent in proportion to achieved results as the only way to preserve the interests of principal. A large portion of the current debate on corporate governance takes its inspiration from the agency theory. However, all these solutions rely on self-interest, and as such they reduce the individual to a utility-maximising mechanism devoid of all ethical scruples. Such a person becomes easy to manipulate because s/he moves according to the structures of remuneration that are put in place. In such a context it is the paying body that commands and holds the reins. The agent, following the example of the head of a major multinational, will simply take a bow and hasten to pocket the cheque offered in return for blind loyalty. When applied to politics, the logic of self-interest can serve as justification of almost every corrupt practice. In the economic sphere, the recent scandals have shown that, when left to its own devices, pecuniary motivation is a devastating force, not only against itself but against society as a whole.

The considerations above tend to suggest that the liberal society's organising principle is not as autonomous and independent of ethics as the utopian but mechanistic ideal would have us believe. Taken to extremes, the principle of self-interest releases the seeds of destruction capable of sapping the foundation of the social system, as the case of Enron suggests. The question of ethics and responsibility, and the role played by the efficient cause cannot be ignored. In other words, if the actors are equipped only with utility-maximising mechanisms and not with values or substantial principles, they will not be able to solve ethical dilemmas or conflicts of interest, and the stability of the whole social system will thereby be at risk.

Beyond 'financiarisation': common good at risk

Far from being a neutral mechanism in terms of finalities, 'financiarisation' carries with it radical transformations of individual and social values and objectives. This may be observed in both substantial and procedural terms, and has a deep impact on the conception of the 'common good' prevailing in contemporary society. Behind finance's role change, there is a fundamental shift in social values. Finance is nothing more than a mirror of social change, and it would be wrong to confuse it with the change itself.

The liberal utopia leaves it up to the real actors – in the exercise of their freedom – to define the space that the market will occupy within their society. While this doctrine states that the market is the most effective means of ensuring the happiness of society's members, the market's natural tendency is to expand and occupy an ever-larger portion of social space. This is certainly true in reality: keeping pace with the specialisation of needs and technological progress, whole areas of human activity switch from the private sphere to the public realm, where they are required to submit to the regulating action of either the market or of public institutions. Consequently, the private sphere is emptied progressively of its content in favour of the public space, in particular the market.

The truth is that the extension of the market's role is fuelled by a very powerful self-justification, according to which the only forseeable remedy for possible market imperfections consists in expanding the very market even further. This is especially visible in innovation-driven finance. As mentioned above, liberal society, consequent to this justification, tends towards a market society. In such a context, the idea of efficiency becomes all-important. In fact the 'efficiency ethos', which makes the relationship between the means employed and the results obtained the primary criterion at both individual and social levels, became widespread within nineteenth-century bourgeois society. The extension of the economic sphere into the heart of liberal societies was made possible by the triumph of rationalism, of which economic efficiency became the most immediate manifestation. The accent on rationality as the common ground between individuals is perfectly compatible with the individualist vision of human nature upon which the liberal utopia rests. However, reliance on cold calculation, of which the economic represents the ideal sphere of application, leads to transactions being favoured above other forms of warmer interaction.

Economics has been on the rise since around the 1950s, while at the same time the 'social link' at the heart of Western societies has weakened. This observation allows us to posit the hypothesis that economics exerts an irresistible attraction over individuals who, seduced, extricate themselves from traditional social links and in doing so empty the private sphere of an important element of its content. Thus it may be that this extension of the domain governed by impersonal relations and procedures (market and administration) culminates in the appropriation of content that, until very recently, was a matter for interpersonal relationships. Such a change increases the importance of functional communities – companies, institutions – based on the interchangeability of actors and the depersonalisation of their relationships, which are by definition ephemeral. At the same time, the importance of living communities, in particular the family and those based on long-lasting personal relationships between members, dwindles. Were this hypothesis to be validated, private life, whose protection is the *raison d'être* of the liberal utopia, would be in the process of being emptied of content. The transfer of private life's essential content into the public space and the market would have drained, in the truest sense, the liberal utopia of its core justification.

The spreading of the market's domain brings our societies closer to the abstract society anticipated by Karl Popper in *The Open Society and its Enemies* (1962). In this vision, the cold, strictly functional transaction governed by procedures occupies the entire space of interaction, to the extent that no space is left for relationships. One may ask whether, if such a stage were reached, society would still exist. Or would it rather be the result of random coincidences of time and place, with no past and no future, like the coming together of quarks in a nuclear experiment. The question of the very existence of the social must be addressed in the face of such atomisation.

At the same time, this market-driven society will tend to eject (marginalise and exclude) those who fail to find a role. This has a twofold effect: traditional societies implode as they find their most dynamic elements constantly drawn away from them; and, on the other hand, open (Western) societies prove unable to combat social exclusion. This process is made possible by the far-reaching demutualisation of shared destinies, and thus of the protection measures against existential risks. Such a framework is highly conducive to opportunistic behaviour, as the Enron case illustrates, and makes the very existence of a 'common good' problematic. If self-interest is the only common ground between the members of a collective, the perspective of shared values or objectives becomes problematic in itself. This holds true for all types of communities, ranging from states to small and medium-sized companies, or even families. Again, the Enron scandal exemplifies the difficulty in identifying common principles and concerns in a context that promotes opportunism and self-interest.

The most commonly invoked remedy in such contexts is the consensual adoption of procedures. In other words, the impossibility of reaching agreements on substantial values is compensated by the common acceptance of procedures. In this case, principles or values find their legitimacy not in themselves, but in the acceptance of their designing procedures. In the concluding part of our chapter, we shall question the relevance of this procedural conception.

Disenchantment with anonymity and cold procedures: the common good in the modern world

The communist experiment came to an end because its project imagined that all involved shared an identical vision of human nature, whereas the liberal system is shaking because, as Auguste Comte tells us, it is based upon a rationally grounded premise of the superiority of cold, impersonal and anonymous procedures. This applies to the political realm, with democratic procedures, as well as to the economic realm with cold market rules.

There are structural similarities between the two utopias, the most important being their anthropocentric character. In the words of the late Russian philosopher, Julij Szrejder,[3] we are witnessing a double 'anthropological catastrophe'. This catastrophe is caused by the fact that both systems attempted to denature humankind – with varying degrees of wholly ephemeral success. These systems falter because at one point or one other, human nature strikes back. The communist system collapsed because it failed to spring the lock of a private sphere whose existence it denied. And the liberal system is faltering because the private sphere, whose defence was its purpose, has dissolved at the same time as the public market space has failed to meet the needs of individuals who are isolated and utterly unequal. For symmetrical reasons, neither approach passes the test of the 'common good'.

The term 'common good' includes the word 'good'. This is a way of making explicit the premise according to which its precise content cannot be described, nor socially constructed, without the fundamental consideration of human beings, of what they seek to accomplish during their existence, and of the true sources of their ultimate happiness. In qualifying 'good' by the addition of the adjective 'common', the expression is focused on the fact that mankind is unable to attain happiness in total solitude and isolation, and that, for an individual and personal being, the pursuit of good necessarily involves the surrounding community.

Whatever the precise definition and institutional arrangement, the notion of the common good expresses the desire of a group of people to lead happy lives. It hints at the tension between the common good's two poles: that of the group, and that of each individual member. From its inception, political philosophy has always set out plans for the perfect society, although without ever offering any definitive solution. Approaches to the subject have varied down the centuries, as Emilio Garcia Estebanez tells us, in referring to Aristotle, Plato and St. Thomas:[4]

> The traditional method started from the idea of a perfect society and defined individual interests according to this idea. The modern method (Habermas, Nozick or Rawls) adopts the opposite perspective, taking individual interests as the starting point in its conception of the perfect society. Individuals may then present, compare and reconcile these interests by projecting them onto a social model upon which they are agreed.

No matter the exact definition, however, writers who have considered the subject agree, implicitly at least, on the fact that living in a community is a necessity, for both material (to guard against poverty) and social (to guard against solitude) reasons. Furthermore, as Hollenbach (2002) writes: 'One of the key elements in the common good of a community or society, therefore,

is the good of being a community or society at all. This shared good is imma-
nent within the relationships that bring this community or society into
being' (p. 9).

Community life, and by extension the common good, can be grounded in
many different things. Modern thinkers emphasise the deliberative procedure that allows community members to reach a consensus. Taking the
operation of American society as an example, Hollenbach shows that, in
reality, the public sphere for debate and confrontation has been emptied of
its content, leaving in its place a widespread indifference that is barely
hidden by the principle of tolerance. Tolerance is therefore the atrophied,
modern version of the common good. Hollenbach goes on to state that
tolerance is not enough to meet contemporary social challenges, notably
those posed by the urban poor or by globalisation. This situation has arisen
because lying at the centre of these phenomena are relationships of economic
and social interdependence established over decades. However, tolerance,
'an ethos whose primary values are independence and autonomy, is not
adequate to address this new interdependence' (Hollenbach, 2002, p. 42).

A common good that restricts itself to tolerance alone therefore demands
not only that the rich and socialised unblinkingly 'tolerate' the poverty and
solitude of the excluded, but additionally that the excluded 'tolerate' the
opulence of the rich that the media display for all the world to see. Thus, if
the common good resides only in tolerance and the procedures that render
it operational, community life – and therefore society – is exposed to the risk
of breakdown, in so far as the tolerance of some becomes intolerable to others. Put another way, the procedure for guaranteeing tolerance alone, no
matter how sophisticated, is an inadequate basis for the common good. It
has to be supported and complemented by solidarity in daily life:

> One of the most important meanings of the concept of common good,
> therefore, is that it is the good that comes into existence in a community
> of solidarity among active and equal agents. The common good, under-
> stood in this way, is not extrinsic to the relationships that prevail among
> members and sub-communities of a society. When these relationships
> form reciprocal ties among equals, solidarity achieved is in itself a good
> that cannot otherwise exist ... When society not only falls short of the
> level of solidarity it could reasonably aspire to but is shaped by institu-
> tions that exclude some members from agency altogether, the resulting
> interdependence becomes a ... 'common bad' that affects the quality of
> life of all members, especially of those who are excluded. (Hollenbach,
> 2002, p. 189)

The common good therefore supposes both interpersonal interactions, a
good in itself – in the pattern of Aristotelian political friendship – and a
reasonable measure of material solidarity, a quality that fellowship in any

case requires. The common good is therefore not a precise institutional project; rather it is a set of principles for life within society. The common good demands the involvement of all, in the respect of individual freedom, and in establishing institutions capable of regulating social life in accordance with the principles of justice and solidarity. Nevertheless, in societies organised in the same way as Western society, it would be pointless to limit the quest for the common good to the establishment of an institutional architecture capable of a degree of material solidarity through the distribution of wealth (distributive justice). The common good also requires that a space is provided within all interpersonal ties, including economic one, for reciprocated fellowship and concern for others (commutative justice). The common good, to use the terms of Etienne Perrot's (1996) elegant definition, lies in the relationship between the individual good and the good of the community; it cannot be reduced to the economists' concept of general interest (the sum of individual goods) nor to a 'public good'. Enron's failure, as well as many other similar wrongdoings, fundamentally result from the lack of understanding of this issue.

Indeed, the reference to the final cause is the very condition and prerequisite for the reflexive capacity, and conscious and responsible action. Left alone, material, formal and efficient causes appear as mere physical and social phenomena which cannot be converted into responsible action. Some of the forces related to the material and formal dimension can certainly be kept in check by procedures, but these procedures will not offer enough resistance if not rooted in substantial values and convictions that extend deeper than the sheer arguments of efficiency and common survival.

Today, at a time when the ruins of the inhuman communist system are of interest to very few, it is vital to learn the lessons of its unprecedented collapse so that we may enrich liberal society's organising principle by integrating concern for the common good. Without such a change of emphasis, the so far superficial cracks in the system – as in the 'Enron affair' – risk expanding to become the fatal fractures of tomorrow.

Notes

1   A similar approach has been elaborated by Jean-Loup, Dherse, *Ethique ou le chaos* (Paris: Presses de la Renaissance, 1999).

2   See 'From Bretton Woods to Basel II', *Finance & the Common Good/Bien Commun*, no. 21 (2005).

3   Szrejder, Julij, 'Chrystianizacja rosyjskiego spoleczenstwa wobec grozby katastrofy antropologicznej', *Znac*, vol. 417–18, no. 2–3 (1990), pp. 107–16.

4   Garcia Estebanez, Emilio, 'Le bien commun, approches philosophiques et politiques', in Espaces, *Le bien commun, approches philosophiques et politiques* (Bruxelles: Espaces, 1997), p. 24.

References

Attali, J. (1988) *Au propre et au figuré: une histoire de la propriété* (Paris: Fayard).

Brooking, A. (1996) *Intellectual Capital. Core Asset for the Third Millennium Enterprise* (London: Thomson Business Press).

Cochoy, F. (1999) *Une histoire du marketing: discipliner l'économie de marché* (Paris: La découverte).

Crump, T. (1995) *Anthropologie des nombres. Savoirs-compter, cultures et sociétés* (Paris: Seuil).

Dembinski, P. H. (1990) *The Logic of the Planned Economy: Seeds of the Collapse* (Oxford: Oxford University Press).

Dembinski, P. H. (1998) 'Le piège de l'économisme: quand l'arithmétique remplace l'éthique', in B. Sitter-Liver and P. Caroni (eds), *Der Mensch – ein Egoist? Für und wider die Ausbreitung des methodischen Utilitarismus in der Kulturwissenschaften* (Fribourg: Swiss Academy of Humanities and Social Sciences), pp. 227–45.

Dembinski, P. H. (2000) 'La globalisation annonce-t-elle la Civilisation de l'Amour?', in J.-P. Fragnière, Y. Fricker and J. Kellerhals (eds), *La vérité est multiple – Hommages au Professeur Patrick de Laubier* (Lausanne: Réalités Sociales), pp. 231–40.

Dembinski, P. H. (2004) 'De l'échec des utopies à la redécouverte du bien commun', in J.-M. Bonvin, G. Kohler and B. Sitter-Liver (eds), *Gemeinwohl – Bien commun: Ein kritisches Plädoyer – Un plaidoyer critique* (Fribourg: Academic Press), pp. 231–57.

Dupuy, J.-P. (2003) *Avons-nous oublié le mal?* (Paris: Bayard Presse).

Enciso, A. G. (2000) 'Valores burgueses y valores aristocràticos en el capitalismo moderno: una reflexión histórica', *Cuadernos Empresa y Humanismo*, no. 78 (June).

Groupement d'intérêt scientifique pour l'étude de la mondialisation et du développement (GEMDEV) (1999), *Mondialisation. Les mots et les choses* (Paris: Karthala).

Hirschman, A. O. (1977) *The Passions and the Interests. Political Arguments for Capitalism Before its Triumph* (Princeton, NJ: Princeton University Press).

Hollenbach, D. (2002) *The Common Good and Christian Ethics. New Studies in Christian Ethics* (Cambridge: Cambridge University Press).

Latouche, S. (1998) *L'autre Afrique, entre don et marché* (Paris: Albin Michel).

Lear, Jonathan (1998) *Aristotle: The Desire to Understand* (Cambridge: Cambridge University Press).

North, D. C. (1990) *Institutions, Institutional Change and Economic Performance. Political Economy of Institutions and Decisions* (Cambridge: Cambridge University Press).

Perrot, E. (1996) *La séduction de l'argent* (Paris: Desclée de Brouwer).

Rifkin, J. (2000) *The Age of Access. The New Culture of Hypercapitalism, Where All of Life Is a Paid-For Experience* (New York: Jeremy P. Tarcher/Putman).

Rosanvallon, P. (1979) *Le capitalisme utopique. Critique de l'idéologie économique* (Paris: Le Seuil).

Sombart, W. (1966) *Le Bourgeois. Contribution à l'histoire morale et intellectuelle de l'homme économique moderne* (Paris: Petite Bibliothèque Payot).

Soros, G. (1998) *The Crisis of Global Capitalism* (London: Little, Brown).

Steger, U. (ed.) (1998) *Wirkmuster des Globalisierung. Nicht geht mehr, aber alles geht* (Landenburg: Gottlieb Daimler- und Karl Benz-Stiftung).

Williamson, O. E. (1975) *Markets and Hierarchies: Analysis and Antitrust Implications. A Study in Economics of Internal Organisation* (New York: The Free Press).

Index